leading a digital school

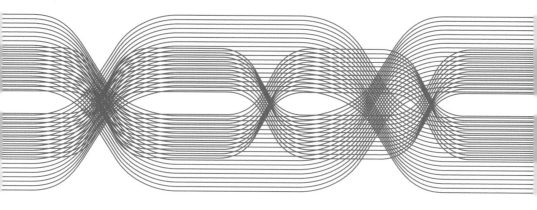

PRINCIPLES AND PRACTICE

Edited by Mal Lee and Michael Gaffney

ACER Press

First published 2008
by ACER Press, an imprint of
Australian Council *for* Educational Research Ltd
19 Prospect Hill Road, Camberwell
Victoria, 3124, Australia

Reprinted 2009

www.acerpress.com.au
sales@acer.edu.au

Edited by Ronél Redman
Cover design by mightyworld
Cover photograph © Andrew Thurtell 2008
Text design based on design by mightyworld
Typeset by Kerry Cooke, eggplant communications
Printed in Australia by Hyde Park Press

National Library of Australia Cataloguing-in-Publication entry

Author:	Lee, M. R. (Malcolm Robert)
Title:	Leading a digital school / Mal Lee ; Michael Gaffney.
ISBN:	9780864318961 (pbk.)
Notes:	Includes index.
	Bibliography.
Subjects:	Education—Australia—Data processing.
	Computer-assisted instruction—Australia
	Computers—Study and teaching—Australia.
	Internet in education—Australia.
	Educational technology—Australia.
	Information technology—Study and teaching—Australia.
	Schools—Australia
Other Authors/Contributors:	
	Gaffney, Michael (Michael Francis)
	Australian Council for Educational Research
Dewey Number:	371.3340994

CONTENTS

5 Fostering digitally based teaching and learning: strategic considerations 51

6 Creating a nexus between homes and schools 68

7 Leading a digital school: a case study—St Leonard's College 80

8 The 'Good Video Game Guide' to successful integration of digital technology: a case study of Ingle Farm Primary School with interactive whiteboards 93

FIGURES
AND TABLES

Figures

Tables

PREFACE

Schools are facing profound challenges. For more than one hundred years, they have been shaped by the thinking of the industrial era of the late nineteenth century, and by and large have been highly effective in serving the needs of that period. However, teachers, principals, system officers and education policy makers now find themselves in increasingly volatile and uncertain social, cultural, and economic times where questions about the quality and relevance of schooling are being raised and demanding answers.

What is taught, how it is taught, who teaches it—and to whom—are contestable issues at this time when the political and education policy spotlights are on matters of national curriculum and international comparisons, teacher quality and standards. Similarly what is learnt, how it is assessed and how it is reported – and to whom—are questions of significant importance to students and parents, and especially to schools, education systems and governments faced with the task of educating young people *as learners*, *as persons* with intellectual, physical, social, emotional, moral and spiritual talents and capabilities, *as community members*, and *as contributors to society* (ACTDET, 2007).

At the same time, as a society we are witnessing far-reaching global technological developments. Thomas Friedman (2006) in his book, **The World is Flat: The globalised world in the twenty-first century** describes these changes in terms of the convergence of three related phenonema: the emergence of the World Wide Web and related digital technologies; the development of a critical mass of people using these technologies and doing business differently; and the broadening of the global marketplace especially through the inclusion of China and India. In fact, Friedman argues that these developments are only the beginning, and predicts that:

As the world starts to move from a primarily vertical – command and control – system for creating value to a more horizontal – connect and collaborate – value creation model, and as we blow away more walls, ceilings and floors ...

*societies are going to find themselves facing a lot of very profound changes
all at once. ... To put it simply, following the great triple convergence that
started right around the year 2000 we are going to experience what I call
'the great sorting out'.*

(Friedman, 2006, p. 234)

Against this background of societal and technological change, we
believe that the publication of this book, *Leading a Digital School*, including
chapters by leading educators engaged in policy, research, consultancy and
day-to-day practices in schools and education systems, is timely. Our aim
is to provide a practical overview of how emerging digital technologies can
be used to engage and support students in their learning— in ways that
take into account the changing nature of learning and teaching, and the
place of school education in a world which is becoming 'flatter and flatter'
(Friedman, 2006).

In Chapter 1, we outline the essential features of schooling in a digital
era, highlighting recent government initiatives in the UK and Australia
and cite examples of effective planning and leadership, and teacher use of
new technology from 'pathfinder schools'. In Chapter 2, *Successful learning
and school design for the knowledge age*, Michael Hough overviews the
characteristics of post-industrial society and compares the characteristics
of today's students with those of previous generations. This provides the
background for his model of 'digital schools' as learning organisations with
distinctive approaches to teaching, learning, school design and planning.

The importance of addressing planning issues associated with digital
technology is examined in more detail by Allan Shaw in Chapter 3 *Planning
in a Digital School*. Digital schools, in contrast to the traditional segmented
school organisation are highly integrated and networked entities. This calls
for holistic models of planning which recognise, for example, that seemingly
small decisions in one area can have profound impacts on other operations.
The message from Allan's experience as a foundation principal in leading
the establishment of a new school is that the days of 'bolt on' plans, and in
particular discrete ICT or technology plans, are over.

In Chapter 4, we emphasise the view that school and system leaders
need an up-to-date 'macro understanding' of the digital technology
available to their schools. Moreover as the senior educational architect
within their school, we argue that principals need to take more direct
responsibility for that technology and its use.

Accompanying this challenge is the complex process of transforming
teaching and learning to take advantage of the increasingly sophisticated

technologies available to students in the networked, digital world experienced in their homes, their daily lives and their classrooms. In Chapter 5 Glenn Finger highlights the strategic considerations required to achieve 'total teacher usage' of digital technologies. Glenn uses the metaphors of the *journey*, *roadmaps* and *signposts* to highlight the learning and the evolving nature of planning associated with implementing digital technologies. He concludes with the set of principles to offer guidance to educators on the journey.

The connection between students' experiences of digital technologies within and outside school is the theme of Chapter 6, *Creating a nexus between homes and schools*. We explore the challenges associated with this nexus and examine options for addressing the *digital divide* between homes and schools.

To provide an insight into the kinds of issues and challenges facing principals leading digital schools, we invited two principals, Roger Hayward and David O'Brien, to write about the paths taken by their respective schools (see Chapters 7 and 8). We deliberately chose two very different situations, at different ends of the socio-economic scale. Roger's school, St Leonard's College, is an independent K-12 school, close to the CBD in Melbourne, Australia. David's school, Ingle Farm Primary is a government primary school located in the northern suburbs of Adelaide, Australia. The school's student population is characterised by significant poverty and a large Aboriginal and English as a Second Language cohort, inclusive of 250 mostly non-English speaking refugees. Despite these differences the commonality of the issues is apparent.

Of primary importance among these issues is the appointment and development of teaching staff. Schools in the digital era require specific teacher attributes and a different staffing mix to what most schools have known. In Chapter 9, Greg Whitby explores the concept of teachers as authentic knowledge workers and offers some ground rules for those charged with the responsibility for selecting and developing staff.

Underpinning the work of these teaching (as well as administrative) staff is an appropriate and reliable ICT infrastructure and access to technical support. Without that infrastructure and support schools simply cannot operate in the digital era. School principals and education authority executives require a working knowledge of what is involved in setting up and maintaining suitable forms of ICT infrastructure and technical support. Peter Murray draws from his school and industry background in Chapters 10 and 11 to provide that insight.

Closely allied to the provision of effective ICT infrastructure and support are information services which are able to manage the escalating information that is generated, assembled, stored and disseminated by school communities and education authorities. Schools and systems over recent decades have developed separate curriculum library, computing and networking groups which at times have tended to compete for control of the digital technology. We believe that these 'sub groups' are important but ought to be working as one.

Karen Bonanno explores this point and the ways of managing and servicing the information needs of schools in Chapter 12. She contends that the handling of information and digital materials will occupy an increasingly significant role in schools, and that therefore, each school will need an organisational arrangement and the expertise to fulfil that role. She makes the point (somewhat ironically) that at a time when some schools are doing away with school libraries, the importance of schools having quality information professionals has never been greater.

As digital technologies develop further, it is likely that a major portion of the school's digital information will be accommodated in a managed learning environment (MLE), virtual learning environment (VLE), course management system (CMS), or what BECTA in the UK has labelled a 'learning platform'. These variously labelled entities have the potential to play a vital part in the teaching and learning undertaken in schools. However as Daniel Ingvarson and Michael Gaffney indicate in Chapter 13, they can also become expensive 'white elephants' unwittingly providing an education alien to the school or system vision. On the other hand, Dan and Mike argue that emerging Web 2.0 technologies and related online social networking opportunities have immense possibilities for supporting quality teaching and enhancing student engagement.

Effecting these desired types of developments in teaching using digital tools requires more than traditional forms of professional development Ongoing, timely and well-informed professional learning is needed for teachers to flourish. In Chapter 14 John Hodgkinson explains that one of the vital professional development elements that all staff need is time— time to get to know the emerging technology, time to collaborate, and time to pause and consider how best to move in the unchartered waters.

Leading a school as it begins to take advantage of the potential of digital technologies, and provide students with an education appropriate for the twenty-first century can be immensely exciting and professionally gratifying. In the concluding Chapter 15, we present a set of principles and guidelines for leading schools into the digital era. But be warned— this is not a job for the faint-hearted! It obliges educational leaders to simultaneously address a host of changing variables, to learn *on the move*, and to develop and maintain an appreciation of the available digital technology, while at the same time fulfilling all their regular administrative roles and responsibilities. Someone once described this type of leadership and organisation of change as like changing a tyre while the car is moving, or building an aircraft in flight!

Throughout the book, the key messages for school and education system leaders are that:

- informed and wise use of digital technology is an indispensable element of quality schooling in the early twenty-first century
- digital technologies are tools in the hands of professional dedicated teachers and it is teachers (not the technology) who can make a positive difference to student learning; and
- teachers need to be supported by principals, system officers and policy makers to explore the potential of digital technologies and develop their capabilities in using those technologies appropriately.

While the challenges are profound, it is clear that if schools are to educate the young for the contemporary world, educational leaders at school, system and government levels have no option other than to develop an informed understanding of the capacity of digital technologies to support quality teaching and learning, and to use those technologies wisely for the students and school communities which they serve. We hope that *Leading a Digital School* is an important contribution to meeting those challenges.

Mal Lee
Michael Gaffney (Editors)

References

Australian Capital Territory Department of Education and Training. (2007). *Every chance to learn*. Canberra: ACTDET.

Friedman, Thomas. (2006). *The world is flat: The globalised world in the twenty-first Century* (2nd edition). New York: Farrar, Straus & Giroux.

THE CONTRIBUTORS

[In chapter order]

Mal Lee

Mal Lee is an educational consultant specialising in the development of digital schools. He is a former director of schools, secondary college principal, technology company director and a member of the Mayer Committee. As a Fellow of the Australian Council for Educational Administration (FACEA), Mal has been closely associated with the use of digital technology in schooling, particularly by the school leadership for the last decade.

A historian by training, Mal has written extensively, particularly for *The Practising Administrator*, *Australian Educational Leaders* and *Access, Educational Technology Guide* on school planning for the Information Age, digital schooling and the effective use of ICT in schooling.

Michael Gaffney

Professor Michael Gaffney is Chair of Educational Leadership at Australian Catholic University. He was formerly Head of Education Services in the Archdiocese of Canberra and Goulburn Catholic Education System. Mike has had a range of senior executive and policy advisory roles with education authorities and governments, including with the National Catholic Education Commission; Commonwealth, State and Territory education departments; and MCEETYA. He has been recognised for his contribution to Australian school education through being awarded Fellowships with the Australian College of Educators, and the Australian Council for Education Leaders. His associated academic experiences include Director of the Educational Leadership and Professional Program, and Convener of Postgraduate Education Research at the University of Canberra. Mike has a deep interest in school and education system transformation and the exercise of leadership at all levels to bring about meaningful, sustainable and high quality learning opportunities for students.

Michael Hough

Dr Michael Hough is a Professorial Fellow at the University of Wollongong, working in both the Graduate School of Business and the Australian Centre for Educational Leadership. He has recently presented on Moral Values and Business Success to conferences in Hong Kong and Australia, written and presented on engaging Gen X and Gen Y, and presented several conference keynote addresses on the issues of leading a digital school. He is a past National President of ACEA and has been awarded the ACEL Gold Medal and appointed a Member of the Order of Australia.

Allan Shaw

Allan Shaw is Chief Executive Association of Heads of Independent Schools of Australia (AHISA), a role that provides pastoral support for members, representing their interests in national forums, and assists with the provision of professional learning. For the last three years, he has been involved in establishing a low-fee, suburban independent school using best practice ICT policy and practice.

Glenn Finger

Dr Glenn Finger is Deputy Dean (Learning and Teaching), Faculty of Education at Griffith University. Prior to his appointment at Griffith University in 1999, Dr Finger served with Education Queensland for more than 24 years as a physical education specialist, primary school teacher, deputy principal and acting principal in a wide variety of educational settings. He has particular expertise in ICT and Technology Education initiatives, research and evaluation, and has extensively researched, published, and provided consultancies in the area of ICT curriculum integration and the Technology Key Learning Area.

Roger Hayward

Roger Hayward was schooled in Edinburgh, Scotland. He began his professional life as a research scientist but soon looked for the richness and satisfaction of a career in education. He has taught at schools in England, Zambia and Australia, and at a teachers' college in Zambia. He used a programmable calculator in teaching physics in 1976 and has been using computers in the classroom since 1983. He claims to be a sceptical early adopter of electronic technologies. He has been Principal of St Leonard's College in Melbourne since 2000.

David O'Brien

David O'Brien is currently Principal of Ingle Farm Primary School in Adelaide. For the past 15 years he has worked as a school leader in a range of educational settings across South Australia. A significant part of this leadership experience has been in disadvantaged communities. David is an experienced facilitator of professional learning aimed at school leaders presenting at a range of local and national conferences.

Greg Whitby

Greg Whitby is the Executive Director of Schools for the Parramatta Catholic Education Office and has extensive experience in K–12 schooling and senior system leadership. He leads a multidisciplinary team enabling the provision of quality learning and teaching in 77 primary and secondary schools. An understanding of how students learn in today's world is driving the development of innovative and sustainable learning frameworks aimed at improving the learning outcomes for all students.

Peter Murray

Peter Murray has been associated with the shaping of whole-school technology programs since his beginning days with the Western Australian Education Department. In 1996, Peter took on an IT mentor role at Christ Church Grammar School in Perth, working with teachers and students to shift their focus on the advantages of ICT in education. In 1999, Peter took on the role of Director of Studies at the school, managing the day-to-day operation of the school's academic program and driving curriculum change within the school. In 2003, Peter was appointed to a newly formed position as Director of Information and Communication Services. He now works as an educational technology adviser.

Karen Bonanno

Karen Bonanno is the managing director of KB Enterprises (Aust) Pty Ltd. Her company provides administration and management support to non-profit professional associations. She has been a secondary teacher, teacher librarian, head of department, regional adviser, and education officer in the public education sector. Karen is currently contracted as the Executive Officer for the Australian School Library Association and the Executive Secretary for the International Association of School Librarianship. She has published articles and book chapters and presented at local, national and international conferences. In 2001, she was awarded the ASLA Citation in recognition of her contribution to teacher librarianship in Australia.

Daniel Ingvarson

Daniel Ingvarson grew up in a family where education was the central theme, as every member of his immediate family was a teacher. Daniel built the first

Education Internet Service Provider (1993) in Australia, he designed and built the first school-specific Internet gateway (1995), and built the first Internet portal that linked logins to Internet activity in one central infrastructure (1998) called SINA. This changed the way the Internet was managed, and at one time his software was used by over 50 per cent of Australian students. Daniel built a VLE and learning content system called myclasses (2001), which won the National Australian Internet Industry Association software innovation award. Daniel's software was arguably one of the most used e-learning platforms in the world, being used by over 2.7 million users in five countries. In the United Kingdom it is part of the BECTA Learning platform. After successfully selling his business (2005), he now assists education systems to understand the balance of policy, technology and teaching while navigating the complexities of dealing with vendors.

John Hodgkinson

John Hodgkinson was a secondary school principal in Queensland for 18 years from 1988 to 2005. In this role, he was heavily involved in projects to embed ICT into teaching and learning. He was Secretary/Treasurer for the Australian Secondary Principals Association (ASPA) from 1995 to 2006 and developed and managed the ASPA Online website from 1997 to 2006. He was an ASPA delegate to the International Confederation of Principals (ICP) from 2002 to 2006.During that time he built and managed the ASPA website—now one of the largest of its type in the world. He now manages websites for a number of national and international principals' associations (including ASPA, APPA, AGPPA, and the International Confederation of Principals).

This involvement has provided John with a rare appreciation of the current level of understanding of school principals and their needs.

CHAPTER 1

LEADING SCHOOLS IN A DIGITAL ERA

Mal Lee & Michael Gaffney

In March 2005, the British Government launched its e-Strategy with the publication of its aptly titled *Harnessing Technology* and the provision of very significant amounts of money to support the implementation of that strategy. That initiative consolidated moves that had been made by successive British governments since the 1990s, and provided a major impetus to the nationwide use of digital technology in all areas of youth education.

Harnessing Technology set four major goals:

- *To transform teaching and learning and help to improve outcomes for children and young people, through shared ideas, more exciting lessons and online help for professionals.*
- *To engage hard-to-reach learners by providing special needs support, more motivating ways of learning, and more choice about how and where to learn.*
- *To build an open and accessible system with more information and services online for parents and carers, children, young people, adult learners and employers, and more cross-organisation collaboration to improve personalised support and choice.*
- *To achieve greater efficiency and effectiveness through online research, access to shared ideas and lesson plans, improved systems and processes in children's services, shared procurement and easier administration.*

(DfES, 2005)

The UK adopted a comprehensive—and notably proactive—approach in its quest to harness the educative power of ever-emerging digital technology, simultaneously addressing the many variables that experience had shown needed attention. The government provided direction and support from the Prime Minister and the Treasurer through to local education authorities. Most importantly, it allocated the vital funding for such diverse variables as the ICT infrastructure, Becta, a national coordinating body, teacher training, leadership development, support networks, teacher purchase of digital teaching resources, and practical, ongoing research and evaluation. Significantly, the government took responsibility for the instructional technology used in its schools, opted to install interactive whiteboards in every British classroom and stimulated the growth of a British interactive, multimedia teaching software industry.

Moreover, the *Harnessing Technology* initiative complemented many other UK education initiatives, not least of which was refurbishment of the nation's schools.

Similar comprehensive, national moves to both harness digital technology and provide a more appropriate education for the digital world were made in nations as diverse as New Zealand, Mexico and Singapore.

In February 2008, the newly appointed Australian Deputy Prime Minister and Minister for Education, Julia Gillard, wrote to all secondary school principals inviting their participation in the recently elected Rudd Labor Government's $1-billion Digital Education Revolution. The media release stated that:

> The Digital Education Revolution will dramatically change classroom education by ensuring that all students in years 9 to 12 have access to information and communication technology.

The remainder of the announcement went on to explain the rationale behind Australian government policy in terms of two foundational principles: first, every Australian child deserves a world-class education; and, second, to be able to compete globally, Australia needs a world-class education system. While the details of the new policy continue to develop, it is clear that the government recognises the value of investing in digital technologies, especially in the provision of computer hardware and broadband connections to schools (see http://www.digital educationrevolution.gov.au).

This policy initiative highlights some significant shifts in thinking about the nature of schooling. Among these is the sense that traditional modes of teaching and models of schooling are becoming obsolete in the face of the rapid, social, economic and technological changes facing individuals, communities and societies. Within this context, the emergence of terms such as 'the digital education revolution' and 'digital schooling' can present an image that these contemporary demands and pressures for change can be accommodated by investing in technology and 'going digital'. But it is not as simple as that.

LEADING A DIGITAL SCHOOL

The purpose of this book is two-fold. First, we and our contributing authors seek to inform educational leaders in schools and school systems about current developments in the use of digital technologies in schools. We present a range of case studies illustrating the value as well as the complexity of school development involving technology. Second, we aim to encourage educational leaders to engage in the processes of successful change with digital technologies for their school communities and education systems by providing guidelines and advice drawn from the case studies and from emerging research and professional literature. Our message is that *leading a digital school* involves far more than investing in hardware and software and implementing a 'technological solution'.

Rather, the change we envisage is about ways to integrate digital technologies creatively and wisely to enliven teaching and support student learning. We have chosen to use the term 'digital technology' in preference to 'information and communications terminology' or 'ICT' because the latter term (like those of 'audio-visual education', 'media education', 'computer education' and 'IT' that preceded it) is becoming dated, and does not cover the range of technology now available for use in teaching, administration and communication in schools and education systems.

The effective use of digital technologies in teaching, administration and communication is a multifaceted challenge. It requires:

- recognition and respect for the place of the student and how they learn, and how we assess and report their learning achievements
- development of quality teaching practices and the digital resources to support those practices
- redesign of school structures and processes in ways that will transform our industrial age schools from that 'curious mix of the factory, the asylum and the prison' (as Cambridge Professor of Education David

Hargreaves puts it) to forms that truly reflect the significant demands and engaging possibilities of schooling in the early twenty-first century; and, finally

- understanding of the nature and potential of emerging digital technologies to the point where they can be sensibly incorporated in discussions and decisions about the vision and plans for schools and education systems.

The challenges of improving student engagement and achievement, developing teaching quality and redesigning schooling are challenges of educational leadership. Developing an understanding of the value and the means by which digital technologies can assist practitioners and policy makers in meeting those challenges is what *leading a digital school* is about.

'THE SCHOOL IS FLAT'

In early 2000, a group of pathfinding schools in different parts of the world became digital. They began to use a fundamentally different mode of schooling to what had been done before. Schools like St Paul's College in Surrey, England, Hillside Primary School, in New Jersey, USA, and, indeed, low socioeconomic schools like Priestic Primary School in the Midlands of the UK, Richardson Primary School in Canberra, Australia and Ingle Farm Primary (featured in Chapter 7) achieved total teacher use of digital technology in everyday teaching, and developed and integrated digital administration, communication and learning systems to support their teachers' work and students' learning. Put simply, these schools moved into a digital operational mode. They entered a world where many of the old assumptions and ways of schooling were no longer applicable. (Lee & Winzenried, 2006)

Schools as we have known them have been heavily paper-based, and shaped by the thinking of the industrial age. At present we are witnessing a shift from this traditional operational paradigm to one that is digital. And while the way forward is just being charted, we believe that this shift holds immense promise.

The possibilities open to educators within the digital mode are considerable and exciting. Schools, like industry and society as a whole, have the opportunity to take advantage of the profound economic, societal and technological changes identified by Thomas Friedman (2006) in his bestselling book, *The World Is Flat: The globalised world in the twenty-first century*. He refers to these changes by using the term 'triple convergence', which he defines as the coming together of three related global developments that began around 2000:

1   A web-enabled platform for multiple forms of collaboration—the Internet, email and digital convergence.
2   A critical mass of people engaged in new ways of doing business involving a change from a 'command and control vertical chain of command' to 'horizontal collaboration and management' for creating value.
3   The addition of China, India, Latin America, Central Asia, Russia and Eastern Europe to the global marketplace.

Friedman believes that this 'triple convergence'—of new players, on a new playing field, developing new processes and habits for collaboration—demands different mindsets. He illustrates the point by contrasting traditional 'vertical thinking', which starts by asking 'Who controls what system?', with 'horizontal thinking', which starts with 'What is the effect or outcome you want to create?' He contends that:

> *Triple convergence ... is the most important force shaping global economics and politics in the early twenty-first century. Giving so many people access to all these tools of collaboration, along with the ability through search engines and the Web to access billions of pages of raw information, ensures that the next generation of innovations will come from all over Planet Flat. The scale of the global community that is soon going to be able to participate in all sorts of discovery and innovation is something the world has simply never seen before.*

(Friedman, 2006, p. 212)

Friedman goes on to advise that:

> *Societies are going to find themselves facing a lot of very profound changes all at once. But those changes won't just affect how business gets done. They will affect how individuals, communities and companies organise themselves, where companies stop and start, how individuals balance their different identities as consumers, employees, shareholders and citizen, how people define themselves politically, and what role government plays in managing all this flux. This won't happen overnight, but over time many roles, habits, political identities, and management practices that we have grown used to in the round world are going to be profoundly adjusted for the age of flatness.*

(Friedman, 2006, p. 234)

These predictions have significant import for education and for schooling, in particular. Industrial models of schooling were very efficient for the mass production economy, which needed groups of mass production workers educated to the level required while—as Friedman explains—'money was poured into the elite who could innovate'. He argues that this was fine while there were 'a lot of bread and butter mass-production jobs, paying decent wages waiting on the other side of the high school gates'.

Unfortunately, as he observes:

> The world has flattened out, those mass production jobs are increasingly being automated or outsourced. There are fewer and fewer decent jobs for those without a lot of knowledge ... So a poorly funded and staffed high school is a pathway to a dead end.

(Friedman, 2006, p. 347)

This confluence of the variables described by Friedman has provided the platform and the necessity for schools to take advantage of digital technology.

Lessons from 'pathfinder schools'

There is much that can be learned from the pathfinder schools to guide the way through the largely uncharted territory of digital technologies in schools. We can also learn from those school and education authorities that lost their way in the wilderness; that is, those schools that have failed to reach the desired destination or have used technology in ways that have been counterproductive to the performance and wellbeing of their community.

Consider, for example, those schools where:

- teachers are deluged by inappropriate, distracting or trivial email
- there is little or no staff development
- administration systems add to, rather than reduce, the workload
- networks are unreliable
- valuable technology is underused.

This list demonstrates that by identifying the pathologies affecting the development and implementation of change in schools, we can sometimes discover the cure. The case studies and policy examples in this book come from a diversity of situations: primary, secondary and K–12 schools— government, religious, and independent, small and large, low and high socioeconomic, and from different parts of the world. They highlight some healthy accounts of school change as well as underline the illnesses that can arise; and, of course, they offer suggestions to maintain wellbeing as well as some prescriptions for cure.

TEACHERS USING NEW TECHNOLOGIES

History shows that getting all teachers to use any type of electronic instructional technology in their everyday teaching needs to be approached thoughtfully. The most common instructional technologies used by teachers to supplement their voice are the pen, paper and the teaching board—be it black, green or white (Lee & Winzenried, 2008). It is sobering to reflect that after almost a century of experience with various forms of electronic instructional technology—all of which were projected to 'revolutionise' teaching—in the main, teachers are still using technologies of the 1800s or earlier. The challenge of getting all the teachers in the school to go digital in their teaching is thus not to be taken lightly.

Ways identified by Lee and Winzenried (2008) to encourage the use of new instructional technologies by teachers are to:

- select technology appropriate for everyday teaching
- supply the requisite content and software
- provide ongoing training, development and support to teachers
- ensure the arrangements are in place to enable use of the technology, including the requisite budgetary allocations
- have school executive and education authority officers who provide leadership, direction and support
- use 'whole school' development and implementation strategies.

An illustration of how these actions can be combined to effect successful change is described in the following vignette about the introduction of Interactive White Boards (IWBs).

ACHIEVING 'DIGITAL TAKE-OFF' THROUGH INTERACTIVE WHITEBOARDS

A primary school in a growing suburb on the outskirts of a major Australian capital city decided to install interactive whiteboards in all teaching rooms. Within several months all teachers were using the technology. In fact, so rapid was the surge in teacher acceptance that the term 'digital take-off' was coined.

Linked to this 'take-off' were teachers' rapidly rising expectations of what they could do with the new digital resources. Interactive multimedia teaching materials prepared six months earlier, and with much pride, became passé as new possibilities emerged. When all teachers' expectations rose (not just those of the few early adopters'), and when the students' expectations also rose, the momentum for development across the whole school community grew.

The teachers soon came to expect much more of the technology and began questioning not only the teaching possibilities, but also the school operations designed to support the teaching. For example, when 100 per cent of teachers were using the network, they expected it to be operational for 100 per cent of teaching time. They expected swift Internet access from their classroom and, most importantly, immediate support when the technology went amiss. They suddenly wanted to be able to communicate electronically with the parents, to store their interactive teaching materials, and to use the emerging Web 2.0 opportunities.

The executive staff at the school appreciated the implications of 'going digital' and gradually came to understand, particularly when they talked to colleagues in similar situations, that they were now working within a very new paradigm, with few of the operational parameters determined. Moreover, they realised that they were being obliged by their community to develop the school in the new paradigm, while having to work within the traditional established structures and processes of their local education system.

The story highlights the value of technology that is suited to the needs and practices of teachers, and the merit in ensuring that adequate resources and priority are given for its use. It also shows that once teaching materials became predominantly digital, this can act as a catalyst for whole-school development. Teachers' expectations of what can be done with technology grow at a pace and can begin to impact on the school operations and system policy. As a consequence, this places responsibility on school executive and other key members of staff to show leadership—not only in the face of internal demands from their school community, but also in their interactions with, and accountabilities to, education system authorities and other external agencies.

The attributes that make a good school and school system transcend the use of digital technologies. The McKinsey Report (Barber & Mourshed, 2007, p. 19) examining factors underpinning the world's best performing school systems noted that 'the quality of a school system rests on the quality of its teachers'. We agree. In fact, contrary to the proposition that digital technologies lessen the importance of teacher quality, we believe that the more sophisticated digital technologies become, the more 'professional potential' these tools can release in teachers.

PRINCIPALS AS RESPONSIBLE LEADERS IN TECHNOLOGY

Along with quality teachers, the effective development of digital schools requires principals with the capability to lead. Without that commitment and knowledge the school has little chance of becoming a digital school. There are simply too many decisions to be made, variables to be addressed and hurdles to overcome to do so without the full support of the principal.

This means that principals, as the key educational leaders in schools, need to not only understand the technology, but also take and maintain responsibility for that technology and its use. Don't worry—we are not talking about principals having the technical expertise to configure ICT systems or trouble-shoot breakdowns. However, we do believe that the leader of a digital school should have significant operator knowledge and hands-on experience with the technologies in order to appreciate the basic requirements and implications associated with the school's use of digital technologies, especially those related to staffing. Gone are the days when school principals could delegate major technology decisions to IT specialists. The costs and implications are now too high to be 'under-informed'. Indeed, one can hypothesise that as the sophistication of the technology rises, so too will the leadership expertise that is needed to make the best use of it.

In this context, recent research by Moyle (2006) and Lee and Winzenried (2008) is of concern, revealing that relatively few existing and prospective Australian school principals have acquired the understanding required to lead a digital school. This underscores the importance of ongoing professional learning—not only for teachers, but also for principals and other members of the school executive; and this needs to be factored into school development planning.

Planning is important

An international think-tank, organised under the auspices of the Macarthur Foundation in Illinois, USA, recently concluded that:

> *Schools need to become network institutions, establishing themselves as the centre of diverse, overlapping networks of learning, which reach out to the fullest possible range of institutions, sources of information, social groups and physical facilities. To solve this problem schools need to become nodes on a network instead of isolated factories.*

(Illinois Institute of Design, p. 25)

These schools are connected to the point where a seemingly small decision in one area (for example, granting or withholding information access to a single staff member, or student) can have profound impact on others and on school operations. Further, because they are so closely linked to the outside world, the opportunities, risks and demands of external events and issues need to be carefully considered for their impact on the design and delivery of education programs and student achievement.

As a consequence these schools, as highly integrated and networked entities, require new, flexible and holistic models of planning. Moreover, while planning in digital technologies is important, it cannot stand alone or develop separately from the plans and vision for the organisation as a whole. Gone are the days of 'bolt on' technology plans. The power and potential benefits of digital technology, as well as its substantial resource demands, mean that it must be considered in relation to the other elements of school and system planning.

There are two further issues related to planning with digital technology. These are the sway that the major technology corporations have had over the choice of the technology for school use over the last century (Lee & Winzenried, 2008), and the related propensity of schools and education systems to waste immense amounts of money on technology that has had little or no positive impact on teaching, learning or the administration of schools. Dealing with these issues is a continuing leadership challenge that requires school principals, education system executives and policy makers to exercise responsible stewardship in the choice of technology and its integration with the educational, administrative and communication dimensions of their organisations. Such stewardship entails decisions such as whether to buy or lease, or whether to host 'in-house' or externally, as well as taking steps to ensure that the technology chosen:

- supports the desired vision for student learning
- integrates with other digital systems within the school or system
- provides easy and reliable storage, retrieval and analysis of information
- is regularly monitored and evaluated for its effectiveness and value for money including through methodologies that calculate the 'total cost of ownership' of that technology.

Existing evidence from Lee and Winzenried (2008) of the tendency of schools to use digital technologies to better perform the tasks of the past was reflected in the propositions of John Naisbitt over 20 years ago in his groundbreaking work, *Megatrends*. Naisbitt (1984, p. 19) explained that 'new information technologies will at first be applied to old industrial tasks, then, gradually, give birth to new activities, processes and products'.

Naisbitt's propositions were also supported by the research conducted by the Illinois Institute of Design (ID), which observed that:

> [Schools] are following the pattern of what other organisations do when faced with disruptive technology. Time and again, the standard pattern is for organisations to initially ignore disruptive technology, claiming it is not relevant to their core needs. Then they adopt it, using it at first as a faster and better way of doing an existing function. Schools are now in the middle of this first stage of adoption, in which they are using digital media to transform the creation and delivery of information and skills.

> (ID, 2007, p. 51)

However, they go on to conclude that:

> Ultimately schools will not be improved if they only transform the medium of delivering content while ignoring the changes in how organisations work and what society needs.

> (ID, 2007, p. 51)

On this basis it is to be expected most schools are only beginning to explore the teaching and learning options of the digital technologies that have become increasingly available since 2000—in Friedman's (2006) terms, since the beginning of the period of the 'triple convergence'.

As the technology and its use becomes more sophisticated, so too will the magnitude of the dangers and the risk to be borne by the school and system leadership. A series of potential planning pitfalls with digital technologies is presented overleaf.

POTENTIAL PLANNING PITFALLS WITH DIGITAL TECHNOLOGIES

- Being 'conned' by adept technology salespeople and acquiring inappropriate technology
- Not considering the total school needs and the total cost of ownership of the technology
- Wasting considerable money by not paying due regard to implementation, training and embedding the technology
- Bankrupting the school by choosing technology that does not deliver
- Using a staffing model that impedes the desired development
- Failing to set appropriate operational parameters for the digital mode
- Sliding into unrealistic working conditions that crush the staff

---

THE PURPOSE AND POSSIBILITIES OF DIGITAL SCHOOLING

Leading a digital school involves taking a school from the traditional paper-based to a digitally based operational paradigm. Along the way leaders will undoubtedly be obliged to work with a model that blends the paper-based with the digital, the old and the new. The contrasting characteristics of these paradigms are presented in Table 1.1.

But the point of such leadership is not to simply replace 'paper and pens' with 'screens and keyboards'. Rather it is to make a positive difference to the learning of young people through taking advantage of the opportunities that digital technologies offer for:
- enhancing student interest, engagement and learning achievement
- enlivening teaching practice and improving the quality and status of the teaching profession
- supporting efficient organisation and knowledge management in schools and education authorities, and
- providing timely communication between parents, schools, education authorities, governments, community agencies, business and industry.

Learning to use digital technologies in these ways will better position educators to anticipate and respond to needs and demands of students and others, to demonstrate effectiveness and accountability, and to continue to attract, if not increase, investment in education.

Table 1.1 *Characteristics of the paper-based and digitally based paradigms of schooling*

PAPER-BASED SCHOOLING	DIGITALLY BASED SCHOOLING
• Industrial age organisational structures	• Information age organisational model
• Schools operating as discrete, largely stand-alone entities	• Networked, incorporating the total school community and its homes
• A segmented organisational structure, with a widespread division of labour	• Integrated synergistic operations
• Discrete and constant instructional technologies in paper, the pen and the teaching board	• Suite of changing, increasingly sophisticated, converging and networked digital instructional technologies
• Individual lesson preparation	• Increasing collaborative lesson development
• Reliance on mass media	• Interactive multimedia
• Staffing hierarchical, with fixed roles	• Changing flexible team-oriented staff roles
• Well-defined and long-lasting jobs	• Uncertainty, untapped potential, rising expectations and frequent job changes
• Slow segmented paper-based internal communication and information management	• Instant communication and management of digital information across the organisation
• Long established operational parameters	• Few established operational parameters

Leading schools and education systems to provide students with learning opportunities appropriate for the twenty-first century through taking advantage of digital technologies can be immensely exciting and professionally gratifying. Such leaders need to simultaneously address a host of variables. They need to learn on the job, and develop and maintain a macro appreciation of the digital tools, while at the same time fulfilling their 'normal' leadership roles and responsibilities.

If schools are to educate the young for this contemporary 'flat' world, they have to develop digitally. The purpose of this book is to assist schools in doing just that.

CHAPTER **2**

SUCCESSFUL LEARNING AND SCHOOL DESIGN FOR THE KNOWLEDGE AGE

Michael Hough

There is no doubt that developed economies are in the forefront of coping with the impact of global change. It is now possible to recognise patterns and trends in the knowledge-based 'service' economy—which is emerging to overlay (and largely replace) what is often called the 'manufacturing' economy that has provided the basis for much of our managerial and accounting practices and conventional wisdoms over the past 200 years or so.

The following major trends are beginning to emerge as features of the knowledge-based service economy:

- The world economy is globalising at the same time as the demand for individualised and localised service is expanding.
- New knowledge-based technologies now lead societal change, in that they develop and provide options before we have even discussed whether they are socially desirable and acceptable.
- New knowledge-based technologies are changing the ways in which we define ourselves, our family units, our work and work units, and challenging our economic and social order assumptions. The 'way schools are' is one of those assumptions.

In this chapter, I will begin by 'setting the scene' and reviewing the global context, and the challenges this global context provides schools. This review is necessary for two reasons. First, schools are usually accepted as preparing young people for adult life and sorting and optimising student readiness for good jobs, but many schools are still structured and operated to prepare students for a previous economy—that of the manufacturing era. Second, a review of the context will illustrate the amount of turbulence experienced by western economies over the last few decades, and support the argument that younger generations have grown up in a period of constant and significant change.

REVIEWING THE GLOBAL CONTEXT— CHALLENGES FOR SCHOOLS

A range of economic, social, environmental and cultural factors are shaping contemporary life and impacting on organisations across the globe—including schools. The following list is illustrative of the context faced by all countries, their leaders and their peoples:

- widening of the gaps between rich and poor between countries, societal groups and individuals
- increasing global capital flows with the growth of e-commerce (for example, noting that Microsoft is now the twelfth largest economy in the world).
- emerging global virtual organisations, which cross national boundaries and employ staff worldwide
- growth of 'planetism thinking' evidenced by global environmental concerns about climate change and access to clean water.

The impacts of these pressures are being felt in various ways. One is the reduced influence of the nation state. Another is the profound influence that technology is exerting on human behaviour, relationships and personal identity.

Given this context, one of the challenges facing schools is to remain relevant to the lives of students, and central to the requirements of a post-industrial economy in which knowledge and knowledge systems have begun to emerge as the new form of competitive advantage.

A defining characteristic of this post-industrial, knowledge-based society is that it will be constituted by individuals, groups and organisations, connected by digital facilities such as the Internet and e-mail to 'electronic communities'. Those with the opportunity and capability to communicate through digital technologies such as the Web, Internet, mobile phones and PDAs will be members of these communities. Those without will be excluded.

Unfortunately many schools have been slow to appreciate the significance of these electronic communities. On the other hand, their students are becoming very used to the idea of rapid change in their societal realities. Adding further challenge to this situation is the emerging evidence that our younger generations are providing quite different skills and capabilities as they enter both learning and work. The challenges for schools of this dichotomy are significant.

At the same time as this global context is evolving, traditional western economy schools and education systems are experiencing:

- an 'out of balance' demographic with many older teachers about to retire, and a missing middle group caused by a decade of teacher surplus and low levels of regular recruitment by employment systems
- a narrowly focused ICT teacher skill base, with the older group of teachers wary or cautious users of technology
- greater parental interest and involvement in monitoring and influencing the progress of the smaller number of children each family now has and sends to school.

Consequently, a successful futures-oriented school is one that is relevant to and valued by a new style economy, because it is able to contribute to both students and to the economy. In simple terms, an effective 'digital school' helps students to make a living in a global economy, while at the same time it helps them to make a life as a member of the various local, regional and global communities to which they already, or desire to, belong.

Features of younger generations

Our younger generations are strikingly different in terms of their awareness of digital technologies, and many of their attributes and characteristics are premised on '24/7' access to electronic capabilities. To highlight these differences, some key generational characteristics are proposed in Table 2.1. These are based on the comparisons suggested by Sheahan (2005, p. 4) between Baby Boomers (over 40 years of age), Generation X (approximately 26–40 years), and Generation Y (approximately 8–25 years).

These young people are different in their attitudes and capacities as workers, consumers and parents. As a consequence, Mackay (2005) provides the following advice to schools.

- Recognise 'tribal herd' needs. Children rely on the school for a sense of community. Therefore, stress the value of groups and group work. Also provide social contexts for parents, such as parent groups, parent choirs and sports teams.
- Recognise students' value needs. Schools are finding increasing need to give moral instruction, going beyond the curriculum for explicit value

Table 2.1 *Comparing Baby Boomers, Generation X and Generation Y against different influences*

INFLUENCE	BABY BOOMERS	GENERATION X	GENERATION Y
Role models	Men of character	Men and women of character	What is character?
Television	*I Love Lucy*	*Happy Days*	*Jerry Springer*
Musical icons	Elvis	Madonna	Eminem
Music mediums	LPs and EPs	Cassettes and CDs	Digital iPods and MP3s
Computer games	*Pong*	*Pacman*	*Counter Strike*
Money	Earn it	It is not everything	Give it to me
Loyalty to employer	Work my way to the top	Shortcut to the top	Give me Saturday off or I will quit
Respecting your elders	Automatic	Is polite	Whatever!
Sex	After marriage	On the back seat	Online
Change	Resist it	Accept it	Want it
Technology	Ignorant of it	Comfortable	Feel it in their gut
Justice	Always prevails	Up to the courts	If you can afford it

training. Therefore, study philosophers as well as religious leaders, and illustrate issues and examples of choice and consequences. Schools will also have to accept some responsibility for educating parents—in part by providing them with a community.

- Recognise the need for flexibility. In answer to students' concerns, such as 'What else can I do?', 'Can I try everything?' and 'I don't want to be committed too soon', schools can respond by broadening fields of study, delaying vocational choices as long as possible, and refocusing on a liberal education.
- Find ways of blending science and humanities. Try to retain students doing both for as long as possible, and aim to produce scientists with strong understanding of the humanities and vice versa.
- Reduce perceived boredom. Students are outraged and angry at what they perceive they have to go through at secondary school. They see school as designed to be boring. To them, school is about relationships that are only permitted outside the classroom. Therefore,

use the principles of flexibility, meeting tribal needs, creating a sense of community, and giving general broad education, in order to make it more interesting.

(Source: Mackay, 2005)

Further evidence (Hough, 2006) suggests that properly handled and encouraged, the move to digital schooling would be welcomed by members of our younger generations.

Work and job challenges in a new economy

The 'old' model of schooling was developed for and suited to a manufacturing society. Schooling was seen as a preliminary stage of preparation for work, while actual adult work was about carrying out 'work routines' rather than engaging new learning.

In contrast, schooling for a new economy should be focused on the learning needs of all students to participate and contribute to the full range of opportunities that a knowledge-based service economy presents and requires. Flexible, cooperative learners who are confident and capable users of digital technologies are intellectual assets for communities, organisations and societies in these new service and information environments. Within this context, old distinctions between learning and work disappear: learning is regarded as a form of work, work is premised on continuous learning and, as a consequence, 'school' might be properly regarded as the first version of what young people experience as a 'learning organisation' (Senge, 2007).

Successful learning in a knowledge-based society

The general requirements for people to survive and thrive—individually and collectively—in this post-industrial era have been described by Ellyard (2004) in terms of the following set of human learning characteristics:

- Being flexible
- Being adaptive
- Developing to a high degree the set of knowledge, skills and understanding relevant to the current context
- Anticipating and coping with change
- Being skilled in information technologies, and
- Being willing to continue learning across a lifetime.

In looking forward and considering the implications for the design of schooling to promote these characteristics, we first need to appreciate that the format of existing schools is a relatively recent societal invention—essentially to meet the needs of a manufacturing era. We should also draw some inspiration from the fact that throughout history new societal eras have required different forms of learning and 'schooling', as illustrated in Table 2.2.

Table 2.2 *Characteristics of learning across societal eras*

ERA	CHARACTERISTICS OF LEARNING
Nomadic	By observation and practice, occurring in one-to-one or small-group learning situations, and focused on skills of survival (i.e. the physical challenges and training of survival experiences while moving around).
Agricultural	By observation, apprenticeships and small-group learning in more stable community structures, focused on the needs of survival in local and static locations, with some emergence of higher-order social learning (e.g. painting, clothing). Very few schools, with access restricted to the elite and to religious and military orders.
Manufacturing	Adapted to the needs of a society in fixed locations over artificial times, directed at the technology of production and a growing range of higher-order understandings, formalised around codified knowledge. Available to most people through specialist organisations (schools and colleges) based on specialist teacher–class interaction.
Post Industrial	Personalised and cooperative with high levels of customer demand and expectations to meet the needs of a society faced with rapid change; increasingly managed by learners themselves (e.g. by interaction with digital technologies).

Not only have these societal-learning relationships changed, there are corresponding changes to the role and needs of schools, and teaching, as shown in Table 2.3 (page 20).

Differences between learning using digital technologies and traditional learning are presented in Table 2.4 (page 20).

Along with these differences there are associated contrasts in the form and use of learning resources. For example, in traditional learning modes where textbooks are used, the processes of author selection of content, review, editing, proofing, legal scrutiny, and publishing in expected formats to a quality standard involve considerable expense and refinement of content. On the other hand, resources available through digital technologies may be less costly but not reviewed or edited, and may be produced anonymously in idiosyncratic formats with little or

Table 2.3 *Changes in schools and teaching across societal eras*

ERA	SCHOOLS	TEACHING
Nomadic	Did not exist, as they were not needed by that form of society.	One-to-one, naturalistic-based teaching, usually within a family group.
Agricultural	Few existed, and only for an elite. A growing system of apprenticeships as ways of passing on sophisticated skills.	Master–pupil small-group or one-to-one teaching, restructured to narrow ranges of need (e.g. Army/Church).
Manufacturing	Emergence of formal schooling, designed to prepare larger numbers for social roles, with features of production lines and standardised output. Full levels of schooling available only to an elite few.	Teaching as organised labour, the emergence of the pupil–teacher class size concept, with some recognition of teaching as a specialist profession.
Post-industrial	Emergence of new education providers and questions about relevance of formal schooling—'everyone needs learning, but we may not need traditional schools'. Full levels of schooling now available to most.	Focus on learning as well as teaching, with associated challenges for teachers to retain a central, professional role in a community where 'everyone learns' and technology can offer direct learning access.

Table 2.4 *Differences between traditional learning and learning with digital technologies*

TRADITIONAL LEARNING	LEARNING WITH DIGITAL TECHNOLOGIES
Content selected and controlled by teachers (e.g. textbooks)	Content available to students from various sources (e.g. Google, Wikipedia)
Teachers are powerful and students are relatively powerless and teacher-directed	Students share power with teachers who exercise less direct control of learning activities
Passive learning aids (e.g. blackboards and textbooks)	Active learning aids (e.g. interactive whiteboards and web-based software)

no legal scrutiny. Related to this, traditional text-based knowledge is classified using agreed systems, logically organised and retrievable, whereas digitally based systems, though possessing enormous retrieval capability, have less-developed systems of classification.

A second area of contrast associated with the use of digital technologies is the impact on teacher time for personalising the learning of their students. In traditional modes, more time tends to be spent on delivering content and directing student learning, whereas with the use of digital technologies the content may be pre-prepared and give the teacher and the student more time for remedial, extension and higher-order 'value-added' learning activities.

Third, the use of digital technologies can extend the ways in which student learning is demonstrated and assessed. By catering to a wider array of student learning styles, digital technologies have the potential to engage students in different ways. Word-processing and multimedia applications introduce a greater range of possibilities for students to demonstrate their learning achievements than the pen and paper, voice presentation and related performance modes of traditional learning environments.

Successful learning in a knowledge-based society requires openness to the possibilities of digital technologies for enhancing student engagement and learning, improving teaching practices, and redesigning schools for the knowledge-based society of the early twenty-first century. I trust that these analyses have enabled you to reflect on the role and future shape of schools and learning.

In reflecting on the overview that has been presented on the changing nature of learning, teaching and schooling across various societal eras, the message is best summarised by Senge (2007) in these terms: 'We may not recognise a twenty-first century school if we are conditioned to believe what a school should be!'

PLANNING SCHOOLING FOR THE KNOWLEDGE AGE

The final section of this chapter presents some ideas on the shape of schooling and learning for the knowledge age, and offers some suggestions for bringing about the desired changes.

As a starting point to understanding the strategic futures thinking required for planning schooling for the knowledge age, a useful construct is that of *preferred* and *probable* futures. The distinction between these concepts was codified into the futurist literature by Ellyard (1998), and essentially consists of the following advice:

- A *preferred future* is the future that we aim to create or influence to some degree. This implies developing deliberate actions that are aimed at improving the likelihood of positive things occurring, and reducing the likelihood of negative things occurring.
- A *probable future* is the future that we can expect to encounter but which is created substantially by others. Among other things, it incorporates the concepts of 'helplessness' and 'reacting to events'.

A listing of preferred future characteristics of schooling is presented in Table 2.5.

In creating a preferred future, you will need to state what you really mean when using terms like 'school as a learning organisation' or 'knowledge age school'. One practical approach is based on a technique developed by a quality management theorist, Philip Crosby (1980). A 'Crosby Grid' provides a way of describing the future in concrete terms that can be easily understood, as well as the stages in the journey in achieving that future. Its development involves generating a matrix of two complementary logics:

- the Y axis listing the key improvement drivers for change, and
- the X axis containing a graded series of statements ranging from 'don't know about or have this feature' through to 'fully have/fully developed for this feature'.

A well-developed Crosby Grid represents the wisdom of the leaders and staff of the organisation evidenced by their judgment in filling in the details in the grid. Once the details are entered, the completed grid can be used to monitor progress of the change process. The details of the grid can be upgraded and altered as targets are reached or circumstances change.

In designing a Crosby Grid, it is important to select the few key 'change drivers' that you plan to use to change the organisation (the original Crosby Grid selected only five), and then describe the stages of the process that needs to be undertaken to achieve the preferred future.

For our purposes, the Crosby Grid approach can be used to describe the key features of a fully developed 'digital school', by treating the final stage of the grid (Certainty) as a statement of the preferred future for a functioning digital school. A sample of a Digital School Crosby Grid is presented in Table 2.6 (page 25).

You are invited to develop your own Crosby Grid logic to create a more specific school development grid from the statements of a preferred future provided in the sample (Table 2.6), so that the steps of your 'change journey' can be forecast and tracked. An outline framework from which you could begin to approach these tasks is given in Table 2.7 (page 27).

Table 2.5 *Preferred future characteristics of schooling*

NOW (TRADITIONAL SCHOOLS)	PREFERRED FUTURE (SCHOOLS AS LEARNING ORGANISATIONS)
Education occurs at scheduled times in deliberate, physical locations called schools, colleges, universities.	Education is 24/7 and partly occurs in deliberate physical locations called schools, colleges, universities.
Funding is premised on input factors based on the class unit, with class sizes in the range 20–30.	Funding is premised on outcome factors based on the student unit. Class sizes range widely depending on the learning outcome envisaged.
Schools are stand-alone learning agencies.	Schools are networked learning agencies.
Minimal data sharing between schools, parents, business and community.	Much data sharing between schools, parents, business and community.
Teaching is an isolated activity conducted by professional teachers in classrooms.	Teaching is a cooperative activity involving professional teachers, teacher aides, and others.
Curricula and learning methods (including assessment) directed towards individual behaviour and achievement, but achieved through group teaching methods and assessing accumulations of past knowledge and understanding.	Curricula and learning methods (including assessment) directed towards cooperative behaviour and both individual and group outcomes. Achieved through digitally based, individual accessed learning systems that also enable group learning.
Learning is preparation for work and done prior to employment. Individual learning is major focus.	Learning is work, and work depends on both individual and team-based learning.
Teachers drive learning as 'content deliverers' and 'child minders'.	Teachers assist learning as 'knowledge navigators', 'tutors' and 'mentors'.
Teacher time and activities driven by 'duty of care' type monitoring and checking. Physical presence of teacher used as proof of activities discharging duty of care.	Some 'duty of care' responsibilities (e.g. roll marking), undertaken by technologies. Digitally based record systems increasingly used as proof of activities discharging duty of care.

(continued)

Table 2.5 *Preferred future characteristics of schooling (continued)*

NOW (TRADITIONAL SCHOOLS)	PREFERRED FUTURE (SCHOOLS AS LEARNING ORGANISATIONS)
Teacher as a skilled tradesperson/ artisan and deliverer of educational content. Student as passive learner.	Teacher as knowledge professional and student as active learner.
Teacher is hierarchically more senior and powerful than a student.	Cooperative learning teams where teacher expertise in coaching/ assisting/directing is basis of power. Students accepted as knowledgeable and powerful in learning.
Libraries and librarians as separate places and providers of resources.	Libraries and librarians as integral part of the learning community. Librarians seen as skilled 'Web pilots' assisting with accessing information with integrity.
Physical architecture and appearance of schools are main concerns of improvement and upgrade.	Virtual electronic architecture of schools is of equal concern with physical infrastructure.
Physical procedures and controls are well developed, while electronic procedures and controls (e.g. computer access and usage) are seen as peripheral	Digital procedures and controls (e.g. computer access and usage) are central part of routine procedures, with library as a key advice and procedures source.
School as a sorting, testing and labelling organisation that acts as preparation and gatekeeper to a manufacturing society job.	School as a learning organisation that simulates and introduces work in the knowledge society through the behaviour of the whole school community.
Parents are relatively uninvolved, entrust their children to school care, and expect the school to make decisions about their children's learning, while the home environment deals with personal disciplines and values.	Parents expect to be involved through continuous communication, are concerned about the progress and care experienced by their (much fewer) numbers of children. Expect that school will discipline the child and instil values rather than the home, but complain if they disagree with what is done.

Table 2.6 Sample Digital School Crosby Grid

MEASUREMENT CATEGORIES	STAGE I: UNCERTAINTY ('WE DON'T HAVE IT')	STAGE II: AWAKENING	STAGE III: ENLIGHTENMENT	STAGE IV: WISDOM	STAGE V: CERTAINTY ('WE HAVE ACHIEVED IT')
Leadership and management understanding and attitude	No comprehension of digital learning as a leadership and management tool. Tend to 'blame technology' (e.g. mobile phones) for problems.	Recognise that digital learning management may be of value but not willing to provide money or time to make it all happen.	While going through digital learning program, learn more about ICT-based capabilities; becoming supportive and helpful.	Participate. Understand absolutes of digitally based learning and learning organisations. Recognise their personal role in continuing ICT emphasis.	Consider digital learning and digital systems an essential part of school system.
ICT-based organisation status	ICT base is hidden in separate activities and departments. ICT-based learning largely absent. Emphasis on teacher-based selection and delivery of content.	A stronger ICT-based learning officer is appointed but main emphasis is still on teacher delivery of content. ICT is still part of individual efforts or subsections of the school.	Chief Information Officer appointed, reports to executive of school, all ICT-based activities are incorporated, and CIO has role in management of school.	CIO is a senior executive member of the school. ICT learning has status and is reported on and preventive action taken. CIO involved with student learning and launches special ICT improvement assignments.	CIO is a key decision maker at school and on school board or district. Prevention is the thought leader.

(continued)

Table 2.6 Sample Digital School Crosby Grid (continued)

MEASUREMENT CATEGORIES	STAGE I: UNCERTAINTY ('WE DON'T HAVE IT')	STAGE II: AWAKENING	STAGE III: ENLIGHTENMENT	STAGE IV: WISDOM	STAGE V: CERTAINTY ('WE HAVE ACHIEVED IT')
Problem handling	Problems are fought as they occur; no resolution; inadequate definition; lots of yelling and accusations.	Teams are set up to attack major problems. Long-range solutions are not solicited.	Corrective action communications established. Problems are faced openly and resolved in an orderly way.	Problems are identified early in their development. All functions are open to suggestion and improvement.	Except in the most unusual cases, problems are prevented.
ICT-based improvement actions	No organised activities. No understanding of such activities.	Trying obvious motivational short-range efforts.	Implementation of an ICT-based change program with thorough understanding and establishment of each step.	Continuing the ICT-based change program. Make certain it is accepted.	ICT-based learning improvement is a normal and continued activity.
Summation of school's digital usage posture	'We don't know why we have problems with digital based systems.'	'Is it absolutely necessary to always have problems with ICT-based digital systems?'	'Through management commitment to improvement of our digital learning and admin systems we are identifying and resolving our problems.'	'Defect prevention in digital systems is a routine part of our operation.'	'We know why we do not have problems with digitally based systems.'

Table 2.7 Features of a partial Crosby Grid

MEASUREMENT CATEGORIES	STAGE I: UNCERTAINTY ('WE DON'T HAVE IT')	STAGE II: AWAKENING	STAGE III: ENLIGHTENMENT	STAGE IV: WISDOM	STAGE V: CERTAINTY ('WE HAVE ACHIEVED IT')
School leadership understanding and attitude	No comprehension of ICT-based education as a leadership tool. Tend to blame others for 'ICT-based problems'.	Recognise that ICT-based schools and learning may be of value, but not willing to provide resources or time to make it all happen.	While going through ICT-based learning improvement program, learn more about benefits of ICT-based education; becoming supportive and helpful.	Participate. Understand principles and benefits of ICT-based learning. Recognise their personal role in continuing emphasis.	Consider ICT-based learning an essential part of school system.
Societal attitudes	Society sees public schools as a cost and invests in them reluctantly.				Society values digital schools highly and resources them well.
Parental attitudes	Parents are uninvolved and disinterested in the school.				Parents see the school as an essential partner for their child's success.
Teacher attitudes	Teachers as 'content deliverers' with classroom control role.				Teachers as 'knowledge navigators' and mentors to students.

(continued)

Table 2.7 Features of a partial Crosby Grid (continued)

MEASUREMENT CATEGORIES	STAGE I: UNCERTAINTY ('WE DON'T HAVE IT')	STAGE II: AWAKENING	STAGE III: ENLIGHTENMENT	STAGE IV: WISDOM	STAGE V: CERTAINTY ('WE HAVE ACHIEVED IT')
Student attitudes	Students see school as divorced from their world and boring.				Students access a fully integrated digital system to underpin their school learning.
Learning characteristics	Traditional teacher- and textbook-based learning.	Introduction of ICT means that existing learning is done more efficiently and effectively.			Learning has explored and used the change potential of technologies to the full.
Architecture	Architecture supports 'factory model' of schooling with fixed class sizes and standard curriculum.				Physical and virtual architecture supports digital learning.

CONCLUSION

Successful learning and school design for the knowledge age is a multifaceted challenge. It requires a contemporary understanding of the nature and potential of digital technology, and a broad appreciation of the context of schooling and how the major features of teaching, learning and school organisation have been shaped by societal trends from earlier times.

This chapter has highlighted possibilities, explained the context and provided some advice on planning tools, such as the Crosby Grid, to assist educational leaders to describe and create the preferred future for their schools and education systems as we move further into the knowledge age.

As educators, 'we live in interesting times', to paraphrase a Confucian curse. The advent of digital technologies, global trends, changing family and societal structures, the demands and opportunities from business and governments, and the vitality and talents of our students will certainly ensure that those engaged with school education over the coming years continue to do so.

CHAPTER 3

PLANNING IN A DIGITAL SCHOOL

Allan Shaw

Planning for a 'digital school' is essentially about achieving high-quality outcomes through the creative and appropriate use of digital technologies. Plans for the digital aspect—that is, the technical infrastructure—are an important part, but just a part, of overall school and system planning that must have high-quality student learning outcomes as the top priority.

The intent of this chapter is to provide guidelines to assist you in the planning process. The key planning elements for a digital school are presented. Some significant dimensions of situational analysis as a process of 'getting to know your present and future environments' are then discussed. These form the basis for considering the planning process in more detail, particularly ways of combining short- and long-term planning to achieve results. Finally some suggestions are made to assist school and education system leaders with the challenge of translating plans into practice.

FOCUS ON PEOPLE NOT MACHINES: PLANNING ELEMENTS FOR A DIGITAL SCHOOL

Planning is a *people process*. The temptation when thinking about digital environments is to believe that planning is primarily about the technology. However, the keys to successful planning for a digital school have more to do with taking account of leadership styles, school culture, politics, relationships and emotions, than they do with engaging in research and analysis, or deciding on the allocation of resources. After all, the focus of a digital school is people, not machines. The experience of those who work and learn in a digital school should be a humanising one, driven by conducive values and school culture towards achieving better learning outcomes for students.

All plans should be designed to have a positive impact on teachers' classroom practices and students' achievements. Further, as a people process, planning must engage the school community, especially staff. The teacher in the classroom is the single most powerful influence within a school on student learning (Barber & Mourshed, 2007). As such, plans need to be developed in consultation with teachers, with expert assistance provided when needed. Implementation has to be well led by the principal and staff, with the outcomes carefully analysed and reflected upon by those in the school community on which they have an effect.

ELEMENTS OF THE PLANNING PROCESS

1   *Vision and goals, values and beliefs:* Where are you going? What will it be like when you get there? Why make the journey? How will you travel?

2   *People:* Who is travelling with you on the planning journey? Who else should be invited along? What do these people bring to the process?

3   *Facts and analysis:* What is the environment in which your school operates—locally, regionally, nationally and globally? What is the actual and ideal learning and teaching environment in your school? What resources have you got? What results are gained from them? What does your school need (rather than want) to 'live its vision' and achieve its goals?

4   *Policy, practice and procedure:* Are current school policies, programs and practices efficiently and effectively supporting teaching and learning? Will they support the desired change?

Notes:

- The term 'you' can apply to you as an educational leader, to your school community, or to your system, whichever is more useful.

- These elements and questions have been expanded into a series of templates that can be adapted and used to support you in your planning journey. (Full information on the templates can be found in Appendix 1. They are also available in digital format on the AHISA website at http://www.ahisa.com.au.)

Planning in a people-rich environment like a school is complex. Although structure and sequence are important, planning is not a linear process. It is a holistic one that should encompass the four elements, described below. Associated with each element is a set of questions to be considered by educational policymakers. These questions can help you, as an educational leader, identify the implicit values and beliefs that influence planning, and describe the environments, understandings and skill sets that form the context for planning. The questions are by no means exhaustive or prescriptive.

Successful planning involves each of these elements. To make your planning efforts worthwhile, you should have a vision of the future—or at least a vision for the process of getting there. Second, you need to know the needs, talents and aspirations of the people affected by the plans, and engage them in the process. Third, you need to collect and analyse relevant data about your school or system, its environment, its day-to-day operation and outcomes, and use this information to challenge your beliefs and ideology, not just confirm them. Finally you need to consider how existing policies, programs and practices will align or conflict with the planning process, and be prepared to adjust one or the other in light of that consideration.

Situational analysis: *What is happening here? What's coming over the hill?*

Planning implies that you are aiming to be somewhere other than where you are now. For schools, envisioning a way forward can be difficult as the staff, students and parents as members of the school community have their own experience of school and, most likely, some entrenched beliefs about what school should or should not be.

Planning is complicated by technological and generational change and global effects that lie beyond the influence of schools. For these reasons, to plan effectively, you need to carefully examine your beliefs and consider not only your current situation but also your possible, probable and preferred future operating environments.

The global scene

When looking to the future from a global perspective, you might think about the impact of increasing numbers of mathematics, science and technology graduates in China and India on the career prospects of your students, on your nation's economic development and on what you can do, in your local situation, to minimise the negative and accentuate the positive effects of these trends for your school community.

The student scene

As a second scenario, you may wish to consider the students who will form your school's intake in (say) 2012, and the world into which they will graduate. For example, students who will form the secondary school intake of 2012 are currently around eight years of age. These children are in Year 3 and (perhaps with exceptions due to levels of affluence) are immersed in mobile phones, the Internet and iPods. What are the characteristics and needs of these students of 'Generation Z'? And for children for whom the Internet is not the norm, how do their characteristics differ, if at all? School leaders and staff of secondary schools need to be talking to the teachers of these students now.

Similarly, the babies of 2008 will join primary schools around 2013 and graduate from school in 2026. As a primary school principal or teacher, you should be researching and discussing the balance of basic skills, attitudes and values these young children need in order to flourish in the adult world of 2026.

Your considerations will continue to be influenced by rapid technological developments. For example, remember back to 2002—iPods were just gathering momentum and MySpace, Bebo and Facebook were unknown in most schools and homes. But regardless of the individual piece of new technology, the issues you confront as educators are inherently human issues.

The staff scene

As a third scenario: what about your own school staff, who are increasingly drawn from Generation X and Generation Y? If you are not one of them, how well do you understand their motivations, their values and beliefs about work? If you are one of them, how do you work through the retirements of the baby boomers, and induct their younger replacements into your school culture?

PLANNING PRAGMATICALLY IN CHANGING TIMES

Plans for short-term projects need to be specific and detailed, whereas plans for a longer period can follow a more strategic approach where the policies, programs, processes, performance indicators, and sometimes even the purposes of the plan, tend to evolve as circumstances change.

Planning with digital technologies requires both short- and long-term thinking and action. Short-term planning, such as that involved with the installation of hardware to support local area networks or the trialling of new software applications, requires clear and agreed project management guidelines. At the same time, articulating and deciding on the ways in which these types of projects connect with one another and, most importantly, with the overall direction for the school community or system, requires a longer and broader planning perspective from policymakers.

Venezky and Davis (2002) reinforce this view with their contention that planning in digital technologies is not simply a technical issue. In fact, they argue that:

> The highest returns on ICT in education appear to come when ICT is seen as part of a strategy for solving an important problem rather than as an end in itself. (p. 46)

Linking the various short-term projects in digital technology that a school or system might have in place to a longer-term strategic plan is not a simple task. You should not presume that each particular piece of the 'project management jigsaw puzzle' will automatically fit together to form a coherent and appealing strategic organisational picture. In fact, to avoid a jumbled mess, you need to have a plan for how all the various project plans can come together.

One means of completing the 'planning jigsaw' successfully is to develop a *scope document* for each short-term project. This is a useful device for describing what will be included and what will not be included in each project. A well-defined project scope not only gives those involved directly and indirectly in the project an opportunity to understand how the proposed initiative fits with other projects and the overall strategy, but also helps to prevent 'specification creep'—that tendency of people to ask for a project to do more and more (without necessarily having to pay for it, of course!)

The sort of planning that combines short- and long-term goals and activities is necessarily pragmatic. Long-term thinking needs to be combined with short-term action—otherwise the thinking remains just somebody's dream, and the action makes no sense. When thinking and action are combined effectively, something practical and strategic happens. It gets the job done!

FROM PLANNING TO IMPLEMENTATION

As we all know, the best-laid plans can go awry. An understanding of key groups of people in your school is essential if you are to translate planning into implementation. Two of the most significant groups are teachers and parents.

Support your teachers

Teaching is a strongly habitual profession and development can subside, with regression back towards the traditional norms, unless teachers see the point of changing their practices and are given appropriate challenges and support.

Some change processes are more effective than others. Vernez, Karam, Mariano and DeMartini (2006) found that teachers who regarded their training as inadequate, reported a lukewarm commitment to adopting their school's reform model. However, in schools where the level of teacher support increased, so too did teachers' adoption of new practices.

Communicate with parents

You need to engage parents in the planning process to increase the likelihood of successful implementation. You need to get to know them, and assist them in understanding the educational needs and experiences of their children.

Many current parents are Generation X. These parents are better educated than previous generations. They have their children later and have fewer of them, and tend to be more 'time poor' than 'resource poor'.

The first of the children of Generation Y are starting school now. These parents have grown up with media that have become increasingly interactive and portable, starting with videos, personal computers, computer games, and moving on to the Internet, mobile phones and so on. The dramatic changes in information content and distribution through their lives to this point mean that Generation Y parents are not as willing to be passive in accepting information or knowledge as the previous generations. They take their childrearing seriously and leave few stones unturned in wanting the absolute best for their children. They have high expectations of schools, with an emphasis on the individualisation of learning for their children.

In fact, Generation Y parents expect to co-create, co-filter or collaborate in knowledge production, rather than accept a 'top-down' distribution of knowledge. The didactic model of the 'expert' informing the 'learner' has less credence with them—so principals and system authorities who are fond of making pronouncements from on high, beware!

One way to encourage parents' support is to develop a parent engagement strategy with long-, medium- and short-term goals and activities that are linked to demonstrate consistency in approach and build parent, staff and student confidence over time. Regular review and 'refreshment' cycles should be built into the strategy to account for student and parent turnover and other changing circumstances.

Other aspects of the strategy to encourage parent engagement might include:

- using a variety of information presentation processes to reach parents, such as workshops, forums, newsletters, Web publications such as wikis and blogs
- developing a parenting resources library and referral services covering areas such as: child development (especially cognitive and social development), communication, discipline, confidence building and relationship building
- focusing on the provision of other services as needs arise, such as grief and loss, rites of passage, sole-parenting and step-parenting.

Engaging parents through good communication and well-targeted support and educational services builds community support, improves planning, encourages implementation and increases the likelihood of successful outcomes for students. A future created with parents is more self-sustaining than one developed by the school alone.

CONCLUSION

The planning of a digital school is complex, involving multiple stakeholders and various factors. *The creation of a digital school is always a work in progress.*

This complex and changing context means that educational planners at school or system levels are well advised to focus on 'the people' at least as much as 'the technology'. Second, any planning related to the technical aspects of the school or system operation must be integrated with the overall vision, structure and processes of the organisation as a whole.

Third, those charged with leading the planning process need to know the environment in which their school or system is situated locally and globally in terms of its present and future opportunities and challenges. Fourth, to make the most of the opportunities and effectively confront the challenges, educational planners have to work pragmatically, balancing short- and long-term perspectives and actions as necessary to get the job done.

Finally, as planning is essentially a people process, those engaged with planning for a digital school should take careful note of those who are most important in bringing those plans to fruition—their teachers and the parents or guardians of their students.

CHAPTER 4

ENGAGEMENT WITH DIGITAL TECHNOLOGY: NEW CHALLENGES FOR SCHOOL AND SYSTEM LEADERS

Mal Lee and Michael Gaffney

School principals and education system officers face new challenges in leading schools into the digital age. These are educational and administrative in nature and concern the need to learn about the potential benefits and costs of new technologies, to build their capability, to take strategic action to maximise the benefits and minimise the costs, and to play an active role in decision making about the planning, implementation and outcomes resulting from investment in digital technology in their school communities and systems.

As the senior educational architects, principals and education authority leaders need not only to understand the building materials they will be working with but, importantly, maintain responsibility for that technology and its use.

To meet these challenges, principals not only need to have a general understanding of the digital technology infrastructure in their school, but also provide effective oversight of how that technology is being used in classrooms to support teaching and learning; in school administration to manage information; and with parents, the school community, the system, other schools, governments and outside agencies to communicate and demonstrate accountability to these key stakeholders.

Digital technology is increasingly being used in teaching, administration and for communication between the school and the outside world. Moreover, that technology is rapidly evolving, becoming more sophisticated and in need of more frequent renovation than the 'bricks and mortar' physical infrastructure of the traditional school. Most school leaders are only too aware that this growing sophistication and need for renovation is usually accompanied by increasing costs and expectations from students, teachers and parents. One sobering aspect of this trend is that as technology evolves, it is likely to take an even larger slice of school and system budgets— unless, of course, the size of the overall school funding cake is increased proportionally or the current funding cake is re-divided.

In practical terms, this means that educational leaders at school and system levels will increasingly be required to make prudent and yet 'predictably novel' decisions about investment in digital technology. One of the most difficult aspects of making decisions about technology is that one is usually faced with new circumstances, options, costs and protocols for which past planning and administrative experience is of limited value. By comparison, developing plans, gaining funding approval, tendering and oversighting the construction of, for instance, a new school classroom block are relatively straightforward exercises. With investment in digital technology there are fewer signposts and established customs, practices and formulas compared with those administered by state and national capital funding authorities for school building projects. Further, investment decisions about digital technology are likely to become even more complicated by the greater potential benefits as well as escalating level of risk associated with the increasing sophistication and use of that technology.

By highlighting that principals and system officers are responsible for the budgeting, selection, deployment, use and evaluation of digital technology, we are not suggesting that they have daily 'hands-on' tasks. Rather, their role is to monitor how that technology is being used to support teaching, manage information, and communicate in ways which align with their school and system vision and mission, organisational arrangements, teaching practices and community characteristics, and which ultimately serve to enhance the learning outcomes of students. Principals and education system officers who are not capable or willing to accept these new leadership challenges are likely to abdicate their responsibility to ICT experts and wear the consequences.

On the other hand, for those who are willing to lead their schools and systems into the digital age, the question is: How might principals and education system decision makers develop their capability to meet the challenges associated with the development, use and investment in digital technology?

Following are some proposed themes and suggested actions that educational leaders in schools and systems might consider. In Chapter 15, we suggest some ways of enhancing one's own understanding of the digital materials with which you could be working.

SHAPING AND SELECTING DIGITAL TECHNOLOGIES

Over the last century, and particularly over more recent times, the 'selection' of the technology used in schools has been strongly influenced de facto by the major technology corporations.

While schools and education authorities have chosen the brands and models, the 'choice' of the technology has invariably been out of their hands (Lee & Winzenried, 2008). From the point of their design and introduction, forms of new technology (including film, radio, television, VCRs, electronic calculators, computer-aided instruction, personal computers, audiocassette recorders and interactive multimedia CD-ROMs) were designed primarily for the wider consumer or office market. Schools were only ever a secondary market, with the consequence that school and education authorities were usually swept along by the hype generated by the marketing arms of those technology corporations.

The prime motive of all technology corporations is—and always has been—making profit. If the technology providers can convince schools and education authorities, as secondary markets, to add to their company profits, so much the better. In retrospect, it should not be a surprise that most of the electronic instructional technology of the last century that was not designed for class use has been so little used by teachers.

In recent years, some education authorities and schools have begun to exert more influence over the selection of the digital technology, and have used their market strength to shape the type of technology they want. Becta, the government body formed by the British Government to oversee the development of digital schooling in the British Isles, has, for example, since the early 2000s very much taken 'control' of the technology used by schools and has had a profound impact on the nature of the interactive whiteboard technology used not only in the UK but globally, the development of interactive, multimedia teaching materials, the development of learning platforms and online student reporting.

All digital technology moves through a life cycle (Lee & Winzenried, 2008). In the initial stage there will be immense hype, usually exaggerated claims about the effectiveness of the technology, invariably glitches and most assuredly inflated pricing. In time, the price will fall and the initial shortcomings will be overcome. All technology has a finite life, but some forms will last longer than others. In this respect, it is wise (as Roger Hayward warns in Chapter 7) to avoid being at the 'bleeding edge' in your purchasing or leasing of new technologies.

It is not easy to exercise influence when the technology is developing at such a pace and major breakthroughs seem to appear from nowhere. Principals and education system officers need to develop their capability to understand technology, ask the hard questions, and shape how technology could be used to enhance their school and education system and outcomes for students.

Exercise 4.1

Require—for a trial period—that all hardware and software decisions be pre-ceded with a brief rationale for the principal/system executive, explaining how the item(s) fit within the school/system total schema of technology acquisitions.

MANAGING ENTHUSIASM: FROM EARLY ADOPTION TO SUSTAINED WIDESPREAD USE

When selecting digital technology to support teaching and learning, the aim should be for that technology to be used by all teachers, and become as accepted as the pen, paper and the traditional teaching board. As part of the selection process, it is important to encourage trialling and development of new technologies, and carefully monitor the effects of those technologies on teaching practice, student outcomes and school costs. Innovative teachers are usually the ones to put their hands up and 'give it a go'.

One of the interesting challenges is managing the enthusiasm of 'early adopters' and their quest to acquire and use every new piece of technology, whether it is the latest communication device, educational software, or social networking facility. While one should not wish to quash the enthusiasm of the early adopters or prevent their exploration of new educational opportunities, these individuals should be encouraged to ask and report on the hard questions about the educational appropriateness of the technology for students, in schools, *at this time*.

The use of new technologies by early adopters does not automatically translate to acceptance by other teachers, most of whom do not share their innate love of technology. Nevertheless, early adopters can play an important 'research' role for schools and education authorities when their enthusiasm and engagement with new technologies are incorporated within a carefully designed research and development framework, based around the broader needs of schools, teachers and students.

Exercise 4.2

Play the devil's advocate with each request for acquiring an emerging techno-logy. Have 'early adopters' submit an explanation of how and why it should be used by all (or at least a significant proportion of) teachers or students.

ACHIEVING DIGITAL INTEGRATION

One of the characteristics of a digital school is the 'seamless' integration of the school's digital information and communication systems, and the facility to provide online access, through one Web portal, to appropriate services for everyone within the school's networked community.

Such integration and facility require deliberate action by principals at the school level, and by education authority executives at system level. As a first step, this might include undertaking an audit of how data is collected and stored, how major software applications are used, and how information is accessed. When carried out effectively, the results can inform strategic decisions about:

- the purchase and use of core applications, and the training required for those applications
- school (or system) website design, presence and access
- content and records management, including data warehousing.

Achieving the technical integration is relatively straightforward compared with the more important challenge of aligning any changes in technical capacity and processes with the needs, interests, capabilities, and work flow patterns of staff. In this respect, careful attention needs to be given to how roles may be redesigned or the organisation restructured to achieve the desired alignment.

It is important to remember that people are more important than technology, and every effort should be made to inform and engage staff in achieving 'digital integration' across a school or school system. For these changes to be successful, people need to work together in the hope of better outcomes for students—rather than defend competing empires in the fear of losing control or organisational prestige.

Exercise 4.3

Consider understanding the digital integration exercise 15.3 in Chapter 15 (page 184).

BALANCING INTERNAL AND EXTERNAL CONTROL

How does one decide which services will be controlled by the school, or system, and which will be delegated to outside bodies?

In a networked world, most digital information and communication systems used by schools and systems could be hosted and controlled by external bodies. For example, the school's website, email system, student information, publications and teaching resources could all be hosted by an external agency—located across the street or across the globe. Where this occurs, there need to be clear contractual arrangements and obligations agreed between the relevant education authority and the external agency to control the use of information.

The question of whether to hand over control is a vexed one for educators. The answer depends on a host of practical as well as policy issues. At a practical level, bandwidth, the cost and expertise to host professional databases, and the cost of developing and sustaining in-house services need to be considered.

On the policy side, technology corporations and government agencies are prone to promising more than they can deliver. These companies and agencies come and go. Can schools trust them with its data?

In most cases schools are tending to opt for an amalgam of in-house and external service providers. Whichever course is taken, the principal remains responsible for taking these decisions—not a network manager.

Exercise 4.4

What technical and non-technical services does your school/system currently outsource? Why were these arrangements put in place? Are they providing overall benefits to your organisation? Which services do you think could be outsourced and which might be brought in-house?

MANAGING RISK

While there are opportunities to be realised in moving into the 'less-charted' waters of the digital mode, there are also potential dangers—even disasters—waiting to occur. One is the failure to manage risk.

Not only can (and undoubtedly, will) principals be held responsible for poor choice and loss of teaching time, they also stand to lose their job for wasting money or as a result of legal action for inappropriate use of the technology. Already the authors have seen principals entering into 'questionable' long-term ICT solutions that have seen the school unable to maintain its repayments. The new intellectual property (IP) laws—unless watched very closely and with appropriate parameters established—could see school principals taken to court in future years, even after they have retired.

Schools (and especially principals!) are putting themselves at severe risk of legal action when they do not have appropriate network redundancy and disaster plans, data backup, exigencies to cover the loss of key staff expertise and appropriate student Internet usage.

Perhaps one of the more surprising risks that all can fall for is the reliance on a key individual, be it for staff support, network design, the digital integration or any other key operation. Unfortunately, like failing to save key documents, the tendency is to learn only from bitter experience the importance of working towards sustainable solutions and minimising the risk.

Exercise 4.5

Ask your network manager to explain how your school (or system) intranet and website are secured, how staff and student internet usage is monitored, and how databases are backed up.

SECURING SCHOOL INFORMATION ASSETS

As schools move further into the digital age, they will build up extensive and valuable information assets that need to be protected, managed and archived.

Among the most valuable of the holdings are digital teaching resources developed by staff. These resources can add to the richness and efficiency of the teaching in the school (and possibly even to its revenue stream). But these will remain only 'potential' resources unless school leaders exercise their responsibility, and put systems in place to collect, categorise, store and regularly review and cull them. The unfortunate alternative is that these resources will either be wiped by well-intentioned network managers, or taken by the teachers when they leave the school.

Exercise 4.6

Ask your teaching staff to identify what digital resources they have developed and are currently sharing or wish to share with colleagues. Engage them in a review, or development, of your school or system policy on intellectual property.

MANAGING INFORMATION

The digital technology can provide school and system leaders with timely valuable information on the workings and outcomes being achieved by the school and the system. This information relates to many of the following areas:

- student census and achievement data
- curriculum and timetable including class size and teaching load
- human resource management including payroll information, staff qualifications and professional development
- program budget planning and control statements
- capital expenditure
- maintenance of the physical plant
- school funding, fees and contributions; and
- use of the library and ICT infrastructure.

Those leading and working in schools require ready access to information relevant to their areas of responsibility. In some instances the information will be mainly for tactical use; for instance, when it is necessary to quickly ascertain when a request was submitted, who has actioned it and when, and what is the current situation. Calls from parents or arranging relief teachers are examples that come to mind.

On other occasions the information needs to be more strategic and presented in the form of a report—perhaps drawing from different databases and areas of the organisation. Examples include information to assist policy and program evaluation and development, annual budgets or major investment decisions.

In either circumstance, schools need the information and knowledge management systems in place to obtain a ready insight into the short- and long-term effectiveness and efficiency of their operation. Principals and education system executives should insist on the selection and use of systems that provide that capability.

Exercise 4.7

Ask your executive staff—educational and administrative—to provide a report to you on the operations of their area of responsibility for the last month, using the information systems available.

OVERSEEING THE TECHNOLOGY AND EDUCATION DIRECTION

Principals and system leaders have the responsibility to ensure that the technology chosen is consonant with the educational goals of the school and the education system.

They have the opportunity to take 'a helicopter view of the educational and digital landscape' in which their schools and systems are situated. They are in a privileged position to view the totality and identify how what is being contemplated, or being done, might enhance school outcomes and student learning. The importance of that perspective will become more important as the range of community expectations and accountabilities and digital offerings increases.

One related area that warrants attention is the nature of some of the emerging learning platforms. Without due consideration, schools may find themselves opting for platforms that promote low-level content-driven learning rather than the creative, higher-order thinking. School leaders need to continue to carefully evaluate the underlying rationale of any educational software.

The other area to watch is the technology and accompanying protocols designed for office use. Principals should be willing to question and vary some of those practices. One example would be to ask:

Why it is educationally appropriate to get early childhood students to change their network password each week?

or:

Might it be more educationally beneficial to get students to use their own name and to teach them the value of respecting each other's property?

Our experience reveals that too many school leaders have been inclined to go with the flow and not pose the educational questions.

Exercise 4.8

Work with your teachers and technical support staff to develop a checklist of characteristics that proposed educational software and organisational protocols should exhibit for implementation in your school.

NETWORKING WITH THE HOME TECHNOLOGY

While the young continue to embrace the everyday use of digital technology and use it to further their learning, the awareness and use of that learning by educators in school and classroom settings are limited.

The amount of digital 'instructional technology' within most homes will always exceed that in most classrooms (Lee & Winzenried, 2008). In a networked world where schools are no longer stand-alone entities but rather part of the larger learning community, it is important for school leaders to take account of the level of technology in students' homes or hands when making decisions regarding the school's acquisition of technology and the design of its instructional program.

Schools obviously cannot control the technology that parents make available to their sons and daughters, but they can work with parents and provide advice about management and choice of hardware and software to support their children's education. Our view is that most parents would welcome guidance.

Better educational and more cost-efficient use can be made of technology within the home and in the school. Current thinking and expenditure appears predicated on trying to duplicate the resources of the home in the school. For example, why should schools, education systems or governments outlay considerable recurrent funding on laptops for students when they can access their personal, online learning space at school *and* at home, and mediate between the two by the use of an inexpensive USB drive?

Exercise 4.9

Audit the hardware and educational software available in the homes of your students. Engage students, parents and school board members in discussion about how these resources can be used to provide more efficient use of teaching and learning time, and investment of digital technology in the home and at school.

FINANCING THE TECHNOLOGY

There are at least two givens for educators seeking to develop the capability for funding investments in digital technology. The first is there is never enough money. The second is that 'going with the flow' will no longer suffice.

The best way for school and system leaders to work with this context is to take strategic investment decisions that maximise the benefits that digital technology holds for the students in their care. This means that they need to set clear operational parameters, review the use of existing technology, question the return on investment, and (as best they can in changing and uncertain times) channel the scarce resources towards the use of technology that will lead their schools and systems into the digital age.

Some tips for approaching these tasks are to:

- look at the *total cost of ownership* of the technology, and not just the upfront cost (see Chapter 11)
- consider, as a priority, those models that provide the appropriate digital technology in *all* teaching rooms
- take account of the technology in students' homes, look for efficiencies and work to address equity issues.

By way of comparison on the international scene, the USA is continuing its quest for 'ubiquitous computing' with the desire to have a 1:1 computer–

student ratio. On the other hand, the UK and Mexico are questioning the educational wisdom of this approach, particularly given the continuing low level of teacher use of personal computers in teaching. Instead, these countries have opted for a model that makes extensive use of interactive whiteboards (IWBs) and digital peripherals. It is also less costly in terms of hardware leasing and licensing arrangements.

Moving schools from a traditional industrially based structure to a digital platform costs money. As schools make greater use of digital technology, they will be obliged to spend a greater proportion of their budget on hardware, software and connectivity associated with that technology. The current proportion of the total education budget in most nations is between 2 and 3 per cent (Anderson & Becker, 1999, p. 6).

That improvement can come from a special infusion of monies by governments, such as seen in the UK in the 2000s, or by diverting some of the existing budget, such as has been evidenced in Singapore. The obvious, albeit contentious source, from which to divert some monies is the staffing allocation. While not wanting to get into a debate about staffing, suffice it say that with the ever-smarter instructional technology it is probably timely to rethink the size of classes (as per the McKinsey study of 2007), or the nature of teaching at the post-compulsory years, to make do with a few less staff and to divert those funds to instructional technology for K–12 schooling.

Exercise 4.10

Audit the total cost of ownership of the digital technology infrastructure in your school or system. Engage your community in discussion about the demonstrated outcomes and the cost benefit resulting from the investment.

CONCLUSION

In leading schools into the digital age, principals and education system officers need to understand the digital technology they will be working with, and maintain oversight of that technology as developments occur.

In his bestselling book, *The World Is Flat*, Thomas Friedman (2006) uses the concept of 'triple convergence' to explain the rapidly changing and powerful forces shaping global economics and politics (see also Chapter 1).

He explains triple convergence as the coming together of *new players* from various parts of the world, particularly China and India, *on a new playing field* largely constructed from recent developments in digital technology, *developing new processes and habits for horizontal collaboration* as they grow more and more accustomed to using that technology.

Friedman goes on to predict that:

> Giving so many people access to all these tools of collaboration, along with the ability through search engines and the Web to access billions of pages of raw information, ensures that the next generation of innovations will come from all over Planet Flat. The scale of the global community that is soon going to be able to participate in all sorts of discovery and innovation is something the world has simply never seen before. (p. 212)

These predictions have tremendous implications for education and the work of educational leaders. The message from them is to engage broadly and deeply with digital technology. The future of your systems and schools—and, more importantly, the life chances of your students—depend on it.

CHAPTER 5

FOSTERING DIGITALLY BASED TEACHING AND LEARNING: STRATEGIC CONSIDERATIONS

Glenn Finger

How can teaching and learning be enriched by the digital technologies becoming available to students in their homes, their classrooms and their everyday lives?

This is a strategic challenge for teachers and education policy makers, and one for which the stakes are high—in terms of the outcomes for students, the expectations and the professional status of teachers, and the levels of investment in technology by schools, systems and governments.

In this chapter, three key strategic considerations are discussed. These are: the changing expectations of teachers associated with the introduction of new technologies; the ways to enable more effective usage of digital technologies (DT); and the new understandings of the relationship between emerging technologies and theories of learning described under the general label of 'connectivism' (Siemens 2004). This concept suggests that technology is, in fact, altering the way people think and learn. From a connectivist perspective, learning to 'know how' and 'know what' is being supplemented by learning to 'know where'.

Achieving 'digital take-off', whereby these strategic considerations are taken into account and the opportunities provided by the digital mode are essed to enrich teaching and learning, requires different. he nature of learning, effective teaching practices, and the eration of schools. In short, it requires understanding and of the potential of the technology and outcomes that one wants to achieve with it, but also of the process or journey to be undertaken to achieve those outcomes.

This metaphor of 'the journey', replete with roadmaps, signposts, strategic intents and principles, is a powerful descriptor of the contemporary context faced by school leaders, system officers and education policy makers. Where are we now? Where do we want to go? And, how will we get there? These aspects of this journey are examined in some detail in the latter sections of this chapter.

NEW TECHNOLOGIES, NEW EXPECTATIONS OF TEACHERS IN A DIGITAL WORLD

In its *Harnessing Technology* review assessing the progress and impact of technology in school education, the British Government digital education authority Becta (2007, p. 71), concluded, 'there is a continuing need to find effective ways to realise the full benefits of technology for the education system'.

This challenge is not new and it reflects a familiar pattern with the introduction of new technologies in school settings. Some years ago, issues associated with the uptake of new technology were highlighted in the book, *Oversold and Underused* by Larry Cuban (2001). Despite significant increases in the provision of computers and Internet access for students and teachers in American schools, Cuban reported that:

> Two decades after the introduction of personal computers ...., with more and more schools being wired, and billions of dollars being spent, less than two of every ten teachers are serious users of computers in their classrooms (several times a week). Three to four are occasional users (about once a month). The rest—four to five teachers of every ten teachers—never use the machines for instruction.

(Cuban, 2000, p. xx)

His criticism went further in lamenting the limited impact that technology had had (at least to that point) in supporting new forms of teaching practice, in stating:

> *When the type of use is examined, these powerful technologies end up being used most often for word processing and low-end applications in classrooms that maintain rather than alter existing teaching practices.*

(Cuban, 2000, p. xx)

On the other hand, we have witnessed some remarkable changes outside the classroom over the last few years. These have to do with the ways people are accessing information, communicating in networks, publishing, and creating and sharing knowledge using digital technologies. For instance, according to Wikipedia, MySpace is attracting new registrations at a rate of 230 000 per day, and 'as of December 18, 2007, there are over 300 million accounts' (Wikipedia, 2008a). In a similar vein, Wikipedia reported that more than 2.7 billion Google searches are performed each month. As well as providing access to more than 25 billion websites and 1.3 billion images in 2006, and growing daily, Google provides an extensive array of tools and services (see Wikipedia, 2008b). To check these claims, I recommend that you visit YouTube and search for 'Shift happens'.

These statistics indicate that we are witnessing some profound changes in the ways people are using digital technologies. In light of the proliferation of Web 2.0 technologies, including wikis and blogs (see Wikipedia, 2008c) and the emergence of Web 3.0 technologies (see Wikipedia, 2008d), it has been predicted that there will be as much change in the next three decades of the twenty-first century as there has been in the last three centuries (NSBA, 2002).

These new technologies have been accompanied by new expectations for teachers. For example, in the Australian state of Queensland, the *Smart Classrooms Professional Development Framework* (Queensland Department of Education, Training and the Arts, 2006) is requiring teachers to develop evidence so that they can obtain their ICT Certificate. Teachers can then progress to achieve the ICT Pedagogical Licence, and finally to the ICT Pedagogical Licence, Advanced level. According to the Department of Education, Training and the Arts (DETA), the *Smart Classrooms Professional Development Framework* is designed to provide:

- clear expectations for schools and teachers about how ICT can be used effectively to support and extend student learning
- assistance for teachers to assess their practices in using ICT
- pathways for teachers to build their professional knowledge, practice, values and relationships in making ICT integral to learning. (DETA, 2006)

Another example of the growing profile being given to incorporating ICT is that the student teachers with whom I work are being asked to demonstrate the alignment of their developing knowledge, skills and attributes with the Queensland College of Teachers (QCT) *Professional Standards for Teachers* (2006). The search for ICT in those standards reveals that ICT is mentioned 28 times, including in statements and expectations such as:

Of paramount importance is the need for education to equip students with the skills required to learn, transfer learning, use ICT, contribute to teams, manage change and be self-aware.

(QCT, 2006, p. 3)

Teachers design and deliver learning experiences, for individuals and groups, that employ a range of developmentally appropriate and flexible teaching, learning and assessment strategies and resources in information and communication technology (ICT) enriched environments.

(QCT, 2006, p. 6)

Along with shifts in expectations by those responsible for teacher registration, professional learning and pre-service teacher education in Australia, we are also seeing more explicit reference to the value and place of ICT in statements by international and national education authorities and agencies over recent times. Education policy makers and practitioners are being called upon to adopt a 'futures perspective' that involves the use of new and emerging technologies in envisioning and enacting those futures.

For example, the 1998 UNESCO World Education Report, *Teachers and Teaching in a Changing World,* in describing some radical implications of the new information and communication technologies for conventional teaching and learning, predicts 'the transformation of the teaching-learning process and the way teachers and learners gain access to knowledge and information' (UNESCO, 2002, p. 10).

The New Zealand Ministry for Education (2003, p. 7) adopts a similar tone in explaining that creating a learning culture for a knowledge society can imply:

- changes to traditional relationships among teachers, learners and communities
- increasing demands for flexibility in meeting learners' aspirations, and
- new approaches to school organisation and management.

The North Central Regional Educational Laboratory (NCREL) reinforces this view in stating that:

> All students should have the opportunity to attend dynamic, high-quality schools designed to meet the challenges of the Digital Age. The implications for pedagogy, teacher and student roles, curriculum, assessment, infrastructure, and the community are significant.

> (NCREL, 2003, p. 11)

Inherent in these statements is the notion of transformation of schooling to meet the demands of the so-called 'knowledge age'. These demands are placing new expectations on teachers, particularly around the use of ICT in their teaching practice.

How teachers go about incorporating ICT can be imagined as a process of moving through certain developmental stages. One way of conceptualising these stages has been proposed by Trinidad, Newhouse and Clarkson (2006). The stages are sequenced in terms of inaction, investigation, application, and then by movement through a 'critical use border' to integration and transformation, as shown in Table 5.1.

Table 5.1 Stages of teacher development

STAGE	DESCRIPTION
Inaction	There is a general lack of action and/or interest.
Investigation	The teacher has developed an interest in using ICT with students and is beginning to act on this interest.
Application	The teacher is regularly using ICT with students and knows how to do so competently and confidently.
	Critical use border
Integration	The use of ICT becomes critical to the support of the learning environment and the opportunity for students to achieve learning outcomes through the learning experiences provided.
Transformation	The teacher is able to take on leadership roles (formal and informal) in the use of ICT and be knowledgeably reflective on its integration by themselves and others.

(Source: Trinidad, Newhouse & Clarkson 2006)

The OECD (2005), in its report, *Are students ready for a technology-rich world? What PISA studies tell us*, indicated that:

ICT is an important part of the policy agendas of OECD countries, with profound implications for education ... because ICT can facilitate new forms of learning. (p. 3)

The OECD also reported that:

On average in OECD countries, students with available computers to use at home performed substantially better in terms of Mathematics proficiency using PISA's six level proficiency scale for Mathematics. (pp. 54–55)

One example of a current strategy related to these calls from international agencies and governments is the enhancing Missouri's Instructional Networked Teaching Strategies (eMINTS) initiative being implemented in Missouri, USA. The strategy is founded on the desire to ensure that significant investments in technology translate into improved student performance. eMINTS classrooms are equipped with teachers' laptops, interactive whiteboards, data projectors, teacher workstation computers, digital cameras, scanners and printers. It aims to promote higher academic performance and better understanding of the world by students through encouraging teachers and students to collaborate in the use of multimedia tools (eMINTS, 2007).

Evidence from studies of the eMINTS initiative indicate that third- and fourth-grade eMINTS students are achieving statistically significant higher scores on statewide tests for Missouri than students not enrolled in eMINTS. Further, these studies are showing that eMINTS is working to 'close the gap' in student achievement. The differences in test scores of students in certain subgroups (special education, low income, Title 1) participating in eMINTS are reduced by up to half of the difference usually attributable to their subgroup classification (eMINTS, 2007).

E-LEARNING APPLICATIONS: NEW TOOLS FOR TEACHING AND LEARNING

Some ways in which digital technologies can be used to support teaching and learning are summarised below:

- **Communication**—email, web conferencing, Internet telephony, desktop conferencing, WebCT and Blackboard
- **Course marketing and administration**—online course promotion, dynamic web registration, and real-time financial transactions
- **Collaboration and networking**—involvement in discussion forums, virtual classrooms, groupware, websites for any time and any place

collaboration, with course designs and flexible learning options to take advantage of networks (for example, students with teachers, with peers and with other online communities)

- **Student publishing and promotion**—digital online publishing through ePortfolios as stories of personal learning and life experience, documents sent as email attachments, use and personalisation of websites, use of browsers, multimedia and hypermedia resource development, use of ICT for employment applications, self- and organisational marketing
- **Research**—finding information through web-based search engines, CD-ROM and DVD information resources, using ICT tools to access, retrieve, store and display resources (including text, audio and video) from research libraries, online databases and electronic journals
- **Virtual and managed learning environments**—involving web-based learning management systems (LMS), video conferencing, webcasting, interactive assessments, student performance tracking, specialised software for tutorials, and customised reporting systems.

(adapted from Roffe, 2004)

One of the potential benefits associated with the use of e-learning applications is the personalisation of learning for the student. This can involve enhanced 'one-to-one' as well as 'one-to-many' forms of communication, in either synchronous or asynchronous mode. These applications can allow greater opportunity for students to interact with teachers, with peers and with others in circumstances that are conducive for their learning. When these forms of ICT are linked to student background details and interests, and then with learning resources and course designs, the possibilities are seriously enlivening for the students—and also for their teachers!

NEW LEARNING THROUGH DIGITAL TECHNOLOGIES: CONNECTIVISM

Established theories of learning such as behaviorism, cognitivism, instructivism, constructivism and social constructivism have each been explored in terms of their implications for the use of ICT. For example, from a constructivist perspective, Jonassen (1999) argues that ICT can be used to facilitate meaningful learning experiences that are active, constructive, collaborative, intentional, complex, contextual, conversational, and reflective.

More recently however, Siemens (2004) has argued that the use of the WWW, the Internet, databases, spreadsheets and visual presentation software tools, and the associated proliferation and easier access to information and communication through a networked, digital world is altering the ways that people think and learn. He argues that the 'know how' and 'know what' dimensions, characteristic of most approaches to learning, is being supplemented by the 'know where' dimension; that is, the understanding of where to find the knowledge needed. He proposes the concept of connectivism to explain this phenomenon (see http://www.elearnspace.org/Articles/connectivism.htm).

Some key principles of connectivism are:

1 Learning and knowledge rest in diversity of opinions.
2 Learning is a process of connecting information sources.
3 Capacity to 'know more' is more critical than what is currently known.
4 Nurturing and maintaining connections are needed to facilitate continual learning.
5 Ability to see connections between fields, ideas and concepts is a core skill.
6 Currency (accurate, up-to-date knowledge) is the intent of all connectivist learning activities.

The theory of connectivism proposed by Siemens has implications for curriculum, for pedagogy, and for assessment. To explain how connectivism may be applied to various teaching and learning settings, he has established wikis, blogs and discussion forums at http://www.connectivism.ca/.

So far we have covered the emerging policy context, the rising expectations on teachers and the stages they go through in using ICT, some possibilities associated with various e-learning applications, and some recent insights of learning theory related to the use of ICT. I would now like to share some ideas on planning for the development of digitally based teaching and learning in your school or system. I use the metaphor of the 'ICT journey', and propose a few 'roadmaps' and 'signposts', along with some strategic intents and principles to give you guidance along the way.

STRATEGIC PLANNING: ROADMAPS, SIGNPOSTS AND INTENTS

Predicting the future of ICT based upon current trends is a tricky business. We know from history that there have been some well-documented and spectacularly incorrect predictions about new technologies. For example, in *The Experts Speak: The definitive compendium of authoritative misinformation* (Cerf & Navasky, 1984), the editor in charge of business books for Prentice Hall in 1957 stated: 'I have traveled the length and breadth of this country and talked with the best people, and I can assure you that data processing is a fad that won't last out the year.'

Predictions based upon existing trends are always limited by what has already been experienced. What if the technologies as we have known them are radically superseded? In such circumstances, trends have little predictive value.

An alternative way of considering the future is through the conversations and language that people use to talk about it. For example, in *Educational Futures: Dominant and contesting visions*, Milojević (2005) analyses the ways in which notions of the future circulate in the media and policy, research and academic literature as contemporary discourses. Through historical analysis of educational policy and change within OECD nations, Milojević notes that the ICT discourse is one of five contemporary discourses, with others being the globalisation, feminist, indigenous and spiritual discourses. Citing the dominance of the ICT discourse, Milojević calls for a shift in thinking *from* considering responses to technological change *to* the possibilities of creating desirable futures. As a consequence, we should not only see ourselves operating within an ICT discourse that requires us to predict the future and respond in ways largely determined by technology, but to envision where we want to go, and then develop the strategies to get there (Inayatullah, 1995).

Taking up the challenge to create a desired future requires planning for change rather than merely responding to demands and expectations. The concept of a policy 'roadmap', takes into account the levels of uncertainty associated with predicting the future. Rather than a 'blueprint' designed around firm assumptions and logical rational sequences, the 'roadmap' provides a more flexible and useful means for anticipating and planning for futures that cannot be totally foreseen.

Current policy roadmaps in education are being informed by trends. For example, recent trends evidenced in American, Australian and New Zealand schools have been identified by the Milken Exchange on Technology Education as follows:

> *States are establishing technology standards for students. If the standards are to have an impact, reliable assessments must be developed and implemented.*

Schools are beginning to use learning technology, but most use it to automate learning rather than to bring students unique learning opportunities never before possible.

Significant funds are being invested in schools, especially those with disadvantaged youth, yet a digital divide based on demographics exists between schools.

Schools and classrooms are rapidly getting wired, but in many cases the connections are not yet robust or high-speed; and

The student-to-computer ratio in schools is decreasing, but with that improvement come the challenges of obsolescence and maintenance.

(Source: METE, 2005, pp. 3–5)

On the basis of these trends, a series of action plans were proposed by METE, (2005, p. 27) for achieving the preferred future and the vision of 'transforming education in the context of a knowledge-based, global age'. These plans built upon the 'Seven Dimensions for Gauging Progress in Learning Technology' proposed by Lemke and Coughlin (1998) for transforming school systems to become 'high-performance enterprises that bring world-class educational opportunities for students in this digital age' (METE, 2005, p. 27). The seven dimensions are:

1　Learners
2　Learning environments
3　Professional competency
4　System capacity
5　Community connections
6　Technology capacity, and
7　Accountability.

These dimensions are seen as the key components of the 'roadmap' to assist students to live, learn and work successfully in a digital communication age. According to METE (2005, p. 27), life in the digital age will require that students have high academic standards, technological fluency, communication skills, interpersonal skills, information literacy, independence in learning and critical thinking abilities.

Another example of a policy roadmap is presented in the Becta (2005) review *Evidence on the Progress of ICT in Education*. This review reported on the progress of the British Government's (DfES, 2004) 'Five Year Strategy for Children and Learners', in terms of infrastructure developments, educational content, institutional development and learning and teaching. Four key areas of impact were addressed: the learner, the educational workforce, educational institutions, and the education system as a whole.

Similarly in New Zealand, the *Digital Horizons: Learning through ICT* initiative developed by the New Zealand Ministry of Education (2003) uses a framework for action built around the following areas: learners, teachers, leaders, Maori, families, communities, businesses and other stakeholders, curriculum and learning resources, and infrastructure.

These policy initiatives have much in common. While each initiative can be understood as a distinctive 'roadmap' for its particular jurisdiction, there are some common elements, or signposts, which identify a focus for action and provide direction for shaping the future. These elements/signposts are people, content and services, infrastructure, and policy and regulatory framework; and are presented in Table 5.2.

Table 5.2 *Signposts for a roadmap for ICT futures*

SIGNPOSTS	SUPPORTING SOURCES
People	People (MCEETYA 2000); Learners (NZ Ministry of Education 2003; Milken Exchange on Technology Education 2005); Teachers (NZ Ministry of Education 2003); Professional competency (Milken Exchange on Technology Education 2005); Leaders, Maori, families, communities, businesses and other (NZ Ministry of Education 2003); Community connections (Milken Exchange on Technology Education 2005); Learning and teaching (Becta 2005); Institutional development (Becta 2005)
Content and services	Content and services (MCEETYA 2000); Curriculum and learning resources (NZ Ministry of Education 2003); Educational content (Becta 2005)
Infrastructure	Infrastructure (MCEETYA 2000; NZ Ministry of Education 2003; Becta 2005); Learning environments, System capacity, Technology capacity (Milken Exchange on Technology Education 2005)
Policy and regulatory framework	Supporting policies, Enabling regulation (MCEETYA 2000); Accountability (Milken Exchange on Technology Education 2005)

(Source: Finger et al. 2007, p. 298)

The signposts and the associated policy resources can be used to assist schools and school systems to develop the roadmaps for their ICT futures.

A further aspect of planning in ICT for schools and systems concerns questions of purpose and intent. As you plan, embark and continue on the ICT journey, it is important to understand and appreciate what you intend to achieve. With this in mind, the four strategic intents are proposed: understand new context, create new learning environments, identify teachers' roles and importance, and meet people's needs related to use of technology. These are explained below.

STRATEGIC INTENT: UNDERSTAND THE NEW CONTEXT

Consider the contexts in which students and teachers are immersed and the pervasiveness of media and related digital technologies.

Considerations of digital natives and digital immigrants (Prensky, 2001; Barlow, in Tunbridge, 1995) are helpful in understanding the 'growing gap between children's experience of computers in their two environments of home and school' (Mumtaz, 2000, p. 347). On the other hand, while access and use of ICT have improved in schools, teachers may resist ICT-related change that disturbs their traditional ways of operating (Hodas, 1993; Downes & Fatouros, 1995; Cuban, 1986). New educational thinking about the different contexts that constitute students' and teachers' worlds is desperately needed.

STRATEGIC INTENT: CREATE NEW LEARNING ENVIRONMENTS

Use new and emerging ICT to create effective learning environments.

These environments should be flexible, enable a diverse range of pedagogies, be characterised by authentic interdisciplinary or transdisciplinary curriculum approaches, and use world-class digital learning resources. These new environments should support students to shape and respond to the 'What if?' questions in ways that can bring their answers to reality and their learning to new levels of commitment and to dealing with increasing complexity.

STRATEGIC INTENT: IDENTIFY THE ROLES AND IMPORTANCE OF TEACHERS

Transform teaching and learning through people, not technology.

The effective use of ICT in learning requires a change *from* a traditional didactic, knowledge provider role of the teacher *to* teacher as learner and mediator of ICT-assisted learning (Masters & Yelland, 1998;

Samaras, 1996). Klein et al. (2000) provide definitions and examples of mediation in referring to focusing (intentionality and reciprocity), affecting (exciting), expanding (transcendence), encouraging (mediated feeling of competence), and regulating (mediated regulation of behaviour).

STRATEGIC INTENT: MEET PEOPLE'S NEEDS RELATED TO USE OF TECHNOLOGY

Recognise the new roles of students and teachers, and the need for new organisational structures and relationships.

Moving from the traditional classroom of 'kids in rows' to more collegial classrooms, where teaching and learning increasingly occurs in an online hypertextual, multimedia world, presents new challenges, difficulties, tensions and needs, which must be addressed.

(adapted from Finger, 2002; Finger et al., 2007)

Table 5.3 ICT strategies associated with Maslow's Hierarchy of Needs

NEEDS	ICT STRATEGIES
Self-actualisation	Use new technologies creatively
	Explore new technologies
	Be innovative and enterprising
	Empower students and teachers
Esteem	Celebrate the acquisition of new knowledge, new skills and using new software
	Publish and display student work
	Participate in website and multimedia design challenges and competitions
	Employ computer mentors, student tutors, class experts
	Capitalise upon student and teacher knowledge and skills
Belonging	Collaborate on Internet projects
	Engage in team multimedia planning, design and production
	Network with peers, teachers, students and the local and wider community
Safety	Support students and teachers with technophobia and cyberphobia and in issues of appropriate use of ICT

(Source: Finger 2002, p. 138)

An approach for identifying and addressing students' and teachers' needs associated with the use of technology has been developed by Norwood (2006) using Maslow's Hierarchy of Needs. Various ICT-related strategies are matched against the various levels of need, as presented in Table 5.3.

Along with the strategies to meet these levels of need, as shown in Table 5.3, are a range of administrative and policy supports that are essentially practical in nature and include appropriate infrastructure, access and technical support as well as sufficient time allowances for training and professional development.

STRATEGIC PRINCIPLES FOR THE ICT JOURNEY

The policy roadmaps, signposts and intents that have been presented to this point are designed to guide the strategic planning process. Underpinning these elements is a series of five key principles that can serve to ground the 'ICT journey' undertaken by schools and systems.

Principle 1: Recognise the importance of people

Educational activity must be seen as a human endeavour. Successful transformation of teaching and learning will always be enabled and judged by people. However, it is the technology that is too often foregrounded rather than the learning.

A technology-centred approach misses the point. Instead, we need to promote people dreaming, imagining, creating, testing, critiquing, debating and telling their personal stories of learning, of challenges met and overcome, and of developing appropriate, innovative design solutions.

Principle 2: Develop an educational rationale for ICT use

ICT strategies need a good educational rationale. The limitation of techno-centric approaches is a lack of an appropriate guiding educational rationale. An educational rationale is based on an informed awareness of learning theories and effective teaching practices, and how these can be effectively integrated and supported by digital technologies to improve outcomes for students.

Basing plans on a good educational rationale means asking questions such as 'What are we trying to achieve?' and 'Why?', and then using the answers to inform technology purchases and infrastructure planning, rather than the technology determining the educational activity. Relevant literature on the use of ICT to inform the educational rationale includes the use of the computer as tutor, tool and tutee (Taylor, 1980, p. 5), Type I and Type II applications (Maddux et al., 2001, pp. 99–120), and productivity tools and mindtools (Jonassen, 1999, p. 4).

Principle 3: Adopt a techno-choice perspective for ICT

The techno-choice perspective (Sachs, Russell & Chataway, 1990, p. 53) acknowledges Principles 1 and 2 recognising the importance of people, and of using an educational rationale to guide decision making with ICT. Adopting a techno-choice perspective differs from the technological determinist perspective that views technology as linear and deterministic. It also differs from the social determinist perspective that assumes that technology is dependent on society.

A techno-choice perspective encourages educators to 'evaluate the appropriateness and effectiveness of available technologies, deciding when and how to use them with their students' (MCEETYA, 2005, p. 4). This is consistent with Roblyer's (2006) call for teachers, rather than others, to determine the relative advantage of using ICT. A techno-choice perspective, supported by the development of an educational rationale provides a solid platform for informing decisions about infrastructure, hardware, software, and other ICT purchases.

Principle 4: Develop an ICT plan as part of an overall school or system development strategy

Strategic planning in ICT needs to be linked to the overall school or system development strategy. The following essential conditions are suggested by UNESCO (2002) for achieving the desired alignment:
- The creation of a shared systemic vision for ICT and education that will afford an understanding of, commitment to and sense of advocacy for the implementation of technology at all levels within and across the system.
- Policy that supports and does not hinder the implementation of ICT in education.
- Adequate access to digital technologies, the Internet and WWW needs to be available to teachers and students wherever and whenever they choose to learn.

- Technical assistance to use and maintain the technology resources at a high standard is required.
- Teachers and students need access to high-quality, meaningful and culturally responsive digital content.
- Teachers need the knowledge and skills to use modern digital technologies and resources to facilitate student-centred approaches to learning for all students.

In summary, an effective plan should incorporate those essential conditions and be based upon the recognition of the importance of people (Principle 1), guided by a defensible educational rationale (Principle 2), and the determination of the relative advantage of ICT guided by a techno-choice perspective (Principle 3).

Principle 5: ICT initiatives should inform and be informed by research

ICT initiatives should both inform and be informed by research, and planning in ICT needs to build in a research component.

MCEETYA (2003, p.4) suggests that research can contribute to education by building on national and global education research priorities, anticipating emerging trends and priorities and creating new possibilities for learning. To illustrate this, the AARE 2005 Conference Symposium 'Measuring the integration of ICT in the classroom' brought together some contemporary Australian approaches being developed to measure the integration of ICT use (Finger, Jamieson-Proctor & Watson, 2006; Fitzallen & Brown, 2006; Lloyd, 2006; Trinidad, Newhouse & Clarkson, 2006). At the symposium, the methodology used to evaluate the Queensland Government's ICT Curriculum Integration Performance Measurement Instrument was presented. This instrument is available for download and use at http://education.qld.gov.au/smartclassrooms/strategy/sp_census_learning.html.

The Queensland Department of Education, Training and the Arts (2006) explains that the tool enables teachers and schools to gauge the extent, depth and quality of their ICT curriculum integration strategies. By using the tool, schools can:

- identify the current and preferred level of ICT curriculum integration in each of their classrooms
- identify each individual class's access to ICT, and
- generate discussion and think strategically about the best ways to use and integrate ICT into the classroom.

MAKING IT HAPPEN

This chapter has presented some strategic considerations for fostering digitally based teaching and learning through proposing the use of roadmaps, signposts, strategic intents and principles. These considerations can assist educational leaders in addressing the increasing expectations of teachers and students working in a digital, networked world.

This is important work as we proceed into the twenty-first century and I wish you well as you map and continue on your ICT journeys. The ultimate challenge and test of the effectiveness of the journey lies in the extent to which we can create inspirational and transformational opportunities of learning for students.

CHAPTER **6**

CREATING A NEXUS BETWEEN HOMES AND SCHOOLS

Mal Lee and Michael Gaffney

Digital technology in students' homes plays a significant part in their learning. Internet access, DVD and MP3 players, multi-function mobile phones and various forms of Web 2.0 social networking tools are providing powerful home-based platforms for young people to launch into all types of learning and exploration—for better or for worse. As the connectivity, applications and gadgets in the home become more prevalent and sophisticated, the need for schools and education system authorities to recognise the place of home technology in the education of our school-age children will become more and more important.

The power of emerging technologies presents new challenges and opportunities for schools, parents and students to create stronger links with one another, to communicate, to collaborate, and to build vibrant and effective networked learning communities. Constructing an enlivening nexus between the school and the home involving the tools of digital technology is a key element of leading schools into the digital age.

In this chapter we will discuss the growing digital divide between schools and homes and give some historical perspective to assist in considerations of how this divide may be addressed. Second, we will outline what some governments are doing to address the related issue of the digital divide between 'information rich' and 'information poor' homes. We then explore recent findings about student learning outside school using digital technologies. Finally we will suggest some strategies for how schools can go about developing a new nexus with the homes of their students.

THE DIGITAL DIVIDE BETWEEN HOMES AND SCHOOLS

We are witnessing a widening gap between the digital learning opportunities available to students in their homes and in their leisure time compared with those in most classrooms. This was reported by the Illinois Institute of Design (2007) in their recent study, which showed that:

Kids lead high-tech lives outside school and decidedly low-tech lives inside school. This new 'divide' is making the activities inside school appear to have less real world relevance to kids. (p. 24)

From the advent of television, the level and use of instructional technology available to the young in the average home began to exceed that in the average classroom. The launch of the World Wide Web in 1994, the hype surrounding the creation of the 'information super highway', the release of free web browsers and the popularisation of email had dramatic effects on the take-up of digital technology in homes in most developed countries , particularly those with school-age children. From the mid 1990s, parents were increasingly of the view that the ownership of a personal computer and web access would enhance their children's education and life chances. This was well before most educators had seriously considered the desirability of these new technologies. In Australia in 1995, 59 per cent of families had a personal computer. (ACMA, 2007, p. 27)

At the same time, the main applications software for the computers (including for word processing, presentations, electronic communication or spreadsheets) became easier and more reliable for use in the home.

While schools were struggling to acquire computers in the 1990s, they were becoming commonplace in the homes of the young (Lee & Winzenried, 2008). Some years back, former American Vice-President Al Gore observed that 'when it comes to telecommunications services, schools are the most impoverished institutions in society' (http://artcontext.com/calendar/1997/superhig.html). By 1996, the average power of the personal computer in the home exceeded those in businesses for the first time according to the IDC, the global market intelligence firm.

Along with developments in personal computing came enhancements in telecommunications. By the late 1990s, homes were beginning to secure faster Internet access and benefit from a rapidly developing mobile phone industry. At this time, most youth in the developed nations had in their homes not only ready access to all of the instructional technology that had been projected to 'revolutionise teaching'—be it radio, video or television, but they also had access to the latest digital information and communications technology.

This led American futures author Don Tapscott (1998) to label the generation of young people at that time as the 'Net Generation', as young people who found it natural to use all manner of technology and expected their schools to use the same kind of technology in their everyday teaching.

The *Real Time* study into the use of information and communication technology in Australia conducted by Meredyth et al. in 1999 reported on their survey of the forms of technology found in Australian homes. The results are presented in Table 6.1. This was a national study commissioned by the Federal Department of Education that involved all Australian states and territories.

Table 6.1 *Forms of technology in the home*

Television	98%
Radio	97%
CD or cassette player	96%
Calculator	94%
Computer	82%
Video player	78%
Printer	75%
Mobile phone	53%
Modem	41%
Video camera	21%
SEGA or Nintendo game	21%
Fax	20%
Scanner	11%

Since the survey the range of technology in the home has continued to expand, become more sophisticated, allow greater integration of the digital technologies and has generally fallen in price. For example, by 2007, according to a recent study by the Australian Communications and Media Authority (ACMA), over 90 per cent of Australian students had a computer at home with Internet access. In other results from their study, ACMA (2007, p. 7) found that, in comparing 2007 to 1995:

- computers had become 'standard issue' in family households, with 98 per cent ownership in 2007, compared with 59 per cent in 1995
- access to the Internet at home had evolved from a rarity in 1995 (7 per cent) to being commonplace in 2007 (91 per cent)
- games consoles are also commonplace in 2007.

With regard to other indicators of 'digital technology provision' in the home, ACMA (2007, p. 49) reported that in 2007, the average Australian family household had the following:

- three mobile phones
- three televisions
- two computers
- two DVD players
- two portable MP3/MP4 players
- one VCR
- two games consoles.

This means that an increasing majority of Australian school students have the use of a flat screen TV, a CD and DVD recorder, a sound system, digital camera, MP3 or MP4 digital player, USB drive, multifunction phone (with digital camera, of course), digital games machine and a plethora of application software. The ACMA study (2007) found that students were using that technology much of their free time—for example, listening to their iPod, texting their friends, using the chat facility, creating their own podcasts, inhabiting Second Life or preparing multimedia presentations for YouTube.

Of particular note was the finding that 'over 40 per cent of children and young people have some of their own material on the Internet and a third has a social networking site. From the age of 14 onwards, 70 per cent or more of teenagers engaged in some form of web authorship'. (ACMA, 2007, p. 9). For the first time in human history, the young of the world are able to publish their work to a global audience. The implications for teaching and learning are immense.

A recent related study conducted in Australia by AAPT (2007) found that eight out of 10 Australians owned a mobile phone. Significantly, 75 per cent had some type of Internet connection. Within the 16–34 age group, 80 per cent were found to keep their mobile or cell phone on 24 hours a day, and on average spend 2.4 hours each day on the Internet.

In contrast, the most commonly used instructional technologies in schools in 2007 were the pen, paper and the teaching board, be it black, green or white. Where the young in the home are learning with the latest digital technology, in the classroom they are in the main being taught with the tools of the nineteenth century or earlier (Lee & Winzenried, 2008).

The point is that the digital divide between home and school is beginning to affect student engagement in learning at school. Too many students are bored, or quietly disengaged. Too few are being given opportunities to develop and realise their talents. That is why schools must change.

THE DIGITAL DIVIDE AMONG HOMES

Despite growing access to digital technology in the developed world, there remains a small but significant number of the young people who either do not have ready Internet access at home or only have low-level dial-up access that precludes their use of the broadband-based offerings.

How great and significant is the divide is a moot point, with the trend line in most developed countries suggesting the pronounced divisions of the 1990s lessening as the technology becomes ever cheaper; however, in a number of developed nations there are significant cultural groupings where that trend is not apparent.

The aforementioned Australian study by ACMA (2007), for example, concludes:

Home Internet access seems to be partly a function of means—94% of households with incomes more than $35,000 are online, compared with 75% of those on less than $35,000. (p. 5)

An analysis of household income suggests that electronic media and communications devices are important to all families, even when their income is low. (p. 6)

The point remains there is likely to be families where the young will not be 'competing' on a level playing field and thus it will always be important to provide some support.

As a means of redressing disadvantage, the British Government allocated 60 million pounds in the 2007–08 financial year for the 'Computers for Pupils' and 'Home Access Project' programs. These programs recognise the educative power of learning in the home and seek to ensure all school-age children have a computer and Internet access in their homes. The

'Computers for Pupils' program is designed to help the most disadvantaged secondary school students improve their education and life skills by putting a computer into their home. It aims to:

- *give these pupils the same opportunities as their peers*
- *provide the conditions that can contribute towards raising educational achievement, narrowing the attainment gap and supporting progress towards these pupils' targets*
- *support the personalising of learning by providing access to ICT whenever or wherever is most appropriate for learning*
- *encourage the development of ICT skills appropriate to the 21st century for the pupils and their families.*

(UK Treasury Briefing Paper, July 2007
http://www.nfer.ac.uk/research-areas/pims-data/outlines/evaluation-of-the-cfp.cfm)

The approach taken by the British Government builds upon their education policy paper, *Harnessing Technology: Transforming learning and children's services* released in 2005. It recognises the link between educational disadvantage and access to digital technology. The government is arguing that:

Putting computers into the home can motivate pupils to learn, help develop key ICT and life skills and give them the same opportunities and experiences as their peers.

(UK Treasury Briefing Paper, July 2007)

STUDENT LEARNING OUTSIDE THE CLASSROOM

Different ways of learning

The Australian study by the team led by Meredyth (1999) indicates that most students learn the bulk of their ICT usage skills in the home and not in the classroom. Comparable studies by Laferrierre (1997), Martinez and Mead (1988) and Kersteen and Linn (1998) found the same elsewhere across the developed world.

Today most students not only have better technology and online access, but also spend more hours using that technology in their homes. Research on student use of computers in schools in the mid and late 1990s (Lee & Winzenried, 2008) and Meredyth (1999) found that students were lucky to use them for an hour a week, while teenage students at home were spending several hours each day on their computers.

In their Australian *Real Time* study, Meredyth et al. (1999) found that:

> Students tend to acquire their advanced information technology skills at home rather than at school. Eighty-five per cent of students use computers outside schools ... There is a significant link between students' information technology skills, confidence and enjoyment, their use of computers outside school, the level of resources in their home and their personal ownership of resources ... Students who do not use a computer outside school had relatively poor attainment of information technology skills. (p. xxviii)

In American studies conducted around the same time, Don Tapscott, in his book *Growing Up Digital* (1998), observed that for the first time in human history the young had an understanding of technology that surpassed that of most of their teachers. Tapscott went on to explain that students were also acquiring and enhancing their knowledge and skills in a very different manner to the way in which they were being taught in the schools.

The term 'chaotic learning' has been used to describe the learning styles favoured by the young in their homes (Lee, 2000). Such learning styles are proposed to include preference for experiential or constructivist learning, emphasis on play, collegial support, multi-tasking and networking—often online. The young, like most working online, preferred to learn by 'jumping on and off task', checking out new situations, and returning to the original task. In other words, as Lee (2000, p. 61) suggests, the young chart their own courses. Each sets his or her own goals. No teacher determines what they learn. The concept of 'chaotic learning' has been elaborated upon in the writings of Marc Prensky (2006), and by Oblinger and Oblinger's 2006 online publication, *Educating the 'Net Generation'* (see http://www.educause.edu/IsItAgeorIT%3AFirstStepsTowardUnderstandingtheNetGeneration/6058).

Impact of Web 2.0 technologies

The recent study by the American-based National School Boards Association (NSBA, 2007) on American teenage use of the Internet reported that 96 per cent of students with online access use social networking technologies, such as chatting, texting, blogging, and visiting online communities such as Facebook, MySpace and Webkinz—and that one of the most common topics of conversation on the social networking scene is education. The most common education-related topics were found to be 'college or college planning, learning outside of school, and careers, with around fifty of online students saying they talk specifically about schoolwork'.

In commenting on the report, Executive Director of the National School Boards Association, Anne L. Bryant, said: 'There is no doubt that these online teen hangouts are having a huge influence on how kids today are creatively thinking and behaving.' She added: 'The challenge for school boards and educators is ... to keep pace with how students are using these tools in positive ways and consider how they might incorporate this technology into the school setting.'

Examples from the NSBA study where creative activities and learning are being supported by social networking internet sites included writing, art, and contributing to collaborative online projects. Significantly students indicated that they were engaging in these creative forms of collaboration and production regardless of whether the activities were related to their schoolwork.

Further, the NSBA (2007) study reported:

Students are spending almost as much time using social networking services and Web sites as they spend watching television. Among teens who use social networking sites, that amounts to about 9 hours a week online, compared to 10 hours a week watching television.

The findings from this American NSBA study support contentions about the need for schools to appreciate the kind of learning happening outside the classroom and in the home.

With the advent of social networking technologies, it is becoming more feasible than ever before for educational leaders at school and system levels to recognise the networked, chaotic learning of the young, to rethink the education offerings delivered through the school, to overcome the home–school dichotomy, and to consider new models of networked learning communities. Such communities would incorporate not only the school and the home, but also would extend beyond these traditional social institutions and into the real and virtual, local and global community that is the learning world of young people.

The findings of Illinois Institute of Design study (2007) powerfully captures this sense of networked learning when they indicate that:

In their lives outside the school, kids increasingly interact in a digital meritocracy that allows them the opportunity to push themselves to solve large complex problems or explore personal passions for subjects beyond the mandated curriculum of schools. (p. 26)

Recognising the need to build a better home–school nexus is about keeping schools, as our key socialising and educational institutions, relevant to the everyday lives of students, and as a consequence increase students' engagement and learning development. The study by Illinois Institute of Design (2007) concluded:

> The learning experiences of the kids outside school are increasingly more relevant to modern life than what is learned inside school ... Kids are increasingly motivated and engaged by what they learn in out-of-school programs and in their virtual online lives, and mechanisms for capturing and enabling them must be found. (p. 24)

In essence, these challenges for leaders of digital schools are really challenges about curriculum relevance and student engagement. An interesting next step will be to work out how students' learning in the home and in 'their networked community' using digital technologies, can be best integrated and aligned with the policies and procedures of the 'high stakes' student assessment and credentialling bodies—and the expectation of those who use those assessments and credentials to sort and select students.

DEVELOPING A HOME–SCHOOL NEXUS

Having presented an overview of the digital divide affecting student access to digital technology, and types of learning that students are experiencing through the use of those technologies, it is clear that there are some significant needs and possibilities. The current digital divide between home and school cannot be allowed to continue. The question is: How does your school build the desired nexus between the school and the home?

The authors should hasten to add that at the start of 2008 there was remarkably little written on this issue. While many schools are 'dabbling' in the area, a concerted analysis of the scene, and the best way forward, has still to be undertaken.

Notwithstanding this, some suggestions for your consideration follow.

Adopt an appropriate whole-school strategy

It may well be timely to adopt a formal whole-school or, indeed, education authority strategy for developing networked school communities that seeks to marry and, where appropriate, shape and recognise developments in the home.

Experience would suggest many schools are 'dabbling' with various home–school links, but often the efforts are sporadic and lack the involvement of all the key players. Recent consultancy experience reveals schools where some teachers are actively taking advantage of the technology and learning in the home, while other teachers are rejecting such moves on the grounds of equity.

Research the home scene

Schools need to gain an appreciation of the situation in the students' homes, the level and nature of the digital technology, how it is used by the students, the nature of the learning process they use, the skills, attributes and values they have developed. The aforementioned 2007 studies suggest the vast majority of families in the developed world are well placed to operate within a networked learning community and believe such a move would enhance the education of their children.

Talk with parents

You might ascertain the parents' aspirations in acquiring the digital technologies. Parents' desire to support children's learning through purchasing new technologies is widely recognised. For example, by the mid 1990s—as indicated by the IDC market research—most parents perceived acquiring a computer for their children would improve their life chances.

These findings were reinforced by research undertaken in the use of interactive whiteboards (IWBs) in a low socioeconomic school (Lee & Boyle, 2004). We found most parents had acquired a computer and Internet access for the children to complement teaching with the IWBs. Of note was that not one of the parents was a tertiary graduate and that they made the decision of their own volition. While this is just one instance, it does provide some insight into the thinking of parents that needs to be further explored.

Those views are still evident today, with the 2007 Australian ACMA study finding 96 per cent of parents believed Internet use was beneficial.

The most commonly cited benefit of internet use is the learning and the educational benefits … (ACMA, 2007, p.28)

Always remember, appropriate and realistic advice from principals is important for parents. They are often as bemused by the ever-changing scene as teachers!

Ask the students

Your strategy might involve talking with and listening to your students, including those who do not have Internet access at home. While students might be confident and proficient in using the various digital technologies, they will have various strengths and deficiencies in their developing knowledge, skills and values. Teachers need to know their students. They need to be aware of students' capabilities and attributes, as well as their hopes and aspirations, to identify how the school can build on the learning and the technology used in the home.

Students can also be invaluable sources of advice about changes in various technologies and which are in favour with the different age cohorts. It is also a good idea to research the scene with them several times a year, and always with a cross-section of age cohorts.

Collaborate with the teachers

Teachers are the most knowledgeable and play the most important role in students' learning.

A recent school consultation by the authors brought these considerations into sharp relief. One of the music staff confiscated a Year 11 girl's mobile phone. The teacher then decided to see what the student was doing with her phone. It transpired the girl—a top student—was sending her friends a pretty raunchy video she had made of herself rapping. The video did not leave much to the imagination. The principal was asked what she was going to do about it. Some might say that this is not a school concern. However, it raised important questions about the role and responsibility that teachers (and parents) have in educating the young in a digital context, and why it is important for digital schools to build a constructive home–school nexus.

On a related note, to appreciate the complexity and possibilities of linking home and school learning more effectively, teachers require a good working knowledge of the emerging technologies and applications. This means that school leaders need to also collaborate with teachers on the design, delivery and support of timely and relevant professional learning.

Open up the infrastructure

While most homes have at least dial-up Internet access, there are still a sizeable number of school and education authority networks that restrict the nature of use of even the keen teachers and school leaders. Many prevent, for example, the use of most of the Web 2.0 and social networking services.

For there to be effective, ever-developing networked learning communities, schools and/or their education authority are going to have to find the way to expedite the desired widespread use of the school networks. It is appreciated that there can be network security challenges, but there are also solutions that the astute network managers can use if obliged to do so. Some network managers occasionally need to be reminded their role is to facilitate the business of the organisation, namely the education of the young.

Check out what is happening in business and industry

In shaping your approach to developing the home–school nexus, you need to be aware that work practices in business and industry are being impacted at least as significantly as the learning in the home by changing digital technology. In his recent work, *Wikinomics* (http://www.wikinomics.com/), Tapscott (2007) explores how industry is making use of Web 2.0 tools, such as wikis and blogs and the related online mass collaboration opportunities these present.

The impact of Web 2.0 tools on school and educational system operations—for example, in areas such as program evaluation and policy development—is still in the early stages but can be expected to grow quickly over coming years. The implications of Web 2.0 technology deserve close consideration by those wishing to develop the home–school nexus within these contexts.

CONCLUSION

The development of a new nexus between the home and the school, using the tools available through digital technology, would represent an historic shift in the nature of schooling.

Most of the digital technology desired by the schools already exists and is being used every day in the home. What is more, student learning in the home can provide schools with valuable insights into how best to educate the young. Therefore, it seems timely that school leaders and educational policy makers give more consideration to developing and using the home–school nexus. Such work can inform teachers and parents about student background knowledge and learning styles, assist school and system policy makers to make prudent decisions about investment in digital technology, and, as a consequence, serve to improve student engagement in school and their learning achievements.

CHAPTER 7

LEADING A DIGITAL SCHOOL: A CASE STUDY— ST LEONARD'S COLLEGE

Roger Hayward

I do not think of myself as leading a digital school; I think of myself as leading a very good school that is getting better. It is a school firmly embedded in the digital age. It uses a great deal of digital technology. Nevertheless, our view of ourselves is first and foremost as a very good school.

When I question how well we *are* doing, the 'performance indicators' relate to student outcomes and community acceptance. I use similar performance indicators when I question how well we *should be* doing. I regularly ask myself *what* we should be doing in preparing students for the future.

This chapter looks back on the last eight years of ICT development at St Leonard's College to draw conclusions on structures and people that have made a difference. The College is well resourced and has had a notebook computer program since 1997. It has made real progress by focusing on its educational aims and by having excellent educators leading the planning, supported by excellent IT specialists. The College has deliberately avoided being at the 'bleeding edge'. Instead it has positioned itself to learn from others, while remaining strongly focused on quality outcomes.

THE CONTEXT

St Leonard's College is a school with 1750 students on two campuses. It is coeducational from Early Childhood to Year 12, with a near perfect gender balance throughout. We follow the International Baccalaureate Primary Years Program (PYP) up to the end of Year 6. We have our home-grown Middle Years programs—a little different on each campus—followed by a choice of International Baccalaureate Diploma or Victorian Certificate of Education (VCE) at Years 11 and 12. The College has strong enrolments and very long waiting lists at all levels. The demographics are most encouraging for the future. There is strong retention from year to year. The academic results, evidenced by the Year 12 indicators, are consistently the best in the bayside region of the city of Melbourne, and have been throughout this century. The results of our Year 12 exit surveys each year are very affirming. In the last two years, the reported dissatisfaction with access to IT dropped from 2 to 1 per cent.

Parent satisfaction, reported anecdotally, is high. We are a 'very local' school—most students travel less than 10 kilometres to either campus. Six years ago, one Sunday morning, I was partway through a major weekend home maintenance project when I needed an electric jig saw. I arrived at the nearest hardware chain-store just as it opened, spent 20 minutes comparing models (I am no expert on power tools) and selected a basic model to take to the checkout. The middle-aged man at the till looked at me and said, 'Roger, that is not the one you need, let me swap it for another.' He came back a few seconds later with another jig saw, with more features but a lower price. It had just gone on special. I was still nonplussed, and he went on: 'You don't know me but I have two daughters at your school. I love the school; you are all doing great work. This is my third job, I need it to pay the fees.' There was no embarrassment or bravado about the statement. We spoke for a couple of minutes and then I left and went back to my project. The jig saw did its job well, and I cannot get the conversation out of my head. It is there as a constant reminder of the responsibility of the College to deliver the best quality of education it can … while not wasting one cent of the funds earned by our parents' third (or second, or first) job.

Old Collegians have very positive attitudes to the school. Reunions are well attended. Some years ago, the major Melbourne newspaper, *The Age*, surveyed university students some years out of school with questions about how well school prepared them for university. St Leonard's College was rated very highly.

Students, parents, prospective parents, Old Collegians, public examination results, retention rates—the range of performance indicators suggests we are a very good school, doing what people expect us to do and doing it well. But I do not want to get hung up on performance indicators. Are we doing well? Apparently we do. Are we doing what people want us to do? Apparently we do. Are we doing what we should be doing? I think so. The expectations of government, of employers, of education departments, of universities are all fairly consistent into the future: they want people who are able to work in teams, communicate well, be lifelong learners, be risk takers (at least be open to change), be creative and so on.

How does this relate to being a digital school? We live in an age that can be described as digital, so a good school must be a digital school in some way. However, a school is not a good school because it is digital. It is a good school if it is doing the right things and doing them well. How well are we doing ICT? I am an optimist. I am by nature an early adopter of technologies. I have a strong sense of responsibility to our students that we should educate them to thrive as ethical citizens in an unimagined future. I have a strong sense of duty towards parents who are working hard to pay our very high tuition fees.

In the last 24 years I have worked in three well-resourced academic schools, each of which has measured its success very broadly. But our efforts to use ICT well are, in my opinion, disappointing. At the very least, they are failing my expectations. I am not alone in this. Under the headline, 'A computer revolution? Or £3 billion spent on gloss?' in the *Times Educational Supplement* dated 20 January 2007, it is asserted that '... education researchers have not been able to prove a direct link between the introduction of ICT and an improvement in standards'. I am usually disappointed when I visit education technology conferences (typically the NECC conference in Atlanta in June 2007) because behind the hype and the universes of possibility, there is not much action on the ground. I have been using computers in education settings for 25 years in three countries. Throughout that time, we have put our hardware and software to use in schools. I cannot shake off a feeling akin to driving around in an Aston Martin in first gear with the handbrake on and the windscreen partially obscured. We are clearly not using the full potential of what we have.

I know that my school is doing some IT very well. We have excellent academic results, our students win prizes in art, music composition, media and visual communication and design, for which they exercised excellent computer skills. I know that they enjoy their years at university confident that they have been well prepared. But our dux of the International Baccalaureate Diploma a couple of years ago joined a public debate in the letters pages of *The Age* with the opinion that our notebook computer program was a waste of time. (Actually it was his view that any school's note-book computer program was a waste of time!) The most consistent complaint we get from parents is that student-owned notebooks are a waste of money, a nuisance to carry to and from school, a distraction and a temptation.

But it is worse than that. I am by training a physical scientist. I know very little economics, but an economist once told me that the cost of anything is the sum total of the opportunities you forgo to have it. For convenience, the cost is usually expressed in dollars and cents. Unless you can resource all options, then every choice is about what to forgo. The dollars and cents are just a way of bringing the opportunities into balance. For a family, the dollars and cents might be the measure of the choice between a family holiday in Bali or a plasma-screen TV. In school, if I cut our information technology bill by $1 million, I could afford 20 support staff to assist students with learning difficulties. ICT choices are not about dollars and cents; they are about the opportunities we forgo in order to allow them. If I leave the $1 million in the ICT budget, it had better be spent well.

Time comes into the equation in exactly the same way. If we spend more time in school learning to read, we have less time available to learn to count. This time pressure is a constant problem in schools and in modern life. The crowded curriculum reminds us that we are 'time poor'. So the time we spend on ICT had better be well spent. I am not suggesting that we enter into the debate about which is better: 700 notebook computers or 20 support staff. But I am suggesting that we should always judge what we do in ICT against the most demanding and scrupulous criteria. The time and money we put into ICT could have been spent elsewhere, so the outcomes had better be extremely good.

WHAT WORKS FOR US, AND WHAT HAVE WE ABANDONED?

As the focus here is St Leonard's College as a case study, I am not about to discuss our progress or the success and failures of our talented and hardworking staff. Rather, I will pick out some of the things that have worked and some that have not, trying to be as general as possible for all of our experiences are different, and schools are rarely so similar that one can import another's solutions directly. I will change detail on occasion to protect the privacy of any individual. Should it seem that anything I describe can be identified negatively with a particular individual, then be assured that I have actually provided a composite description of two or more persons and situations.

So, what works? I will describe briefly a few things that, in my opinion, are good things to do.

Have a good ICT Infrastructure

We live in a digital age and will use information technology because it is the norm. We have to use email well—our parents expect it. We have to use computer-based reporting systems—our parents expect it. Our database must be user friendly and used well by staff—our parents expect us to have information about them and their students at our finger tips. Our website must have some useful information for parents and students. Our intranet had better give access to appropriate information—our students and staff expect it.

These five uses give ample reason to have a good ICT infrastructure; they establish minima for infrastructure and skill sets. The last bastion of resistance by teachers to the use of ICT disappeared a few years ago as a result of establishing these minima. Teachers learned keyboarding skills, the user interface and file organisation, and this rapidly flowed through into uses of Word and PowerPoint.

There are positive educational outcomes from an excellent student database system. It works to have computer-only reporting integrated into student records. In the 1990s, we were using Word or Filemaker for report writing, with templates carefully constructed. When we adopted Synergetic about five years ago, we took a real step forward. It integrated the reporting process into the student record system; it allowed both online and offline access; and it provided a web interface to open up online access off-site. This system is quite popular in Victorian schools. Email and computerised reporting really tipped the balance in getting the last few reluctant users onboard.

Develop educational leadership and teamwork in learning technologies

A few years ago we made significant progress under the leadership of a really good Director of Learning Technologies. I strongly believe that the most important word in that title is 'learning'. The person in that position must be first and foremost an educator.

When I advertised for a head of learning technologies in 2001, most applicants were ICT professionals, many had been maths or science teachers, but their recent skills and interests were in ICT. None could demonstrate the communication skills or pedagogical perspective I required. After much thought, I persuaded my head of primary curriculum to take on the position, offering him the support required to get enough technical knowledge to work with the IT specialists. In nearly four years in that position, he successfully directed many advances in the deployment of ICT at St Leonard's and then, according to plan, returned to mainstream education. He is now a deputy principal in a large school overseas.

We no longer have a director of learning technologies. The role of strategically directing learning technologies is now the responsibility of the director of curriculum. The role of implementing learning technologies is the responsibility of the director of finance and corporate services, and the role of directing the professional learning of all staff is the responsibility of the director of professional learning. This is now our third year of the new model. Why? Because we feel we have moved on. Learning technologies are now a part of the educational infrastructure. Our ICT needs must be derived from the curriculum and articulated through heads of faculty and the director of curriculum. The responsibility of meeting the needs is borne by corporate services. There is an implication here of very strong teamwork in senior management.

Find a reason to use the technology

Let me return to issues relating to the use of technology in the classroom. Late adopters will take readily to technology when they see a purpose. The use of 'technology' in its broadest sense has been catalysed in classrooms by the widespread use of PowerPoint for show and tell, and of digital cameras for documentation. Our early learning centre teachers, driven by the *Reggio Emilia* philosophy, place a high priority on documenting the progress of each child. This has encouraged them to become excellent users of digital cameras and digital video.

As an aside, I am convinced that many older people first learn how to use email attachments and digital cameras when they become grandparents. I am convinced that the highest proportion of my staff who is using Skype with video are grandmothers. Our primary Japanese teacher has had a real interest in developing video conferencing, with more reason to do so than most other primary teachers. At her initiative, she has set up a simple web-based conferencing facility. Her skills are now of interest to other primary teachers, whose international focus is enhanced by the aforementioned IB Primary Years Program (PYP).

Beware of technology as a Trojan horse

Notebook (or also called laptop) computer programs disappoint me. Throughout the 1990s—and to some extent, today—I hear people justify their use as the Trojan horse that will bring constructivist pedagogy into schools, or will force teachers to change their style. It is my belief that where schools have become more constructivist it is through other factors than the notebook computer programs or other technologies. Schools change pedagogy by changing pedagogy, not by changing technology.

Last year, I watched a Year 9 maths lesson taught by an exemplary teacher in front of a large class of engaged students in a school in Kunming, China. She was quite young, very passionate about her subject matter, she was clearly engaging the large class very well and she was using the latest technology. All of her standard worksheets and overhead transparencies had been carefully converted into PowerPoint slides viewed on a data projector. She was a first-rate, very conventional, very didactic teacher. The technology made no difference to her methodology. It was simply an expensive page-turning mechanism. I mean no criticism of her methodology. She was by no means relying on pure rote learning. China is producing well-educated students at the highest world standards in many institutions. The point is that the pedagogy adapted the technology to itself, not vice versa.

In our case, adopting the International Baccalaureate PYP made an honest, coherent, widely accepted, well-implemented change to our teaching and learning practices. There was no Trojan horse; there was no sense of a hidden agenda. Teachers realised from the start that, despite the inevitable implementation hump and the need for hard work, they would have tangible professional gains at the end of the process. Our innovative programs at Years 7 and 8 at our smaller campus, and at Year 9 at our larger campus, have been described elsewhere and acknowledged through, for example, the award of Teaching Team of the Year. These programs were very success-ful and benefited from the use of readily available information technologies, but the technologies did not drive or even 'leverage' the change.

Be on the lookout for better technology

There are other reasons for notebook computers. In the early 1990s, access to information meant owning some hardware. The attraction of notebook computers was clear. Once public access to the Internet began in the mid 1990s, this case began to weaken. Access and ownership of one's information no longer meant owning the screen, hard disk and keyboard.

In the 1990s, to put ICT power into the hands of the students meant notebooks or very big classrooms with desktops. Nowadays, it is simply through whatever technology you can get your hands on and choose to use. About four years ago, it seemed to me that students started carrying their flash drives rather than their notebooks. These drives were cheap enough to become ubiquitous and had adequate capacity. More recently, I noticed that students have moved on: they use their iPods to transfer their files—and they ALL have iPods! Who needs a dedicated flash drive?

I look forward to a practical sub-notebook computer for schools—a low-cost, lightweight, robust unit with wireless networking, no mechanical disk drive and long battery life with just basic open-source productivity and web-browsing software would meet the vast majority of our needs. Specialist labs with high-end equipment for art, music and design will suffice for the rest.

Design the right learning spaces

ICT is a real estate issue. We earned a good outcome when we rebuilt our junior school with very large classrooms. The extra space was provided so that we could have a wet area in each classroom and eight desktop computers, and still have space for groups to form and re-form. The rooms are paired, with operable walls between them so that the two classes at each grade can combine on occasion. The inquiry pedagogy of the International Baccalaureate PYP is enhanced by the improved real estate. The sage is never on the stage in these classrooms, but is always guiding at the side. There is some interest in using interactive whiteboards in these classrooms, which may develop over the next couple of years.

We have just opened our new upper school building, which also has big classrooms relative to class sizes. We required that most of the classrooms be big enough for some desktop computers in each room. This arrangement encourages teachers to have students being more active and cooperative in their learning. There are data projectors in every room. Interactive whiteboards can be easily accommodated where required. The very large study centre has readily available desktop computers. Some students bring their own notebook computers.

There are labs of desktop computers, some of which are a little more specialised: the music technology lab, visual communication and design, and media are all very well resourced with desktop computers. Oh yes, and we still have 400 notebooks available to our students. It is only in Year 9 that there are individually allocated notebooks for students.

Consider the educational value of interactive whiteboards

Interactive whiteboards (IWBs) can be of use. Our first two were installed in science labs in 2003. Barry Hill, one of our ICT mentors and a physics teacher who has used them throughout that time, offers the following insights.

IWBs give me the ability to access demonstrations of physics principles on the web, allowing me to replace text-based snapshots with time-variable examples. This prevents the students getting false pictures in their heads when topics are introduced that are often hard to fix. We can compare and share work, building libraries of resources that are always current. Distribution of materials tailored specifically to a course or group of students is easier.

We use data loggers to analyse experiments that are too difficult to observe with normal school-based techniques. A current might be induced in a conductor in a fraction of a second, but we can display and analyse a graph with time increments of 1/50th of a second. Recording temperature overnight or getting distance–time graphs directly from the data logger allows analysis and explanation rather than laborious lower-order skills like graph plotting.

In senior classes the IWB allows me to draw diagrams to illustrate the concepts being covered. The elements of these drawings can be moved to show changes over time. For example, we can draw two sine waves to show interference of waves. Students misconceive this as two static waves with the peaks combining to form an antinode. By moving the waves across the IW, I can show the variations that actually cause the antinode.

Being able to add an explanation, or refer to an earlier screen, is a great bonus. This could be done from the keyboard, but the flexibility of being able to do this seamlessly with the IWB is great.

I often open a past exam paper on the VCAA website to find a question that a student will then attempt. This can't be done effectively with paper as the opportunities for collaboration are reduced.

In Year 10, in addition to the above, the students are motivated to present their work and use the IWB operations to highlight their points.

While science has had IWBs for four years, our English teachers have only been using them for one year. A senior English teacher wrote this summary of her first year of using an IWB.

> I started off using the IWB very enthusiastically. I was lucky enough to have Tim in my class last year and he was well trained by Barry (a physics teacher) and helped me. I also attended several of Barry's physics classes. However, I gradually gave up using the actual IW software. I found it slowed down my ability to write/scribble rapidly as kids verbalised their ideas and I didn't really need to save the notes as students were recording them anyway. Having said that, I make great use of the IWB for sharing materials/notes with students. It is wonderful for working through sample essays, using the highlighter to annotate media texts or for students to display their own work. I like preparing PowerPoint as well to guide students through tasks.

We have recently deployed two IWBs in the music school, one in the music ensemble room and the other in the music technology room. Teachers use music programs such as Auralia, Musition, Sibelius and Groovy Music. Teachers and students of all ages are enjoying the interactivity of each of the music programs. The group work on the IWB, combined with individual work in the music technology lab, is proving very exciting to all music staff.

Our primary teachers are not using IWBs to any great extent. There are data projectors in regular use and there is a primary computer lab in addition to the computers in every classroom. Primary staff members have some interest in using IWBs in the future, with the following expectations:

- increased enjoyment of lessons for both students and teachers with associated gains in motivation
- versatility with applications across all areas of the curriculum
- allowing teachers to present web-based and other resources more effectively
- more opportunities for interaction and discussion in the classroom
- encouraging teachers to use more ICT, encouraging professional development
- assisting students to understand concepts more clearly through more effective and dynamic presentations
- different learning styles can be accommodated more readily.

Many of these expectations can be met with a data projector and wireless mouse or tablet. I am concerned that IWBs may reduce the flexibility of the classroom space, and I wish to prevent the IWB from becoming an altar for the high priest of learning—far worse than the sage on the stage!

Employ technicians with people skills

Moving beyond hardware and software, it works to have technicians with people skills on the help desk. Their people skills are usually more important than their ICT knowledge, which is rarely tested in depth. Those with pure ICT skills can stay in the back room and maintain the infrastructure to the highest levels.

Use good teachers as mentors

It works to have staff mentors, but the choice of mentors is problematic. Often the staff who know most about the technology are not particularly good at putting it across. Similarly, it is not unusual for the best teacher to be the one who has had to struggle with the subject matter, rather than the person to whom the concepts are very obvious. I have learned painfully and often that I am hopeless as an IT teacher or mentor because IT is so easy with my background, I cannot relate to the difficulties some people have. The only generalisation I can make about staff mentors is that they should be good teachers, not good technicians. Our latest approach to staff mentors is to have a small number of staff with time release working in appropriate parts of the College and in appropriate learning areas. It is not hard for the physics teacher to help the literature teacher with a technical issue, but the literature teachers seem to want to be helped by someone from the humanities rather than from the sciences. So we are trying this.

Don't hold back the innovators and early adopters

It works to be prepared to let those with ideas and initiative get way ahead of others, setting aside equity considerations for a while. Playing with a recent slogan and turning it on its head, I espouse the notion 'No person held back'. Let the innovators and early adopters rush ahead. It is going to happen anyway, so do not hold them back. And do not worry about it. The visual communication teacher is always going to be better at Adobe Illustrator than the drama teacher. The teacher with the tired old worksheet will find that students no longer accept his offering that pales into insignificance compared with the web-based interactive resources produced by his colleague next door. The laggards will be motivated into catching up or will head off elsewhere for a quieter life. When an innovation has become commonplace, most people will have discovered ways of making it simple and routine. At this time the reluctant learner/teachers can easily get on the bandwagon.

Offer a variety of professional learning opportunities

An appropriate range of professional learning works. It must be speculative and exploratory on occasion, but mostly it should be very focused. It is my opinion that the best professional learning is neither 'just in case' nor 'just in time'. It is 'on the task' and 'at the time'. It is important to spend time exploring what technology is available, having brilliant presenters like Gary Stager, Jamie McKenzie and Tom March opening people's eyes to possibilities. We use internal opportunities, too, such as the head of art showing what is possible with high-end software. It is important to allocate time for learning skills for which the user has discovered an immediate personal need. I enjoy wide-ranging professional learning once in a while, but I want to do my detailed learning on the task, when I have an appropriate task to undertake. We have two staff conferences each year—in January before the academic year starts, and in July. Faculties are able to undertake 'on the task, at the time' work during these sessions.

It is not easy to know when the balance is right. This is a matter of continuing debate at the senior management level.

THE FUTURE

The future requires the appropriate balance of resources that are fit-for-purpose and yet flexible. Our purposes are clear enough; our architecture is about right; and our infrastructure is about right.

The driver will be our vision of the learner and of the future into which the learner will journey as a thriving and contributing member of the community. This vision shapes our educational goals and our curriculum. It is completely compatible with the International Baccalaureate profile of the learner as an inquirer, a thinker, a communicator and a risk taker, who will be knowledgeable, principled, caring, open-minded, well balanced and reflective. It is completely compatible with the Victorian Essential Learning Standards.

We must continue to provide good access to information and resources and to tools for creation, expression and communication. Our balance of desktops and notebooks will evolve, our portal will evolve, and we expect to implement a learning management system. Quite soon there will be data projectors in every classroom. Depending on need, a proportion will be linked to interactive whiteboards. We have no plans at present for tablet computers or PDAs, but we constantly review these possibilities. A low-cost, lightweight sub-notebook computer with about two gigabytes of user memory would be more than adequate at present, given the other technology infrastructure available at school, in the home and in public libraries.

St Leonard's College is a very good school. It is a digital school. We do many things very well and we should do some things better. It has been useful to me to reflect on our journey and I am grateful to a number of my staff who have assisted with material, in particular Mark Blake, Information Services Manager, James Digby, Director of Finance and Corporate Services, Tom Fisher, Director of Curriculum, and Barry Hill, Head of House, physics teacher and ICT mentor. The errors, opinions and assessments are all mine.

CHAPTER 8

THE 'GOOD VIDEO GAME GUIDE' TO SUCCESSFUL INTEGRATION OF DIGITAL TECHNOLOGY:
A CASE STUDY OF INGLE FARM PRIMARY SCHOOL WITH INTERACTIVE WHITEBOARDS

David O'Brien

Our journey to explore digital technology or, more particularly, the use of interactive whiteboard (IWB) technology began in 2003. At this point there was no 'grand vision' for the buy-in or support of this new technology. The school community had worked through a two-year process of identifying a common vision and purpose for our work. This vision included an emphasis on developing our students' knowledge and use of new technologies, but there was no clear picture of how this might be achieved or what it may look like in practice. What had been discussed were the new political, social and economic contexts in which we now live and work, and how we might organise ourselves to best meet the complexities and challenges we now faced as an educational community.

SCHOOL CONTEXT AND APPROACH TO CHANGE

Our school, Ingle Farm Primary, is unique in terms of primary schooling in South Australia. It is comprised of three sectors:

- a **Primary sector,** which caters for students from five to 13 years of age. This group is characterised by significant poverty and large cohorts of Aboriginal and English as a Second Language (ESL) students.
- a **New Arrivals Program,** which serves the needs of young people from five to 13 years of age who are newly arrived in Australia and require intensive English language support. Many of these students have come to Australia through refugee or humanitarian placement programs.
- the **Special Education sector** catering for students from five to eight years of age with communication and language disorders, and students from eight to 13 years of age with intellectual disabilities.

With such a complex and diverse student population there is no shortage of challenges, dilemmas and issues that confront us in the development and implementation of an effective educational program.

In his book, *Solving Tough Problems*, Adam Kahane (2004, p. 30) describes contexts like ours at Ingle Farm Primary as having high 'dynamic, generative and social complexity' where the solutions to problems require a systemic view, a tolerance of emerging solutions, and a commitment to what Fielding (1999) refers to as 'radical collegiality'. We have used these ideas to work through issues in our school and to focus our thoughts around educational improvement and what needs to be done.

We adopted a model of collaborative research and inquiry based on the belief that professional learning and student outcomes will be enhanced through opportunities for teachers to share ideas and critically interrogate practice in an ongoing, reflective and collaborative manner. We also agreed that in these uncertain and complex times we needed to be open to new ideas and flexible in our response to the opportunities that may arise.

Following a demonstration of IWB technology in 2003, we had three teachers request IWBs for their classrooms. Teachers were told that the IWBs were available on request and that any 'take-up' would not be mandated. Since then, IWBs have been installed in over 30 classrooms, with teachers organising themselves to meet regularly to share ideas, lesson plans, dilemmas and knowledge gained through their experiences. This leadership and commitment by our teachers to professional learning were further evidenced in 2006 by the visits of over 70 schools to Ingle Farm

Primary to participate in training and development, which were developed and provided by our staff.

Our school context is unique and challenging. We believed that the best way to meet the needs of our students and community in these circumstances was through encouraging professional collaboration and learning among our teachers. The integration of interactive whiteboard (IWB) technology into our pedagogical practice, and more recent moves towards a digital resource base for our teaching, are examples of how a sustained commitment to collaborative research and inquiry by teachers can bring about successful change.

I will now turn to the principles that we used to develop, trial and evaluate the use of IWBs in teaching and learning. The basis for these principles may be surprising to some!

'GOOD VIDEO GAMES' AS GUIDES FOR TEACHING AND LEARNING WITH DIGITAL TECHNOLOGY

At the 2006 Curriculum Corporation Conference in Adelaide, I had the pleasure of listening to Professor James Paul Gee give a keynote address on what we can discover about 'learning' from video games. He argued that popular culture often organises learning for problem solving in deep and effective ways and that good video games can teach us much about how to reform learning not only in schools, but for adult learning as well. He went on to state that the real message we should take from good video games is not necessarily to use games for learning, but to use the sorts of learning principles that good games incorporate in our teaching.

The principles that he outlined resonated deeply with the beliefs, principles and methods that have guided our work in equipping our teachers with the knowledge, skills and strategies to use digital technologies in their teaching. These are as follows.

Search for meaning and purpose

Video games always situate or show the meaning of words and how they vary across different actions, images and dialogues (Gee, 2006). They do not just offer words for words, which we understand as 'definitions'. Games give words situated meanings, not just verbal ones.

Any learning in an educational setting is a complex and many-faceted phenomenon. It is not static: it comprises vital, dynamic processes operating in changing contexts. To promote and sustain learning in digital technology, it has to be situated within:

- a shared understanding of the contexts in which we work and live, and
- a collective vision that directs the learning of all members of our school community.

In creating our vision we drew on the work of Layton (2000), who argues that we should not begin our planning for the future by starting where we are at today and imagining how to move forward. He states that this approach encourages people to drag along a great deal of excess baggage. Instead we carefully considered where we wanted to be, and where we think we will be, and worked back through all the steps necessary to get to that point. This process culminated in a statement that epitomises what we stand for and believe in as a school community. It states the principles that guide and inform our teaching practice, the qualities we are seeking to develop in each student and the values that underpin our work in the educational community.

Contextual issues play a major role in finding situated meaning. What may be best practice here may not be within another school setting. Acknowledging this, we realised that we need to be continually asking critical questions, putting ideas into place and then playing with them. We have had to think thoughtfully and rigorously about our work, questioning our assumptions and drawing on research, while continually reflecting on and inquiring into our practice. The contesting of ideas and the capacity to learn from one another has been crucial. We are continually asking whose interests do our schooling structures, teaching methodologies and curriculum currently serve.

Distributed intelligence and cross-functional teams

Good video games use 'smart tools', have distributed knowledge and recruit cross-functional teams, just like in modern high-tech workplaces (Gee, 2006). Often each player must master a specialty, but must also understand enough about the other specialised skill sets to coordinate with other team members. Thus, the core knowledge needed to play video games is distributed among a set of real people.

The process that has had the most significant influence on our professional learning has been the release of staff from their classroom duties to join cross-functional groups to share ideas and perspectives and conduct research. This form of collaborative inquiry has had a positive impact on teaching and learning by providing a lens for examining the technology and teaching practices, as well as developing a deeper sense of efficacy and hope through the conversations and collegial support offered by the group (Weinbaum et al., 2004, p. 78; Mawhinney et al., 2005, p. 36).

Darling-Hammond (1998) argues that this form of collaborative inquiry builds intellectual capital, developing more professional roles for teachers as they construct knowledge that is useful for both practice and ongoing theory building, and aligning professional development with current learning theory. Certainly, our school has sought to marshal the thoughts and talents of the staff to guide our strategies with digital technology in holistic, creative and constructive ways. The inquiry process is about encouraging others' questions, facilitating conversation, initiating investigations and welcoming multiple points of view. It offers staff a way to synthesise different kinds of knowledge, experience and ideas with the intention that this will ultimately make a difference for student learning.

The process of collaborative inquiry has parallels with constructivist and sociocultural theories of learning and encourages our teachers to 'live' the principle that forms the basis of our approach to student learning. This view is supported by Johnson and Golombek (2002) in stating that:

> If we view teacher learning from a socially situated perspective, it follows that teachers need multiple opportunities to examine the theoretical knowledge they are exposed to in their professional development opportunities within the familiar context of their own teaching and learning experiences. It must be understood against the backdrop of teachers' professional lives, within the settings where they work, and within the circumstances of that work. (p. 8)

Evidence has shown that schools that have found ways of embedding democratic learning into their daily practice with a strong focus on teaching that emphasises disciplined inquiry and substantive conversation, not only improve learning outcomes for students but do so in a manner more equitable than traditional schooling processes (Ladwig & Gore, 1998, p. 21).

From my observations and conversation with staff, our collaborative groupings are providing opportunities for teachers to exchange ideas and develop strategies for what they want to try next in a more consistent and long-term approach to learning. Our discussions have also identified that reflection and inquiry into teaching and the integration of digital technology will not easily cut through the teacher's basic assumptions and beliefs and open up new possibilities. Our experience is showing that this will only take place when there is time to build relationships, mutual understanding and trust, as well as productive facilitation that draws the conversation into a deeper analysis of the beliefs and assumptions that group members bring to this forum.

Simulations of experience and preparation for action

Good video games operate on a principle of performance before competence (Gee, 2006). Players can perform before they are competent, supported by the design of the game, the 'smart tools' that the game offers and, often, other more advanced players (in the game or in chat rooms). On the other hand, schools traditionally want competence before performance.

Our professional development and support for staff have placed a high priority on this principle of performance before competence. If we waited for competence before the use of IWBs, they would still be in storage! There is a strong need for 'play' and a 'just in time' approach to staff learning. At the same time, this 'play' needs to be informed by the beliefs, principles and values that guide our actions as a school community.

Second, learning is best structured by goals and preparation for action with comprehension grounded in perceptual simulations that prepare you for that learning (Gee, 2006). Staff can easily be seduced by the visual and colourful nature of digital technology, but still find themselves delivering a curriculum that shows little regard for our stated beliefs and principles in regards to preparing our students for the twenty-first century. Like the discerning video game player who dismisses the 'eye candy' in order to achieve their goal, teachers also need to constantly reflect on the principles that guide their practice and assess whether certain hardware and software programs align with more contemporary beliefs about learning.

Teacher agency, ownership and control

Good video games are built on a cycle where players hypothesise, probe the world, get a reaction, reflect on the results, re-probe to get better results—a cycle typical of experimental science and of reflective practice (Gee, 2006). These games let players act as producers, not just consumers. They often have different levels of difficulty, and good games allow problems to be solved in multiple ways. Good games also allow players to customise the game to fit their learning and playing styles. Thanks to these features, players feel a real sense of agency, ownership and control. It's their game!

Along similar lines, I believe that educational improvement requires a truly democratic environment characterised by trust and respect among colleagues and mutual support. This is best summarised by Elmore (2006) where he states:

> *If I, as leader, induce collective action through control, I have in effect taken responsibility for telling you what to do, which is the equivalent of a teacher assuming full responsibility for imparting to the student what he or she needs to know. Control falls apart as a strategy of collective action for the same reasons that 'telling' falls apart as a strategy of teaching. For the 'teller' to tell you what to do requires (a) that the teller knows what to tell you to do; (b) that you are willing to consent to what the teller tells you what to do; and (c) that you actually know how to do what the teller tells you to do. (p. 285)*

He goes on to explain that if any of these conditions are not present, the power to produce collective action is lost. Adapting Elmore's (2006) example (p. 285) to the implementation of digital technology:

If I, as principal, were to tell every teacher to use the IWB in particular ways, there is no guarantee that these would be the best ways to use IWBs, or that if they were, that I would be able to effectively communicate that to teachers. Since I am not the one doing the teaching, the teacher can choose, within limits, whether or how to consent to my request; if the teacher chooses to resist, he or she substantially decreases my ability to be an effective leader. My directive also assumes that the teacher actually knows what to do, and implies that at the present time the teacher is not doing it. In these circumstances it may be that the teacher could not do what I want him or her to do because the teacher doesn't know how to do it; the fact that I tell the teacher to do something doesn't mean that the teacher is able to learn. This conundrum sounds suspiciously like 'I can teach you, but I can't learn you'.

In contrast to this example, our professional growth and development as a 'digital school' has been characterised by choice, collaborative and collegial support, and authority based on moral and intellectual grounds and personal agency rather than hierarchical commands from the principal. There is individual ownership and control of the learning program that is complemented by expertise and knowledge from both within and outside the organisation.

When we first engaged with IWBs there was little outside expertise on which we could draw. Consequently we had to organise our professional learning in a way that allowed for an emergent knowledge base supported mainly by the 'doers' or early engagers in our school. We also received valuable support from an interstate school, with visits coordinated between the sites to share knowledge, ideas and resources. At the local level, our efforts have been sustained by peer coaching, mentoring, team teaching, inquiry groups and networking with teachers from other schools as we sought to develop a new resource base to inform our teaching.

Consolidation and challenge

Good video games offer players a set of challenging problems and then let them practise these until they have achieved mastery (Gee, 2006). Then the game throws a new class of problem at the player, requiring them to rethink their taken-for-granted mastery. In turn, this new mastery is consolidated through repetition (with variation), only to be challenged again. This cycle of consolidation and challenge is the basis for the development of expertise in any domain. Good games stay within, but at the outer edge, of the player's regime of competence. That is, they feel 'do-able' but challenging.

Similarly, our professional development needed to be deep and fair—at first appearing relatively simple, then becoming more complex. Staff should not feel that professional learning opportunities are set up to make them fail, but rather to encourage them to feel that they can do better. Put another way, effective professional learning should be pleasantly frustrating, on the outer edge of a teacher's competence. This can lead teachers to experience 'flow'—so named by Csikszentmihalyi (1990) as an optimal state of intrinsic motivation, where the person is fully immersed in what he or she is doing.

Consolidation of professional learning has been a constant challenge as we continually have sought to develop our capacity to make the best use of IWBs. Length of tenure, knowledge and expertise in the use of digital technologies, interest and confidence, personal networks, access to professional development, and the knowledge base of our students all play a role in the ability of our staff to use the IWBs effectively. Our peer mentors play a key role in providing the necessary support to both consolidate and challenge learning. Each individual has a different starting point and areas of interest they wish to pursue and develop. By building social networks and linking staff with common interests we have been able to individualise our professional development programs to meet teachers' needs and consolidate their learning.

Low cost of failure

Good video games lower the consequences of failure (Gee, 2006). When players fail, they can start from their last saved game. Players are encouraged to take risks, explore and try new things.

In school contexts, people experience a lower cost of failure when trust is present. Research by Byrk and Schneider (2002) shows that schools in which trust exists are more likely to improve than schools without it. Drawing on the literature of 'social capital', they argue that when trusting relationships develop and are sustained, schools are more likely to have relationships that support collaboration and collective effort to improve over time.

Certainly our professional growth seems to have benefited from the willingness of staff to back their professional judgement and consider the multiple perspectives that exist across our school groupings. In the initial stages of our 'take-up', many staff who asked for IWBs prefaced their inquiry with a statement about their 'lack of expertise' and limited ability to effectively integrate digital technology in their teaching.

Teachers have spent a 'lifetime' in cultures that promote and value 'judgement' rather than 'risk taking' and mutual support. Byrk and Schneider (2002) remind school leaders:

As public criticism focuses on schools' inadequacies, teachers need to know that their principal values their efforts and senses their good intentions. (p. 129)

We have been very careful to make sure that our words and actions show that our staff can be trusted to do what is best for their students. In environments where teachers feel unsupported, mistrusted or constantly on the verge of reprimand, there will be very little risk taking and very little learning. To my understanding, this has not been the case at Ingle Farm Primary.

Reflective practice

Good video games encourage players to reflect on their results and work out ways to get better results (Gee, 2006).

Like these games, the form of collaborative inquiry that we have established and supported at Ingle Farm Primary provides an effective means for teachers to reflect and learn from their experiences in classrooms with students. When combined with insights for external experts and advisers, curriculum support personnel and professional reading, this multifaceted and reflective approach provides rich and deep professional growth for those involved. It not only enables teachers to develop a sense of agency about their practice, but also reaps learning gains for students, especially in the kinds of learning that are going to serve their future needs.

In summary, the principles that we have taken and adapted from 'good video games' developed by Gee (2006) encourage creativity, experimentation and collaboration. They have provided opportunities to reconsider long-held beliefs about teaching, learning, curriculum design and the role of digital technology. Teachers have found our approach to change based on these principles to be informative, challenging and supportive in confronting complex issues in our day-to-day work. Our experiences are reflected in the observations by Lemke (2002) about the consequences of collaborative, community-based change and development:

> As we learn we gradually become our villages: we internalise the diversity of viewpoints that collectively make sense of all that goes on in the community. At the same time, we develop values and identities: in small tasks and large projects, we discover ways we like to work, the people we want to be, [and] the accomplishments that make us proud. (p. 34)

OUTCOMES FROM OUR JOURNEY WITH IWBs

Our journey with IWBs has had important outcomes for teachers and teaching practices, for student engagement and for our school community.

Many experienced teachers speak openly about how the IWBs have rekindled their passion for teaching and broadened their perspectives in regards to curriculum delivery—and their ICT competence has improved markedly! Teachers comment that IWBs have created a more engaging and challenging learning environment for what we term 'children of the screen'. They provide a different scope and quality to their teaching and learning programs. Feedback from students supports this view as well as the tremendous advantage offered by the IWBs in terms of 'just-in-time' learning and the flexibility and spontaneity they offer.

IWBs provide a fundamentally different teaching resource base, and significant amounts of student work are now produced in a digital format. Since the introduction of IWBs, we have seen our pedagogical practices become more digitally based as teachers make increasing use of ICT peripherals such as digital cameras, scanners, audio facilities, infra-red keyboards, slates and new software. More use of digital media is also being made in celebrations and ceremonies as students and staff see the possibilities for more engaging modes of presentation and communication.

In these ways, IWBs have been a vehicle for refreshing and stimulating discussions about pedagogy and relevant curriculum. Moreover, IWBs have brought staff and students together in collegial ways to solve problems, and allowed students to move from being spectators to participants in the game of knowledge creation. Most significantly, our students are developing greater 'agency' of their learning. The use of these new technologies has given them more power over their learning and promoted a greater sense of partnership in teaching and learning with their teachers. Furthermore, as teachers acknowledge the value of these partnerships and students' expertise in the use of new technologies, we are seeing students become producers (rather than just consumers) of knowledge, with increased ownership and control of their learning.

And what's more, our tentative conclusion is that IWBs are having a significant impact on student achievement, at least in terms of the trends in results of statewide literacy and numeracy testing.

Finally, the approaches that we have taken to the implementation of the IWBs and the associated professional learning have encouraged teacher leadership in very significant ways. This and the range of outcomes described above have led to an acknowledgement within the school community that we are striving to prepare students for *their* future, not *our* past.

REFLECTIONS AND CONCLUSIONS

What we have engaged in at Ingle Farm Primary over the past four years reflects the stages of technological use identified by Naisbitt (1984) in his bestselling work, *Megatrends*. In Stage 1, the technology is used to replicate the existing ways, gradually varying over time to a situation in Stage 3 where it is used in new and previously unimagined ways. We have moved through these stages as Naisbitt described, with our move to a predominantly digital mode of teaching and learning fuelled by the rising expectations and competencies of the teachers as well as rapid technological advances.

For those seeking to move further into the digital mode, I would offer the following words of warning based on our experience. New tools for communicating, learning, collaborating and information gathering are available to schools at an ever-increasing rate. With this comes growing reliance on mobile phones, PDAs, email, video-conferencing, IWBs and other technologies to keep us connected. This, in turn, increases pressure on schools to adopt new approaches to teaching and learning as access to information becomes faster and wider and deeper. Herein lies the danger of equating learning with knowledge acquisition and reducing the learning process to information gathering in the form of text, images, video and audio.

Learning has more to do with understanding and making connections between ideas and concepts. While technology can be used to communicate information about these ideas and concepts, it takes reflective thought and dialogue to make meaning of these connections. As educators we need to focus on teaching and learning first, and then selectively integrate those technologies that can best support our instructional objectives—not the other way around.

In this sense, I find it helpful to reflect on the question posed by Sanders (2006), namely: 'What is the problem for which this technology is the solution?' Achieving successful change in school settings, especially those concerning the integration of digital technologies, requires careful attention to questions such as this. In my view, the outcomes that we have accomplished so far have been due to our preparedness to question and to develop and collaborate in school processes and activities that are characterised by trust, a shared vision for change and an emphasis on developing collegial relationships.

There is still a way to go in the video game!

CHAPTER 9

STAFFING THE DIGITAL SCHOOL: IN SEARCH OF GROUND RULES

Greg Whitby

The speaker was just getting started but, already, he had lost his audience of young teachers.

'Education is an industry,' he said. 'It is just like other industries. Teachers are the workers in the process of production; education is the commodity with which they work; they are judged by the edge they have in a competitive marketplace.'

Images and metaphors reveal much about the beliefs and assumptions of those who use them. In this case the speaker lost his audience because its members understood exactly where he was coming from—the past!

Such old-style thinking identifies the teacher as the sole controller of the process, the dispenser of knowledge that he or she had already deconstructed and pre-digested. The role of the student is to internalise this knowledge. ('Sit still and listen! How else will you learn anything?')

The teachers may well have been thinking of their own students back in their classrooms. They knew only too well that these young people do not live in a world characterised by the mindset of the industrial age. On the contrary, they live in a world in which technology envelopes them (Beare, 2001). Immersed in the virtual world, they have never known a time without the mobile phone, laptop, MP3 player and the Internet. Like Mark Twain, they sometimes feel that school interrupts a good education.

While such relational technologies have made significant impact on traditional structures and organisations such as media and politics, it has had little effect on the process and outcomes of schooling.

TEACHING PRACTICE IN AN INDUSTRIAL AGE

In many ways, schools as we have all experienced them, are offspring of the industrial age. So powerfully influential were industrial processes and their effects on all aspects of society, that schooling was actually modelled on these processes, designed to meet the needs of a particular society in a particular point in history. This is not a new realisation. As far back as the early twentieth century, schools and systems operated under a business model, which demanded efficiency and value for money. The language of schooling changed to reflect this; anti-intellectualism grew and decisions were made on 'economic or non-educational grounds' (Callahan, 1962, p. 246).

Headly Beare wrote:

The content of schooling, the curriculum itself, became modelled on factory production lines. Children were divided into year groups; knowledge was subdivided into subjects; teachers became specialists and credentialed (literally certified like tradespersons) and ordered into hierarchies; the students were controlled in class groups or batches, moving in linear progression through graded curricula, from easy to more complex, from lower grades to higher grades, 'promoted' (as are workers in factories) up the steps ...

(Beare, 2001, p. 46)

The industrial mindset structured an understanding of the nature of the school and the work of the teacher. It still affects industrial awards and expectations of how teachers should behave and how schools should operate. Teachers are expected, for instance, to teach deconstructed parts of knowledge in set units of time. The typical time allotted as a 'period' of learning reflects this: *so much time to settle the class ... check the homework ... present some new knowledge or teach a new skill ... practise some activity ... set new homework ... settle class ... move on to next lesson.*

This pattern reflects a strong commitment to control and organisational smoothness. It is predicated on the belief that this is the best structure for learning to occur. This is how adults have traditionally worked in an industrial enterprise with time and space clearly defined. However, it does not have a lot to do with how children grow and learn most efficiently in a world that is changing around them.

The same mindset also encompasses the measurement and assessment of learning, which, in turn, has a profound effect on the understanding of appropriate pedagogy. The most valued aspect of deconstructed knowledge—so the thinking goes—is that which can be separated and measured. Once this sort of reasoning becomes the basis for determining teaching efficiency, it drives pedagogy in a set direction.

And there's more. It also influences the understanding of school effectiveness. In the end, reform hinges on competition among schools, with each striving to achieve mandated and measurable goals. 'Top schools' are the ones with the highest scores. Yet, as every reflective teacher and parent knows, the quality of authentic education does not lend itself to simple measures. Research shows that a 'focus on learning can enhance performance, whereas a focus on performance can depress performance' (Watkins, 2001).

This industrial mindset was reinforced by the classical management theory, which held sway through most of the twentieth century. It is reflected today in proposals for performance pay for teachers and monetary incentives for schools.

It is all very attractive, as well as being deceptive, in its simplicity. People accept it because it is the way things have always been.

A POST-INDUSTRIAL AGE

The digital revolution has fuelled an increasingly global economy. Thomas Friedman (2006) describes this phenomenon as a 'flat world' in which developed and developing nations now compete on an economically level playing field.

While China and India have become the new labour markets, developed nations strive to compete in a knowledge-based economy where creativity, innovation and skill carry economic premium. In this context, competence in accessing, reconfiguring and applying knowledge becomes a vital contributor to progress. This competence is very often exercised collaboratively in both formal and informal contexts so that communication becomes fundamental to knowledge generation and dissemination.

All of this marks the shift from an industrial age and its industrial economy, which relied on labour, machines, physical resources and standardisation, to a knowledge age which now relies on intellectual resources, technical competence and creativity.

Knowledge workers

The new era has produced a new type of worker with new capabilities and expectations. The task of these new knowledge workers is to apply emerging information and knowledge in the workplace. Their natural context is the knowledge networks that feed from and back into a variety of sources. Essential skills for operating effectively in this environment include: self-management, collaboration, analysis, flexibility, facility in integrating new knowledge, and working on different tasks at the one time.

Employers must embrace the new workplace if they wish to retain employees who are no longer 'anchored' to careers and employers as they once were. Rather, these new knowledge workers are connected to like-minded people and groups through online communities—free to move between virtual networks and collaborative teams.

At their best, these workers are able to operate at levels of increasing complexity in response to the changing challenges of work. And they are able to lead others in making similar adjustments.

TEACHING IN THE KNOWLEDGE AGE

Schooling is one of society's key institutions for inducting young people into the contemporary culture. It can no longer be appropriately conceptualised using the mindset of the industrial age.

If they are to be relevant, schools must respond to the realities of the twenty-first century, learning to thrive in a knowledge-based society. Teachers must be new knowledge workers. This requires much more than the widespread use of technology in schools. It calls for systematic change in both organisation and environment, and transformative change in ways of imagining what schooling yet might be. It requires a dramatic shift from control to collaboration and co-learning.

We have always had good teachers, yet the old industrial model tended to de-professionalise them. It assumed that they could not be fully trusted to take control of their own professional lives. There was always the need for awards and classifications, for close supervision and reports on progress. In the knowledge age, teachers must be seen as professionals who operate within frameworks that take full account of the extensive research base that supports their contemporary pedagogy.

A pervasive sense of change, reflecting societal and environmental turbulence on an unprecedented scale, has stimulated the quest for new ways of understanding schools and for new models of school organisation. In the mid 1990s, for instance, Caldwell (1995) was arguing for 'a new organisational image of school' as a starting point for a new agenda (p. 7). And Wallace (1995) was suggesting that 'school communities … need to reconceptualise the means by which they go about educating children' (p. 14).

Over the last decade this has been a recurring theme in the professional literature, both in Australia and elsewhere. A strong consensus is that schools are at something of a crisis point; an 'educational revolution' is long overdue.

Certain assumptions about schooling and learning are being proposed as foundation beliefs underpinning the re-imagining of schools for the contemporary era; each is loaded with implications in the search for new ground rules around the employment and development of teachers. These assumptions include the following:

- Students are at the centre of the process of schooling. The rapidity of change requires them to be prepared for lifelong learning. The best context for this is a learning community—both a community of learners and a community that is ever learning.

- This community must develop its capacity to use new information, to share learning beyond its physical boundaries, to be open to change. It must see both time and space as negotiable. It must create a climate where both innovation and diversity can flourish.

- Teaching is viewed, essentially, as a relational process. This belief has a powerful impact on the ways in which learning is organised and fostered, and on the ways in which students and teachers interact.

- Students learn to construct new knowledge, not just receive it. This construction is enhanced by interaction and collaboration. It employs Web 2.0 social and collaborative tools where appropriate.

- Teachers are learners. They learn by reflection on action, from each other, from the wider experience of their profession, from life—and from their students.

- Among the central aims of schooling is the development of the autonomy of learners who develop the capacity to take responsibility for their own learning. This becomes more important the deeper we move into the knowledge age.

- Authentic learning transcends the barriers of disciplines, timetables and organisational convenience. It is both interdisciplinary and integrated.
- Transparency, rather than testing regimes, is the new accountability. The rightful place of testing is within the context of the learning processes.

In their research on top performing systems of education, Barber and Mourshed (2007) suggest that two of the keys to success are getting the right people to become teachers and then developing them professionally so that they are able to make a quality contribution.

This commonsense finding raises important questions: Who are the right people—that is, the best teachers for schools of the information age? What are the qualities such people should possess? And how can a system, a school, a learning community, recognise these people and develop these qualities? These questions are worth reflecting on because they may well lead us some distance along the road in our search for ground rules.

As in every generation, the 'right people' to become teachers are those who, first of all, love children and delight in working with them. Their value is enhanced to the degree to which they are intelligent, curious, open-minded and creative.

All of these are desirable—dare I say, essential?—qualities of teachers in the knowledge age. To be fully effective in the school of the twenty-first century, teachers need to feel at home with emerging technologies, comfortable with innovation and change, and accepting of ambiguity and occasional setbacks.

They are good learners and good team members, able to work collaboratively with colleagues while taking a practical interest in their development.

THEMES AND GROUND RULES FOR STAFFING OF TWENTY-FIRST CENTURY SCHOOLS

The digital era has opened a world of opportunities that many educators are only beginning to appreciate. In this world there is no single roadmap for taking education forward, no one set of specific criteria for selecting staff, no manual offering simple step-by-step processes for professional development.

What we do have are emerging themes. Features of these set the stage for the creation of signposts or pointers that might stimulate our imagination.

Here, then, are seven themes that can be explored when considering the successful staffing of schools of the twenty-first century. There are many others, of course, but seven are enough to get the essential conversation started. Following an outline of each theme, I suggest a few ground rules that may give rise to fruitful reflection and discussion by those responsible for selecting and developing teachers—teachers who will be authentic knowledge workers in schools of the knowledge age.

1 Shared purpose and understanding of school culture

Teaching is purposeful work. Its focus is the individual student; its task is to promote quality learning outcomes for every student. Effective school structures and processes support teachers' work and serve the school's purpose through being grounded in a deeply reflective culture that teachers come to share, and which reminds them, in a variety of ways, of the significance of what they do.

Such a culture reflects a broad understanding of the most effective learning processes and the conditions that facilitate them. It draws a clear distinction between deep understanding and the superficial mastery of facts and skills. When teachers have internalised the principles of this culture, they employ pedagogies that match basic theories of learning with a knowledge of students' characteristics and backgrounds.

Some ground rules for building shared purpose and understanding of school culture

- The teacher is able to articulate an understanding of both the purpose of schooling and the ways in which learning occurs.
- The teacher is a co-learner who is willing to be inducted into an ethos of reflective practice that is strongly personal as well as communal.
- The school makes provision for serious staff exploration of emerging pedagogies and a sharing of best practice reflecting sound theory.
- The school protects time-on-task, encouraging teachers to distance themselves from the many distractions that can obscure the real purpose of the school. Consistent with this, it limits the amount of clerical work that is not seen as serving the core purpose of the school.

2 Alignment of values

The values of the teachers, the school and the system should reflect the shared sense of purpose and are appropriately aligned. These values would include student-centredness, curiosity, innovation, collaboration, critical discernment and respect for intellectual integrity. All of the parties sharing such values would be linked in a supportive relationship.

Frameworks and strategies supporting these values, both local and system-wide, would be aligned.

Some ground rules for aligning values

- The teacher is able to relate his or her own core professional values with those of the school and system.
- The school only undertakes initiatives that can be aligned with the purpose and values that link its teachers and the wider system.
- Both school and system provide infrastructures and resources that support the shared purpose and values.
- Many across-school opportunities are taken to reinforce the alignment.

3 Professional teams

While teachers work with a specific group and with individual students, they do so in the context of collaborative teamwork. They are members of a group of colleagues and fellow learners, reflecting together, planning, and researching as they go, up-to-date in practice and unconstrained by old barriers. In this context, connectivity becomes the norm, not the exception.

The teams may reconfigure for particular purposes, coming together for a certain time in order to meet a specific challenge or to plan a special task. The teams will often be cross-disciplinary with a focus on integrating the curriculum and removing unnecessary barriers that isolate the disciplines. Some teams may well work across the primary/secondary divide. Always the purpose is to ensure coherence and continuity in the students' learning.

One of the tasks of such teams is to share a growing understanding of the students themselves—their cognitive development, their life experiences and their social and cultural backgrounds.

An issue that is often focused on by professional teams is assessment that is under continual pressure and scrutiny by interests that are external to the school community. The teams are challenged to ensure that assessment frameworks reflect sound educational theory and a thorough understanding of cognitive processes, including critical thinking, reasoning, understanding and problem solving. The team ensures that assessment retains its correct place within the learning/teaching cycle where it influences planning, promotes student development and informs useful and intelligent reporting. Here, as in all areas of the curriculum and school life generally, technology can play a major supportive role.

Teaching would thus become more de-privatised as more teachers pursue their core tasks within a collaborative culture. This culture would invite students, parents, non-teaching staff and community members to participate in appropriate ways.

At a very practical level, this would open up questions of respons-ibilities, tasks and time allocations as well as salary scales. It would require organisational structures and arrangements that would serve this pro-fessional culture. As part of this, it would foster skills of self-management, teamwork and the use of technology in collaborative ways.

Some ground rules for promoting professional teamwork

- The teacher demonstrates a capacity for and commitment to teamwork.
- The school creates structures that encourage teamwork and recognise team achievement.
- The team is often the locus for professional development (for example, induction of staff, peer tutoring or mentoring, sharing of particular skills and experiences).
- The profession itself revisits custom and practice relating to remuneration, roles and responsibilities, and the use of time.

4 Flexibility

When change is the norm, flexibility becomes an essential quality of individuals, groups and school communities seeking to thrive.

Those who are able to respond creatively to changing circumstances and to grasp and incorporate new opportunities become creators of the future. In education, this can apply to teachers, to school communities and to systems.

A flood of new opportunities have accompanied the emerging and converging technologies, and the advent of the knowledge age. Interaction, for instance, has become integrally associated with the social technologies. In educational settings this is seen in the work of the professional teams I have just been discussing. It is at its most productive when it focuses on the processes of learning.

In the classroom, the new technology has stimulated the perceptive teacher to move from being a controller of knowledge to a mentor and fellow learner. The curriculum itself is under scrutiny, now beginning to be seen as more of a dynamic construct than a flat, linear one that sets out courses for everyone to follow.

This leads inevitably to a new consideration of flexibility in the use of time, space and people, which may be reflected in timetables, staffing arrangements and the processes of grouping students for learning. It may see teachers negotiating the use of their time within a framework provided by the system. It may see the existing models of cohorts, classes and disciplines actually replaced. Mobility of teachers and diverse career pathways and opportunities need to be more widely considered.

Some ground rules for creating flexibility

- The teacher demonstrates a capacity for creative adaptation and innovation.
- The school is prepared to implement flexible teaching arrangements, different options in timetabling, and permeable boundaries between disciplines.
- There is ready sharing of the strengths and talents of staff, especially in the area of emerging technologies.
- Throughout the system, there is an acceptance of different forms of staff utilisation, always within a framework that ensures genuine equity.
- The system assists schools to make full use of the potential of the emerging technologies in creating more effective learning and teaching.

5 Research-based practice

Contemporary teaching practice must be based on professional research and the reflected-upon experience of effective teachers.

Today, the ever-increasing research knowledge base provides a strong foundation for guiding pedagogy. While such practices need to be enlivened by individual teacher creativity and intuition, it is important that research is used to inform the creation of dynamic and interactive environments, where:

- the learner is at the centre
- learning is individualised yet connected to the learning of others, and
- learners and teachers interact constructively in significant learning experiences.

Further research is needed on the value of technology as a tool of learning for both students and teachers. 'Valuable' technology is not simply the latest aid to conventional teaching, but rather an evidence-based tool for attaining and expressing deeper understanding, and for enhancing cognitive and social learning outcomes. In this way, technology can provide better opportunities for personalising learning and communicating progress to parents/caregivers than have been available in the past.

When teaching practice is based on sound research, teachers can be more confident in subjecting their pedagogy, including the assessment that is an integral part of it, to constructive critique.

Some ground rules for using research to inform practice

- The teacher demonstrates an understanding of the general principles of learning that emerge from and are validated by contemporary research.
- The school and system promote or provide professional development opportunities that explore the practical implications of research on learning, particularly in the area of technology.
- The school and system ensure teaching practices that are promoted through formal networks and professional development opportunities that are reflective of contemporary research.

6 Connection with other agencies

To be truly effective, teachers and schools must work in partnership with other agencies.

The first, most obvious of these is, of course, the home. School has its most positive and significant impact on student development when it shares understandings and expectations in a supportive relationship with the families of its students.

Second, students are also members of other networks that link them—via Web 2.0 technologies—with other students within and beyond the school, and to community resources such as libraries, government offices and local businesses, and to organisations and groups within other states and countries. Teachers are well advised to account for the networks to which their students belong, and how these memberships may support class-based learning.

Third, teachers also have access to a wide range of professional, community, business, industry and government agency networks. For instance, membership of professional associations and teacher unions, and engagement with university-, government- or system-sponsored professional development programs afford teachers the opportunity to connect and learn from peers and experts external to their local situation.

Some ground rules for connecting with other agencies

- The teacher demonstrates an understanding of the importance of the familial, social and cultural backgrounds and networks of students.
- The teacher demonstrates an interest in and familiarity with various agencies and networks that contribute to extending the school learning community.
- The teacher is familiar with current technology and open to new learning opportunities.
- The school provides support for teachers in accessing networks beyond the school.
- The system links teachers and schools in collaboration around ways of improving pedagogy, especially through the creative use of technology.

7 Balance

Contemporary school life should be characterised by balance—a balanced curriculum where all aspects of learning are present and, as far as possible, integrated; a balance of time and responsibilities; a balance of desirable freedoms and essential constraints; and a balance of the various strengths of teachers.

One of the dangers of the digital age is over-commitment and burnout, because of the 24/7 availability of the technology. The culture of the school must ensure that students develop skills in balancing their responsibilities, managing their time and working in an efficient and economical way. Teachers, too, will do their most effective work when they are in control of their lives and have a healthy sense of self-worth and professional satisfaction. This requires that teachers have a manageable workload, opportunities to make significant decisions regarding their work, and the motivation that comes from viewing oneself as a lifelong learner.

Some ground rules for achieving balance

- The teacher demonstrates personal and professional maturity, a range of life interests and a sense of proportion.
- The school protects teachers from unnecessary and unreasonable expectations and pressures.
- The system leads a wider reflection on flexibility in conditions and arrangements relating to the employment of teachers and other staff.

CONCLUSION

It is clear that schools have moved into a new and challenging era. The knowledge age, serviced by a range of converging technologies, presents a new world of opportunities for learning, working and living.

The invitation to schools to play a leading role in this age is accompanied by many challenges. One of the most pressing is around the selection and development of appropriate staff. There is no quick and easy response one can make to this challenge. Nowhere is the old industrial mentality more entrenched than in the ways we conceptualise the nature of work. Of one thing we can be certain, however: the old industrial mentality is totally inappropriate for re-imagining schools of the knowledge age.

We cannot drive forward with our eyes fixed on the rear-vision mirror.

What is needed is a widespread and open conversation. To stimulate such a conversation, I have offered a framework of seven themes and some ground rules relevant to each.

Much of the change we are facing will be driven by our understanding of today's learner; how they learn and what are the emerging technologies. The manner in which we shape this change will depend on our imagination and the courage we have to consider the hard questions.

CHAPTER 10

ICT INFRASTRUCTURE:
THE CORE COMPONENTS

Peter Murray

There is considerable mythology—and not a little jargon—associated with the ICT infrastructure used in schools. The reality is that technology is but a set of tools, albeit a vital and potentially expensive component of the school. As such it is important that school leaders have a sound macro understanding of the main elements of the infrastructure and the facility to ask ICT staff pertinent questions about the development and effectiveness of the school network.

The aim in this chapter is to provide that understanding and to explore various options that schools have for implementing a suitable ICT infrastructure. The intent is not to make one recommendation or propose 'one best way', but rather to discuss different approaches highlighting the positives and negatives, and indicating the type of school environment to which a particular style of ICT infrastructure is best suited. Every school is unique in terms of its ICT budget allocation, staffing, leadership and strategic intent. Each of these elements makes a difference to the ICT infrastructure that a school or school system chooses to adopt.

THE CHANGING NATURE AND EXPECTATIONS OF ICT INFRASTRUCTURE

The word that best sums up the nature of ICT infrastructure in schools is *change*!

Until recent times, the ICT infrastructure model in many schools was dictated by the needs of administration, and based on long-term business-centric principles. This 'top-down' approach meant that the teachers, and the school's main clients—its students, were at the bottom of the pile and had little say in what their digital environment looked like and what they could or could not access. The general pattern has been that more consideration has been given to matters of security (for example, protecting the network from 'invasion' or other forms of misuse) and business applications (for example, those dealing with school finances), than to issues relating to teaching practices, curriculum resources and student learning.

Fortunately this pattern is changing. Teachers and students are demanding more flexibility in their ICT environment and are questioning the policy decisions of ICT managers. One of the reasons for this may be the growing awareness and capability of teachers and students in digital technologies, developed from their experiences outside of the school. These people have begun to notice the massive discrepancy between what they can do on-site at school versus what they can do at home; and they are demanding ICT environments where teaching and learning take precedence.

School leaders are also becoming aware of this divide and are encouraging their ICT staff to 'open up' access, while at the same time continue to provide protection from the Internet 'nasties'. This is a difficult challenge for ICT departments and often involves a 'ground up' rebuilding of their ICT infrastructure, as well as some reassessment and prioritisation in thinking.

ICT infrastructure—new priorities, better capability and more diversity

A traditional ICT infrastructure and management model in schools is focused around a standard environment, often based on one operating system and with little flexibility in terms of hardware choice by the user.

Fortunately this model is also changing. Not only are users wanting more open access, they are also having influence over the platform and other design features they want their hardware to take. Principals and teachers are now looking for the best instructional technologies available and then insisting that their IT departments accommodate their needs within the ICT infrastructure. Examples of this shift in thinking and control include the lessening dominance of Microsoft 'Office' software, and increasing numbers of schools embracing Web 2.0 technologies, like wikis and podcasting, and using creative technologies such as digital story telling, digital music creation and robotics.

Along with these trends are profound developments in the sophistication of the hardware and software. Some argue that we are on the verge of a 'platform revolution' in schools, citing the growth of Apple being deployed into schools around Australia as well as the growing use of 'Open Source' software.

CORE COMPONENTS OF ICT INFRASTRUCTURE

The core components of a school or system ICT infrastructure are:
- Identity management
- IT services
- Platform
- Storage
- Network
- Internet Protocol addresses, and
- Ports.

These are discussed in more detail below.

Identity management

Identity management (IdM) deals with identifying individuals in a system (such as a country, a network or an enterprise) and controlling their access to resources within that system by associating user rights and restrictions with the established identity. It is also a way of tracking user access to internal systems to ensure they are acting responsibly and within the 'Acceptable Use Guidelines' of the organisation.

A major component of IdM is authentication. There are a number of options available to schools, with Active Directory being a widely used domain controller. Each option has benefits. Openness and flexibility of the authentication system are very important. Most schools tend to deploy a number of systems that require authentication. Having different usernames, passwords and processes for different applications is confusing and inefficient. The ideal is to have a 'single sign-on'. If a school's authentication system is not open, or the system deployed does not use the same standards, then it may not be possible to unify usernames and passwords.

IT services

IT services are the systems required to effectively operate in a technological environment. These will include services such as:

- Email
- Administration system—student records
- Web services—Internet site
- File storage/authentication
- Learning management system (LMS)—learning portal
- Enterprise virus management
- Backup system
- Remote access
- Print services.

In some situations these services will be delivered by the school, in some cases by the education system, and in others by an external provider.

IT services should also encompass data storage, disaster recovery (DR) and business continuity (BC). The school or system office IT department may run reliable and efficient systems, but when disaster strikes without proper DR and BC policies and processes in place, the consequences can be catastrophic! Schools that have encountered natural disasters like floods, fire or hurricanes, or indeed human disasters like vandalism, have learned from bitter experience the importance of risk management, disaster recovery, and having 'backup off-site'. Fire can occur in any school.

Platform

Schools have a choice of platform or operating system on which to host IT services, including Microsoft Windows, Linux (Open Source) and Apple's OSX server environments. These days it is not unusual for schools to run a hybrid of all three operating systems (OSs), making the decision on what is best for the designated task. Each system has advantages and disadvantages. Typically schools are dominated by Microsoft-centric solutions, but schools can be clever with their technology expenditure by looking at non-Microsoft options. For example, Apple's OSX server environment has an enterprise-based email system included at no additional cost with the following features: group email, blogging servers, personal serving, group calendaring, wiki server, and podcasting server.

Storage

Data storage is an emerging issue for schools and systems. Staff and students continue to demand more storage capacity. They need to store data for long-term retrieval as part of the school's information management system. The trend line is surging upwards, placing ever additional burden on school systems. The traditional view had storage located on hard drives in individual servers. While this is still an adequate method, larger schools are implementing centralised storage solutions, in particular with Network Attached Storage (NAS) and Storage Area Network (SAN). Both warrant close consideration.

Network

A typical network environment will consist of some form of core switch, which provides central distribution of network services. Depending on the size of the school or system, this could be a single switch, a stack of switches or a chassis-based core switch. A switch enables network traffic to be distributed to various devices that are connected to the network. It can be used to isolate network traffic to various zones. Typically, optic fibre will radiate from the core to outlining buildings where edge switches will be located to further distribute network services.

Networking is a complex topic and there are many ways they can be designed and implemented. Experience with 'amateur' network efforts in schools points to the need for experts to design the system. A common approach is to divide the network up into 'virtual zones' called VLANs (Virtual Local Area Networks). A VLAN is a method of creating individual logical networks within a physical network. Multiple VLANs can co-exist in

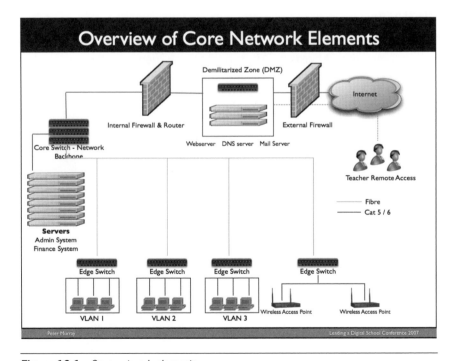

Figure 10.1 *Core network elements*

such a network. The main advantages of VLANs are that they reduce data traffic congestion across the network and isolate it just to the VLAN; can assist in managing LAN security; and aid in the management of computer labs through remote access and software deployment systems.

The network elements found in a typical school environment are shown in Figure 10.1.

Internet Protocol address

An Internet Protocol address (IP address) is a unique address that certain electronic devices use in order to identify and communicate with each other on a computer network utilising the Internet Protocol standard (IP)—in simpler terms, a computer address. Any participating network device— including routers, computers, time-servers, printers, Internet fax machines, and some telephones—can have their own unique address.

An IP address can also be thought of as the equivalent of a street address or a phone number (compare: VoIP [voice over (the) Internet Protocol]) for a computer or other network device on the Internet. Just as each street address and phone number uniquely identifies a building or telephone, an IP address can uniquely identify a specific computer or other network device on a network. For further reading I suggest that you visit http://computer.howstuffworks.com/internet-infrastructure5.htm.

Ports

A port is a special number present in the header of a data packet. Ports are typically used to map data to a particular process running on a computer. Ports can be readily explained with an analogy: think of IP addresses as the street address of a block of flats, and the port number as the number of a particular flat within that building. If a letter (a data packet) is sent to the flats (IP) without a flat number (port number) on it, then nobody knows who it is for (which service it is for). In order for the delivery to work, the sender needs to include a flat number along with the address of the flats to ensure the letter gets to the correct destination. Port numbers work in the same way for delivery data packets.

CONCLUSION

School and system ICT environments are highly complex. Even the smallest schools require most of the services listed.

Understanding the core components of ICT infrastructure—at least to the level presented in this chapter—is vital for school and system leaders. Having this appreciation increases the likelihood that relevant questions can be asked of IT staff and ICT companies to ensure appropriate decisions are made about digital technology.

One thing is certain: ICT infrastructure will continue to develop quickly and with increasing sophistication and importance. Therefore, existing goals and aspirations need to be rethought continuously, and educational leaders need to be part of that development process.

In closing, to learn more about the topics or the terms used in this chapter, call them up on Wikipedia, the free online encyclopedia. It is a useful, up-to-date source of information on digital technology.

CHAPTER 11

ICT SUPPORT

Peter Murray

Having the right people in an organisation is critical. Schools are no different, and for most school and school system leaders having the right staff in information and communication technology (ICT) areas is a major challenge. Attracting good ICT staff and keeping them is a major challenge for schools. While salaries are important, there are other factors that can assist in employing and retaining quality personnel. In this chapter we explore different methods for providing ICT support to a digital school and associated strategies for staffing.

'24/7/365' DEMANDS

One of the changes that has occurred in schools over the last few years is the expectation that ICT systems are always available. The old concept was that schools would only operate between (say) 9am to 4pm and therefore the ICT systems only needed to be available during those hours.

That is now a distant memory. Students, staff, parents and the wider community expect to access the school network, like all other networks, 24 hours a day, seven days a week, 365 days a year (24/7/365). Teachers and students in a digital school will rightly expect to have the network available for use 100 per cent of the time.

As the demands to provide relevant ICT services grow, so too does the need for schools to support the increasingly complex environments. No matter what size the school, some form of ICT support is required. This can range from providing desktop support for users to providing support for complex network and server environments. It is no longer acceptable that school ICT systems are down for long periods of time, nor is it acceptable for staff and students to wait long periods of time for their IT problems to be resolved.

TECHNICAL SUPPORT—INTERNAL OR OUTSOURCED?

Schools can choose to manage their entire ICT support through internal staff, outsource to companies that specialise in ICT support, or use a combination of the two. In some situations schools do not have the budget to pay the 'market' rate for IT professionals and outsourcing is their only means of getting the necessary higher-level technical support. The success of outsourcing very much depends on who is providing the support and the quality of the SLAs (Service Level Agreement) that have been put in place.

The concern with outsourcing has been the lack of ownership of the problem by IT companies and a lack of understanding of how schools use ICT. In recent years, some of these companies have just focused on schools and have made an effort to understand their technology needs.

There is no one perfect solution to IT staffing in terms of outsourcing or employing internal staff. However, some trends that seem to have been successful across many schools include:

- Have at least one technical person employed by the school. Even if this is a low-level position, it provides a point of contact for staff. In some cases this person may be a teacher with allocated time; however, this is not ideal.
- IT support in schools is cyclic, and during busy times (start of year, reporting) a good approach is to outsource additional technical support. In this way, IT people feel valued and teaching staff can have their IT support effectively dealt with during stressful times.
- Many vendors provide phone support on hardware, and in some cases on software. Apple Computer, for example, provides an optional Apple Care Protection Plan where, at a small cost, users have access to a help line to gain support on hardware issues, operating system questions and other Apple applications such as iLife. This type of vendor support can take pressure off IT staff and the small upfront cost can be aggregated across the hardware purchase over the life of the hardware.

Types of ICT support positions

What kind of ICT personnel you opt to use will depend very much on your situation, with factors like size, type of technology used, funding and degree of school control over the employment of staff impacting on the best mix. Below are some typical ICT support positions. In smaller schools, one person might need to take on several of these roles.

- **Help Desk Officer**—The Help Desk position is the face of ICT support in a school. It should be the central point where IT incidents are reported. Even small schools should have some form of Help Desk, even if it is staffed for only a few hours a day.
- **Technical Support**—Larger schools should have technical support staff, in addition to the Help Desk, who are available to provide 'Level 1' support to users. Typically these are roaming roles and can assist staff in their classroom or in their office.
- **System Administrator**—The Systems Administrator is responsible for ensuring ICT services are operating effectively, and for implementing new services. Their duties include updating operating systems on servers, updating services as new versions are released, integration and authentication and the like. In some situations, Systems Administrators are responsible for SOE (Standard Operating Environment) build and deployment.
- **Network Administrator**—The Network Administrator is responsible for the effective running of the school network. This includes switch configuration and deployment, VLAN (Virtual Local Area Network) set-up, network security (internal and external) and Internet connectivity.
- **Computer Manager**—The Computer Manager is usually responsible for the day-to-day running of the technical team, establishing work priorities and project timelines. The Computer Manager will usually also have some technical work to carry out.
- **Director of ICT**—Large schools should have some form of strategic ICT position, a role that should bridge the gap between ICT support and the ICT academic needs of the school. The position will usually manage the ICT budget and inform the strategic ICT direction of the school.

ATTRACTING AND RETAINING QUALITY IT STAFF

Salaries are an important component in schools finding good IT staff and then retaining them. However, in many situations schools do not have the budget to pay the market rate. If schools do have control over salaries, then accurate benchmarking is the first step. Find out what a similar position is being paid in the market place and then attempt to match this as closely as possible.

There are a number of other factors that are useful in negotiating with potential IT employees or for retaining your IT staff:

- The cyclic nature of schools can be used to your advantage. IT people like the fact that there is some 'quieter' time during school holidays where they will have time to work on new projects, rebuild systems or update SOEs.
- Professional development and certification are important—where possible offer this as part of the annual package. Those who have not had to pay the bill for IT support training will soon appreciate the significant difference to those paid for teacher development. Several schools pulling together to employ a course instructor to train a group of staff can offset costs for these courses.
- Many IT staff love 'tech toys'. Keep their equipment up-to-date; ensure they have the latest and best gear to use. Where possible, give them extra gear to use, like a SmartPhone or an iPod that could be used also as a portable hard drive for technical work. In the overall scheme of things these are small costs to pay. If it keeps them working happily for another year, then it is worth the cost compared with that of having to replace a staff member.

ICT TECHNICAL STAFF CERTIFICATION AND RE-SKILLING

ICT systems change rapidly. For instance, a new operating system will be released, a major mail upgrade will be made available, and the backup software the school is using will be updated. School-based technical staff may have been originally employed based on the certifications they hold. Three years on, those certifications will invariably be out of date, and in some cases irrelevant. Therefore, schools need to recognise the importance of ensuring ICT staff have appropriate up-to-date certification and professional development opportunities.

Unfortunately, as mentioned, ICT certification and training courses are very expensive and schools are often reluctant to commit precious funds. However, without that ongoing investment your sustained digital school development is put at significant risk. Moreover, in some situations, schools may have to re-skill technical staff if old systems have been replaced with new ones.

TCO—TOTAL COST OF OWNERSHIP

Too often schools just focus on the cost of the computer hardware. It is all too easy to be 'blinded' by a bargain whereby computer vendor Y indicates he can replace your computer laboratory of 24 machines for $20 000. How many schools or education authorities have you seen that have opted initially for 'cheap gear' only to spend significant monies redressing that problem. The lesson of PC clones should still be remembered.

Schools need to take into account many factors in the total cost of ownership (TCO). For example, what capabilities do the computers in the laboratory have, what extras will need to be added, what software is included, how reliable is it, how much technical support will be required to maintain it. TCO should be calculated on the life of the laboratory—in many cases three to four years.

One example of TCO is with Apple technology. Included with every Apple computer is an extensive range of software suited to a digital classroom. The Apple operating system (OSX) is inherently stable and basically free of attack by viruses. It is easy to support and over a three year period, the TCO is lower than an equivalent Windows environment, which upfront may have cost a couple of thousand dollars less to purchase.

BUDGET ALLOCATION

Following the total cost of ownership theme, it is important that schools recognise the need to spend effectively in 'backend' technology. The trend in some schools is to focus on what is visible—desktops and laptops—and put cheaper, lower-quality infrastructure in place behind the scenes. It is often hard for a school leader to see value in spending an extra $5000 on a network switch or another $1000 per annum on server maintenance. Unfortunately this approach can lead to ongoing infrastructure problems, with teachers and students getting frustrated, and all the money spent on the desktops and laptops being wasted because the network is down 50 per cent of the time!

Depending on the size of your IT department and the trust you have in them to make large IT hardware purchasing decisions, you may want to consider committee-based decision-making processes. Alternatively, you may wish to use a consultant you can trust to assist in the process. Bear in mind the observations made in Chapter 5 about being 'in control' of the spending. There are also a number of excellent Australian email lists and forums focused on technology in education where opinions on hardware selections can be sought.

DOCUMENTATION, DISASTER RECOVERY AND BUSINESS CONTINUITY PLANNING

ICT technical people are generally poor at documentation, in particular with disaster recovery planning and updating as system configuration changes. The importance of appropriate documentation on the working of the various systems and their integration markedly increases when you lose a key member of the ICT team and someone new to the technology has to be quickly brought up to speed. Quality documentation is one way of managing—and, indeed, markedly reducing—the level of risk borne by the principal. School leaders should implement procedures where there are twice yearly audits of ICT documentation. In some situations it may be appropriate to engage an external consultant to review this documentation.

'TECHNICAL VERSUS ACADEMIC' SUPPORT

There should be no such concept as 'technical versus academic' support. The two should go hand in hand. Technical support staff must recognise that teaching and learning are central to all that they do, and supporting the teacher or student in the classroom is critical. Too often barriers are put in place by technical people because they fear the academic needs might compromise IT security. In almost all situations there are alternative ways of working, and some ICT staff may need to shift their mindset to ensure they always support the curriculum requirements of the school. This culture needs to be fostered. If your IT department is not supporting the needs of the students and staff, then there should be some accountability for their action. Don't be afraid to 'let incompatible staff go'. While there might be some short-term pain while replacement staff are found, the 'breath of fresh air' that will result when the 'right' IT person is found will be well worth it.

CONCLUSION

A quality ICT infrastructure and an ICT support team that can both maintain and consistently develop the digital technology are fundamental to the sustained development of a digital school.

Arranging effective ICT infrastructure and staffing support requires commitment from school and system leaders. Getting the 'right' technical people is crucial. Radical as it might first appear, by spending less on equipment and more on ICT support staffing, you will likely achieve the higher-quality services that make staff and students want to engage with the technology.

CHAPTER **12**

MANAGING AND SERVICING THE INFORMATION NEEDS OF A DIGITAL SCHOOL

Karen Bonanno

With the advent of the personal computer (PC), the Internet, the World Wide Web and Web 2.0 applications, millions of people are now creators and sharers of information in a digitally connected world. The early vision of the WWW by its inventor, Tim Berners-Lee, was for a single, global, collaborative information environment. An extension of this vision has been facilitated by the Web 2.0 technologies that enable users from around the world to connect online and share knowledge and expertise through blogs, wikis, multimedia sharing services, social networking and community tagging tools. Web 2.0 is about 'conversations, interpersonal networking, personalisation and individualism' (Abram, 2005). It is likely this level of communication, collaboration, community and contribution will be an expectation of our students within the digital school environment. Virtual places and spaces, preferably within an educational context and hosted locally, will need to be established to facilitate teaching and learning approaches that cater for this level of activity.

Prensky (2001) argues that the students of the twenty-first century are not like the Baby Boomers who represent the majority of the current teaching profession. Today's students—the Net Generation—think, behave and process information very differently. Prensky coined the phrase 'digital natives' and clarified this by stating:

> Our students today are all native speakers of the digital language of computers, video games and the Internet.

This student generation has grown up with computers and the enabling information and communication technologies (ICTs) that have changed the way we share and exchange information and collaboratively construct and create knowledge. These are the students who have been 'born with the chip' (Abram & Luther, 2004) and whose digital toolkit allows them to move adventurously through the maze of a hi-tech, socially-networked, virtual environment that entertains and informs.

CHALLENGES

The attributes of the Net Generation, as identified by Prensky (2001) and Abram and Luther (2004), provide multiple challenges for the digital school in the area of managing and servicing the information needs of the school community.

Students' 'nomadic' nature of receiving information, preferably in multimodal format, at really fast (twitch) speed via multiple connections from multiple locations, challenges the bandwidth, equitable access to and availability of high-end computers hosting the latest suite of software applications. School policy on connectivity to external applications and the use of mobile phones, iPods and the like are further challenges.

Multitasking and agnostic behaviour, whereby the Net Generation are capable of distributing their attention across multiple applications to randomly access information in a variety of formats, are challenging school information management and collection development policy. Also challenged are the concept of the school library as being a place and space for teaching and learning, and the importance of developing information literacy skills to improve the quality of the question asked by students to successfully link them to the best information.

For example, the overzealous blocking of Web 2.0 applications may need to be reconsidered as these students work best when they are networked with others in their 'collaborator' mode. This may also challenge how schools deal with shared authorship under the current assessment methods, but it will most definitely challenge the digital school when it comes to who owns the information generated in the collaborative Web 2.0 environment. Issues of copyright, intellectual property and plagiarism will haunt every school.

As experiential learners, these students crave interactivity, immediate response and instant gratification. These behaviours will challenge how teacher librarians service students' information needs through the provision of virtual reference services, personalised attention for research support at the point of need, and the adoption of Web 2.0 applications such as Real Simple Syndication (RSS) to filter the information flow. This will also challenge how teachers interact with their students in the information-creation process through their responsiveness and feedback to students, and their coordination of the cognitive process in a virtual environment.

What is more, the student's principled and direct beliefs and values, which are often exhibited through risky online behaviour or practices, are already beginning to challenge how schools deal with privacy, social responsibility and ethical behaviour in a digital environment.

RISING TO MEET THE CHALLENGES

In an attempt to address the challenges, school executive and educational policy makers will need to consider how to:
- effectively manage the productivity, discovery and usability of information
- identify and apply standards to ensure 'interoperability'
- source, manage and disseminate multiple, dynamic formats of information
- actively address and apply copyright, intellectual property and privacy requirements, and
- develop information fluency in every student.
  These considerations are discussed below.

Manage the productivity, discovery and usability of information

The development of information management policy within schools and education systems is essential. The scope of such policy might include, for example, online publishing standards, acceptable use of digital tools and spaces, copyright and intellectual property rights, collection development, resource management, filtered and disputed materials and plagiarism.

The purpose of the policy is to guide, direct and protect the user and the school or education system. It should exhibit the following characteristics:

- accountability
- compliance
- information exchange
- information accessibility
- preservation
- enhancement, and
- privacy.

(Bonanno, 2006, pp. 27–28)

These characteristics address the responsibility of the creator of the information, the *life* of the information, legislative requirements, application of standards, intellectual property, access rights, the process for collaborative engagement, publishing standards, preservation and archiving of valuable information, information enhancement for continuity and sustainability, and confidentiality.

The policy needs to address the adoption of specific standards. The use of metadata to manage and service information needs is crucial. Metadata is defined as:

> *structured, encoded data that describe characteristics of information-bearing entities to aid in the identification, discovery, assessment and management of the described entities.*

(Association for Library Collections and Technical Services, 1999)

Basically, metadata is information about information. Table 12.1 gives an example of a simple metadata record.

The elements in Table 12.1 (page 136) are based on the standards of the Dublin Core metadata scheme which has widespread acceptance across the library sector. The Anglo-American Cataloguing Rules (AACR2) provides the framework for the allocation of the values. The primary aim of metadata in an education context is to improve discovery. Additional elements and the related values can be added to increase the discovery rate and to assist the user in identifying how useful the information is likely to be.

Access to digital information, resources and objects can be improved by the application of metadata, either at the time of creation and/or at the

Table 12.1 *Simple metadata record*

ELEMENT NAME	VALUE
Title	An introduction to metadata
Author/Creator	Chris Taylor
Date	29 July 2003
Publisher	University of Queensland Library
Format	Text/html
Identifier	http://www.library.uq.edu.au/iad/ctmeta4.html
Language	English
Relation	Library website

time the item is catalogued, usually within the library and information management system (LIMS). If the digital information is valuable, then it is worth making the information available by describing it with metadata.

In addition, metadata is extremely useful for the management of the information in respect to security, storage, archiving and preservation. As Anderson (2007) states:

> The characteristics of the Web and the way it has developed are not conducive to traditional collection and archiving methods ... It therefore becomes necessary to think about how the traditional skills and expertise of professional library and information staff could be harnessed in order to rise to these challenges. (p. 44)

Creators, authors and contributors of websites, blogs, wikis, multimedia sharing services and social networking applications apply 'fuzzy' metadata. Therefore, to make this type of information available, if considered valuable under a collection development policy, the record is catalogued with metadata on the LIMS with a link to the information hosted on a separate server. A search of the LIMS then provides access to a wider range of information formats within a given discipline or subject area. One disadvantage of this separation of metadata from the original information item is that the linkage will be lost should the item be moved, deleted or modified.

Changes in technology also mean the preservation of digital information can be extremely difficult as the hardware and software used can become obsolete within a three-year cycle. A great deal of content can be produced by the individual student and stored with services outside the school network. As these services are owned by private organisations, there are questions about what happens to these repositories if the organisation decides to remove the service, charge for the service, or change the service significantly. This means additional expense to transfer the digital information into a file format that can be accessed. One means of addressing this issue is to maintain the content at its lowest level, such as ASCII text, and to apply cataloguing standards and controlled vocabulary within a LIMS to make the information accessible and useful. Further development of virtual learning environments (VLEs) should help to address this fragmentation of information while retaining metadata standards and preservation requirements.

Identify and apply standards to ensure interoperability

Interoperability refers to the capacity of digital information systems to transfer or exchange information among its various components, or data sources. An effective metadata scheme supports interoperability by providing a formal structure to identify the knowledge structure of a given discipline, and to link that structure to the information of the discipline through the creation of an information system that will assist the identification, discovery and use of information within that discipline (Association for Library Collections and Technical Services, 1999).

To explain a metadata scheme in simpler terms one can refer to the purpose of applying controlled vocabulary to created or sourced information during the allocation of metadata elements. A controlled vocabulary is a selected list of words and phrases usually chosen by trained professionals who possess expertise in the subject area. The *Schools Catalogue Information Service (SCIS) subject headings* (SCIS, 2007) is a controlled vocabulary designed specifically for a school environment. The linkage of controlled vocabulary to an information item is essential for high-level precision and recall of information.

The Internet does not operate under a recognised metadata scheme; therefore, there is no controlled vocabulary to assist in the management of the information. Meta keywords can be inserted into the web page, but these are applied at random by the creator who can manipulate the keyword entry so the web page ranks better in a search result and insert words that have no relevance at all to the body content. There is differing opinion as to whether search engines actually recognise and use the meta-tags in the delivery of search results. The practice of 'tagging' a keyword to a digital object (especially in Web 2.0 applications) to describe it is not part of a formal classification system. In most cases a collection of tags has been created by an individual for their own personal use.

Information resources available on the World Wide Web suffer from feral cataloguing. There is incongruent use of subject identifiers and keyword vocabulary, multiple styles of in-house developed metadata schemes and no common search domain. Minimal standards apply when it comes to classifying or categorising to assist in the retrieval of relevant information. Taylor (2003) refers to the outcome of this structure for a user as an experience of 'high recall and low precision', where:

> The high recall refers to well-known (and frustrating) experience of using an Internet search engine and receiving thousands of hits. It is popularly known as information overload. The low precision refers to not being able to locate the most useful documents. The search engine companies do not view the high hit rates as a problem. Indeed, they market their products on the basis of their coverage of the web, not on the precision of the search results. (Taylor, 2003)

In these circumstances, interoperability is compromised as the LIMS cannot exchange information seamlessly or make the information easily available for further use without double handling. A fully integrated VLE that accommodates the library or 'knowledge centre', related online learning and community areas, and the personal learning environment (PLE) will help to improve the interoperability of information systems for schools and education authorities.

Source, manage and disseminate multiple, dynamic formats of information

In the 1980s, many school libraries began to embrace the automation of the school's resource collection, which was primarily print-based. Use of the PC and, initially, Windows-based library automation software, supported by online public access catalogues (OPACs), which replaced the card catalogue, provided multiple points of access to the school's resources. A decade later, these systems migrated to web-based library and information management systems providing access to the school's resource collection, online databases and a richer content base of information formats via the OPACs and, at times, via remote web-based access.

As early as the 1990s, it was recognised by the library information service sector that libraries would need to change. While the digital era had not yet fully arrived, there were calls for doing away with 'physical libraries'. However, Crawford and Gorman (1995) argued that a 'library without walls' made no sense as a replacement for a real library:

> Libraries will increasingly offer services to remote users as well as users in the library ... [and] must continue to seek innovative ways to provide access to information and materials not locally held. (p. 165)

They added:

> Although the physical collection will continue to be a primary tool, [libraries] need to adopt tools and techniques that will make extended libraries work. There are many such tools already in existence and many more will evolve in the years to come. (p. 165)

The longer-term aim was therefore to consider information produced in digital environments, such as online databases, websites and Web 2.0 applications, as just another format to collect within an overall collection development policy of the school community.

A VLE of the future will host the next-generation LIMS that embraces the information complexity of Web 2.0 applications by including features that will cater for tagging, social bookmarking, learner-centric search and browse facilities, virtual reference, RSS, Semantic Web, visual and touch-screen OPACs.

Research by Mallan et al. (2002) investigating the impact of new technologies on the role of teacher librarians in Queensland highlighted that advancements in technology continually challenge the knowledge, skills and practices of the school library profession, particularly in the area of information access and processing. Their research also identified a feature of school libraries that has not changed significantly over the years—students and staff see the school library as 'both a *work place* and a *play space*' (Mallan et al., 2002, p. 5). This view was reinforced in the research by Hay conducted during 2004–05 with Years 5–12 students from 46 metropolitan and regional public schools in Queensland and Victoria. When students were asked to identify how their school library helped them with their learning, Hay (2006) reported:

> A positive learning environment that supports student learning where students feel comfortable and can pursue their own information, ICT and recreational interests, was central to students' view of the school library. (p. 30)

The physical facilities, access to a range of resources, computers and related technologies and school library personnel were also viewed as important. Hay states:

> Just under half of the student responses regarding ICT use and assistance specifically referred to the importance of having access to computers in the school library to complete a broad range of information seeking, information selection, transfer and storage, knowledge creation and production tasks. (p. 31)

These research findings support the view that the dominant ethic of librarianship is service. It is from this focus that a school library in a digital school will continue to draw on all forms by which information is communicated, use technology creatively and intelligently to enhance the services to the end user, promote access to information within a safe and ethical environment, and draw on the past to create the future in servicing the information needs of teachers and students.

Address and apply copyright, intellectual property and privacy requirements

Being a good steward of copyright compliance within a digital school is a difficult, and sometimes traumatic, task. Copyright infringement is often the result of ignorance or confusion as to the legitimate rights of the user of the information. Displays of this ignorance or confusion abound in the school environment, ranging from 'I found it on the Internet so I thought I could just drop the image into my presentation without needing to acknowledge the source' to 'I thought I could just forward the article I found on the Internet rather than just sending my friend the web link'. These examples of copyright abuse are mainly due to the current thinking that any material that is provided digitally or is available on the Internet is copyright free. But a word of caution: the absence of a copyright statement on a web page does not automatically mean that copyright does not exist.

Clear conditions on the use of information gathered from any source are vital. Most digitally published materials do carry terms and conditions on how the information can be used. These conditions are provided through a copyright notice or a licence agreement. Unfortunately, most users of the Internet—and, in particular, Web 2.0 applications—rarely make it to the end of the web page where these terms and conditions are clearly hyperlinked to documentation. For example, one clause from YouTube states: 'You agree not to distribute in any medium any part of the Website, including but not limited to User Submissions (defined below), without YouTube's prior written authorization' (YouTube, 2007). A major downfall with the documentation provided on the sites is that it is usually text-centric and is unlikely to be read by the user.

The concepts of fair dealing and library exceptions need to be communicated and must definitely be endorsed and supported by the school leaders. Teacher librarians play a vital role in providing advice on copyright compliance and the proper use of copyright materials in a digital school. With the increasing complexity of copyright and the diverse formats of information now emerging, it is also wise to call on additional support to clarify copyright issues within a school-based context. The information sheets for educational institutions within Australia produced by the Copyright Agency Limited (2007) and the Australian Copyright Council (1994–2008) are a good starting point as well as providing contact details for further communication on copyright matters.

Even an alternative to copyright, Creative Commons (Creative Commons n.d.), claims flexible use but still carries a term 'Some Rights Reserved'. The catchphrase, 'Share, Remix, Reuse—Legally', promotes Creative Commons licences that allow for more freedom of use, but with reservations. The core element appears to be exercising respect for another person's work by giving them credit where credit is due. Is this not acting in a socially responsible way? This is the attitude that needs to be fostered in a digital school at the point of retrieval of information and at the point of creation of information.

In addition, socially responsible behaviour needs to be encouraged to protect the student's personal profile. Students need to understand that online publishing has its hazards and it comes with responsibilities. Posting information about inappropriate behaviour may have ramifications.

Develop information fluency of every student

Concerns have been expressed about the techno-centric assumptions of the Net Generation, especially when it comes to how information savvy or digitally naive they really are. An initial literature review by Combes (2007, p. 23) into the information seeking behaviour of the Net Generation questions whether these assumptions are 'based on fact or merely observations that describe what young people appear to be doing when using ICTs, rather than their actual skill levels and achievements'. Her research with over 1000 students aged between 17 and 22 indicated that 'while students are confident in their ability to use technology to find information, they are less confident in their ability to manipulate [or] use the information they have' (p. 31).

The change in the information landscape over the last several years requires more attention to helping students understand and navigate the digital information environment. The term 'information fluency' has recently emerged as an extension to the focus on information literacy and skills development. Lorenzo (2007) defines the term as the 'acquisition of three primary skills: basic information technology skills (including computer literacy); information literacy skills; and critical thinking skills' (p. 2). Today's students need to become information-fluent. This means being able to:

- ask the right questions to identify the most appropriate search terms to effectively transact a successful search query;
- develop and apply high-level online research skills that require responsiveness to search results and utilising decision-making skills to revise the information-seeking process;
- be discerning users and understand the limitations of various search tools and the idiosyncrasies of specialised search facilities;
- check the reliability and validity of the information sourced;
- use information ethically and know when and how to give credit to an information source; and
- actively engage in constructive knowledge creation knowing how to integrate sourced information to expand their understanding and knowledge of the world.

BRINGING IT TOGETHER—DESIGNING QUALITY VIRTUAL LEARNING ENVIRONMENTS

The core components for the development of a virtual learning environment (VLE) are shown in Figure 12.1. Such environments should be built around a learner-centric infrastructure and provide for smooth workflow between web-based modules. This means that students and teachers are able to move seamlessly between LIMS, curriculum, online communities, assessment and their personal learning environment (PLE).

A well-designed VLE is characterised by the following:

- an effective and efficient collaborative environment
- provision of quality information to improve decision making and critical thinking

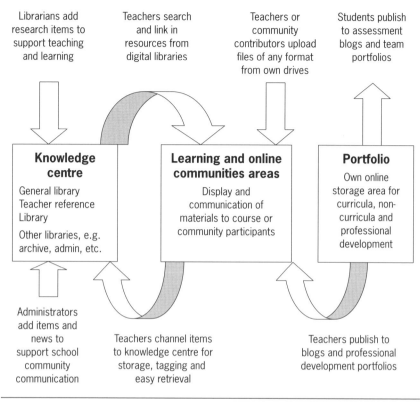

Figure 12.1   *The integration of personal, communal and organisational knowledge (Concord Australia Pty Ltd. Used with permission)*

- facilities for responsiveness, review, feedback and interactivity
- accessibility to information and data
- reduced costs, lower handling and robust storage
- flexible integration of information from various sources and in dynamic formats
- portability of information.

Anderson (2007) highlights some of the broader implications of personal spaces within VLEs:

These collections will become extremely important to people, developing into a form of personal archive of a lifetime. They may well contain content from a person's educational experience and have direct links with Personal Learning Environments. ... [and therefore] a person's personal path through the information space will become profoundly important. This path might include a record of the history of interaction with information sources, the setting up and continual modification of personal filtering mechanisms, records of group interactions ... and the use of other people's filters and knowledge. (p. 46)

One further potential aspect of a school's VLE is the establishment of a 'tribal community'. For the student, this shared space provides peer-to-peer connections and interaction, caters for the coordination of cognitive activity and development of personal learning plans, provides access to resources and personnel to assist with the information retrieval and knowledge creation, and accommodates the need for responsiveness and feedback between teacher and student. Through the use of these tribal community spaces, students' educational experiences (formal and informal) are captured as a record of their learning journey and achievements, and as a foundation for further development.

CONCLUSION

Policy development for the provision and management of information services is crucial. Such policies at school and education system level can help to sort and sift information from misinformation, guide the handling of disputed or filtered materials, and provide criteria for determining access to applications that may have been previously blocked. Information processing standards, as a key component of the policy, need to be clearly stated and applied to facilitate the identification, retrieval and use of quality information. If an information item is worthy of creation, it needs to be processed accordingly. Ethical practice and social responsibility in the creation and use of information need to be documented and integrated across the curriculum and carefully aligned with the copyright, intellectual property and privacy requirements of an educational institution. A policy position on a whole-school approach to information fluency across current and emerging technology environments is essential. Educators cannot assume that 'technology-immersed' students are automatically 'information-smart' users.

These policy issues are not new. Library and information professionals, including teacher librarians, have been dealing with these issues, and the relevant services to address policy, for decades. It is surprising that at a time when the information landscape is becoming more complex, some school principals and education system officers are endorsing the replacement of teacher librarians with personnel who are unqualified and ill-prepared to effectively and efficiently manage and service the information needs of the school. Hay's (2006) research offers a strong counter argument in concluding that

> Students value the flexibility of access provided by the school library, as well as the expertise of the teacher librarian as an information and technology specialist who can help meet their needs. The students in this study identified the school library as a dynamic and unique place, compared to classrooms, PC labs and other specialist rooms within the precinct, because of the availability and flexibility of [its] resources and services ..., and the individualised and customised attention the teacher librarian and library staff could provide students at the point-of-need. (p. 37)

Any moves towards the under-funding and demise of school libraries will have serious implications for the future of schooling. It would be unthinkable to have to consider the re-establishment of a school library, or its futures equivalent, in later years. New, informed commitment by educational leaders and policy makers is needed to manage and service the digital information needs of schools and education systems. The development and implementation of strategic planning in this area would certainly exemplify 'smart-information' thinking and practice.

CHAPTER 13

DEVELOPING AND SUSTAINING THE DIGITAL EDUCATION ECOSYSTEM: THE VALUE AND POSSIBILITIES OF ONLINE ENVIRONMENTS FOR STUDENT LEARNING

Dan Ingvarson & Michael Gaffney

Over recent years, there has been an increasing variety and sophistication of educational software and related ICT systems available to support and manage student learning. This digital technology comes in many guises—from software that is highly specific in content and directed in terms of instructional approach, to more complex multifaceted applications that have broader scope and offer choice and flexibility in the ways students and teachers communicate, learn and develop knowledge.

In this chapter we will overview recent developments in online, or virtual, learning environments and offer a framework for considering their appropriateness and value in contemporary school settings. We will look at the implications of these developments on teaching practices and suggest guidelines for school and system leaders for making decisions about the form of virtual learning environment (VLE) suited to their context.

Decisions about VLEs need to consider two fundamental questions:
* What is the purpose of creating a VLE in your school or education system?

- How does the VLE align with other components of your ICT planning?

Answers to these questions should always be based around the educational value of ICT, and the need to carefully integrate investment and implementation of digital technology with the purpose and vision, organisation and work practices, and community characteristics of your school or system. These are the premises underlying this chapter.

THE EMERGING ELECTRONIC LEARNING ENVIRONMENT

The detailed history of virtual learning environments is provided in Wikipedia, the free online encyclopedia (http://en.wikipedia.org/wiki/History_of_virtual_learning_environments). They are discussed in brief below.

Computer-assisted learning
The earliest forms of electronic learning environments were described under the label 'computer aided learning' (CAL). This term was used from the early 1980s in school contexts to refer to computer programs that were installed mostly in computer laboratories or on individual machines by 'tech-savvy' teachers, and led students through a specific topic or skill development process.

Learning management system
In the early 1990s, the ideas and practices of CAL began to evolve into the concept of the 'learning management system' (LMS). In early LMSs, content and delivery were essentially the same thing. Content was selected and developed by publishers to be processed by teachers and students in specific ways. Schools were faced with the situation of choosing various forms of content, usually from different publishers and which may or may not be appropriately aligned with their local or prescribed curricula. Further, it was often not possible to transfer or integrate content between different publisher products. This lack of interoperability caused difficulty for schools and publishers.

Learning content management system
The 'open standards' movement emerged as a response to the problems highlighted above. It was focused on ways to share content across different

LMS applications and led to the rise of the 'learning content management system' (LCMS) or Content Repository.

The LCMS is an online library with a range of digital content provided by teachers, government departments, education authorities or other agencies, or purchased from publishers, which is stored and made available to and by schools and education authorities. However, these tend to be complicated and labour-intensive systems, requiring staff dedicated to managing the content.

Intranets

Intranets are web-based systems where content and tools are made available via a login. They may or may not be automatically organised into classes. Intranets are used for navigation and as indexes to other tools. In this way intranets serve as 'portals'.

Local area network

The model of the 'local area network' (LAN) being accessed with username and password 'logins' has persisted as the most common way for educational organisations to store and share files. This design has advantages and disadvantages.

On the positive side, the capacity to share digital files has made for faster development and sharing of information. On the downside, there is a tendency for file servers to become messy and clogged. This is because information has been stored with insufficient labels or 'metadata', making retrieval and use of that information more difficult. To this point, it has been the organisational ability of individual teachers and the technical skill of the LAN administrator that have determined the effectiveness and efficiency of local networks.

The LAN has been and will continue to be a significant component of the virtual learning environment. As more consistent ways to 'tag' and store information are developed and agreed, the digital content created and used by teachers and students will be more readily available for supporting quality teaching and learning.

Virtual learning environment

Over recent years, education authorities in the United Kingdom decided that the concept and practice of the 'learning management system' were too restrictive and focused on 'controlling' learning. In response, they coined the term 'virtual learning environment' (VLE). This is meant to convey a less didactic, more open application of digital technology, which is more directed at learning and less about management and control.

As a consequence, a range of open and dynamic VLEs have been created in the UK. These VLEs are web-based applications, meaning that they are used through a web browser and provide 'anywhere, any time' access. However, having reduced the focus on content management and being relatively independent, free-flowing web applications meant that important integration with the school and system administration systems was poor. Hence, what emerged was the same problem that had been experienced years before with content management.

From 'virtual' to 'managed' learning environments

As some schools and education authorities began to realise that VLEs were unable to work with their other digital information systems, they began looking for alternatives. The result was the idea of the managed learning environment (MLE). The underlying notion here is to link student management information with the learning environment. Put simply, this means being able to use information from the student administration system in the design, monitoring and assessment of student learning being supported through the learning systems. More and more school and education system leaders are realising that they need to have inter-operability between the administration systems and the learning systems within the school, and across the education system as a whole.

Towards 'learning platforms' and 'digital ecosystems'

The term emerging as the most likely next phase in the development of online learning environments is 'learning platform'. Underlying this concept is the desire to keep students' learning central to the provision and outcomes of K–12 education, to have 'interoperability' between different, digitally based information and communication systems, and form a base that can be built upon into the future as both the technology and our ability to use it in education develop.

The elements or pieces of the emerging learning workspace for students and teachers that have been described to this point make up the digital ecosystem for a school. Examples of software associated with various elements are listed in Table 13.1 (page 150).

While there are other components that may be present or can be added at a particular site, the most important aspect of a digital ecosystem is that

Table 13.1 *Examples of software in school 'digital ecosystems'*

SOFTWARE	DESCRIPTION
Blackboard	Learning management system with a structured approach to how a 'course' (rather than a 'student') is put online
myInternet myClasses	Virtual learning environment
Moodle	Simple open source virtual learning environment
Drupal	Website content management system, used as a portal
SharePoint	An intranet
D-Space	Learning content management system
'Well-organised file server'	A basic virtual learning environment

one component can both 'feed', and 'feed off', another. This quality is called interoperability and should underpin the design of digital technology at school and system level. The ways in which information might move between the various elements of a school's digital ecosystem is shown in Figure 13.1.

From a school or education authority leader's perspective, the concept of the digital ecosystem focuses attention on what various parts of the technological infrastructure can provide, and how each part relates to others in support of student learning. For example, at class level it is important for teachers to know and be able to link individual student and whole cohort achievement information to the design of programs. This can assist in achieving a higher degree of personalisation for each student in the learning opportunities that are provided to them.

Similarly at school level, there are various forms of student information that are vital to students' engagement and development, including their health, attendance, family situation, academic history, personal development, interests and aspirations. The use of such information can have a significant impact on the design of teaching programs as well as the broader curriculum, structures and policies of the school. Effective school

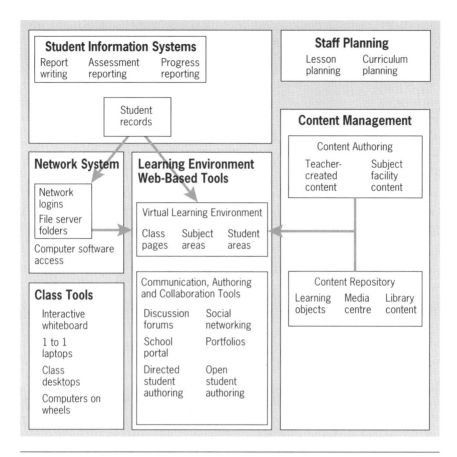

Student Information Systems
Report writing   Assessment reporting   Progress reporting

Student records

Staff Planning
Lesson planning   Curriculum planning

Content Management

Content Authoring
Teacher-created content   Subject facility content

Network System
Network logins
File server folders
Computer software access

Learning Environment Web-Based Tools

Virtual Learning Environment
Class pages   Subject areas   Student areas

Class Tools
Interactive whiteboard
1 to 1 laptops
Class desktops
Computers on wheels

Communication, Authoring and Collaboration Tools
Discussion forums   Social networking
School portal   Portfolios
Directed student authoring   Open student authoring

Content Repository
Learning objects   Media centre   Library content

Figure 13.1 *Elements of a school digital ecosystem (Vrasidas & Glass, 2005)*

leaders understand that the different stages, departments and subject areas of the school have different needs. This also applies to their use and needs in relation to the digital learning environment. Hence, while there may be a single 'ecosystem' for each school, it will have many distinct parts whose needs and potential need to be recognised and considered.

Finally, at the level of the system or education authority, the significance of the concept of digital ecosystem can apply to ways in which information about student engagement and achievement is used to inform decisions about individual school resourcing and staffing, as well as develop strategies for networking schools and supporting the growth of the intellectual, social, financial and spiritual capital available across the system (Caldwell, 2007). In this sense, the interoperability of information about the student, the home, the curriculum, the school and the school system, characteristic of a healthy digital ecosystem, can provide a more responsive, personalised, effective, equitable and efficient learning experience for each student.

To this point, the aspiration of a healthy digital ecosystem remains largely unrealised in schools and systems. And while there may be many reasons for this, some of the lingering questions in the minds of educators include:

- Why are we investing in online technology?
- What do we expect to happen as a consequence?
- What does 'success' actually look like?

The issue is whether teachers, principals, system officers and education policymakers have taken enough time to understand the possibilities and be explicit about their expectations of online environments.

Questions about how these environments are designed to operate and what they are supposed to achieve must be carefully considered. Otherwise we may end up wasting resources and developing 'sick digital ecosystems' that contain pathological entities intent on undermining the vision and culture of the school or system. Examples of the latter would include software applications that are introduced to monitor or control processes or performance with no appreciable benefit in effectiveness, efficiency or esprit de corps for staff or students.

In summary, the point about these emerging learning workspaces—from the earliest computer-assisted learning to the emergence of learning platforms and digital ecosystems—is that we need to understand the online environment that we are creating, or intend to create. And we need to take time to consider how the various digital components that constitute that environment can be brought together to form a cohesive, healthy digital ecosystem where information flows in timely and useful ways in support of student learning.

TECHNOLOGY AS TOOLS FOR TEACHING AND LEARNING

Whatever their technical design or sophistication, every piece of software or computer application used in education should be regarded as a tool to support student learning. Nowhere is this more evident than in the classroom where these digital tools can either support or straitjacket teaching.

One way of describing the interplay between the tools available and teaching approaches is shown in Figure 13.2. The vertical axis is about the

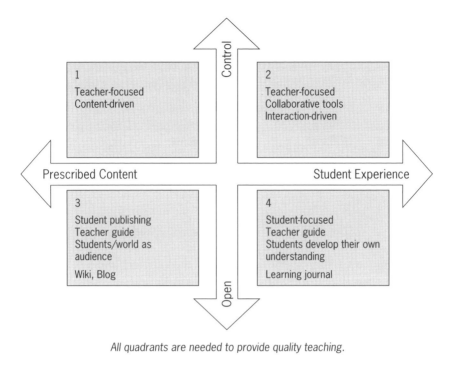

All quadrants are needed to provide quality teaching.

Figure 13.2 *Relationships between 'open versus closed' teaching practice and 'predetermined versus experience-based' content, and the use of digital tools*

teaching process and shows a continuum from tightly teacher-controlled (that is, focused on 'what suits the teacher') to more open teaching practices (that is, where there is more two-way teacher–student involvement in deciding the direction of the learning). At one extreme is where the learning path taken by students is predetermined by the teacher; at the other it is designed and reviewed by teachers and students in light of progress. The horizontal axis is concerned with content and illustrates a continuum from the use of externally predetermined content to drawing on content chosen and researched on the basis of students' experiences. At one end, teaching and learning is about working with content determined elsewhere; at the other it is concerned with finding and developing content of relevance and significance to students' personal contexts.

All four quadrants can be used effectively by teachers, depending however on the circumstances. They are generalisations about teaching practice and, for our purposes, serve as bases for considering how digital technologies can be used in classroom settings.

One way of gaining an understanding of the framework is to consider some 'offline' and 'online' teaching and learning artifacts and experiences associated with each quadrant. These are shown in Table 13.2.

Table 13.2 *Comparing 'offline' and 'online' examples across teaching practice—content quadrants*

QUADRANT	OFFLINE	ONLINE
1	Textbook	Static content VLE
2	Small group	Forum, Mindmap
3	Newsletter	Interactive global posting
4	School camp	Learning journal with digital footprints

In Quadrant 1, the focus is on predetermined content and a high degree of teacher control. This is the area where most VLEs live! Teachers choose the content, determine the order in which every student will work through that content, and set the learning and assessment tasks. The selection and control of content are the key features of the teacher's work and VLEs are designed to assist with this. However, VLEs have high overheads in terms of content entry, training and other set-up costs before teachers can use them effectively. As a consequence, many teachers are reluctant to start, and those early adopters who do, have tended to give up and move on to other possibilities.

In Quadrant 2, teacher-directed use of collaborative tools and techniques are evident. The focus shifts from predetermined content towards topics and issues drawn from students' experiences. These are discovered and discussed through dialogue among students and between students and teachers, rather than by static textual review. Tools that represent the online version of these types of teacher-driven student discussions include chats and forums.

Many VLEs have simple basic versions of these tools. Unfortunately, some teachers have found that they need to do more work to get the same result as they would through the usual, offline class group discussion. On the other hand, they have also observed that there are different dynamics that occur in online interactions to those that happen in normal face-to-face classroom situations. There is still a way to go with these tools. They need to capture the nuances of classroom interactions and be able to summarise for the teacher what has occurred with the interactions in a way that can reduce the teacher's work, rather than the teacher having to read every post and comment to try to glean what is important.

In Quadrant 3, there is an open approach to teaching the predetermined content used for learning. The validity of the content from particular media is questioned and assessed through student feedback and critical thinking. The wiki has shown itself to be an effective medium for this process. Interestingly, Wikipedia is the best example of its success, and not only because of its accuracy content (yes, we need to get over our fears of incorrect content, but it has been shown to be as accurate as any other source!). In fact, the main benefit is that students who are involved in the authorship of wiki pages and who have suitable guidance from their teachers learn to come up with accurate and agreed answers gleaned from multiple sources. It is that process of review and reflection around the content that provides for deeper and longer-lasting learning.

In Quadrant 4, teaching practices support student exploration and self-generation of the path to learn. It highlights the constructivist approach to learning, with students' experiences being the key means for engendering adventurous, creative problem solving and critical thinking. Buzz words aside, students cannot work in Quadrant 4 without a solid basis in literacy and numeracy or an effective scaffold designed by teachers to support their students.

A recent Australian study (ACMA, 2007) highlighted some important implications for Quadrant 4 teaching and learning in reporting that

> Over 40% of children and young people have some of their own material on the Internet and one third have a social networking site. From the age of 14 onwards 70% or more of teenagers have engaged in some form of web authorship. (p. 9)

This reflects an historic change in publishing. Never before have so many young people had the chance to publish to a world audience on such a scale.

In this context it is important for educators to realise that new, digital forms of self-directed learning are burgeoning among school-age students. This learning needs to be recognised, informed and guided by the school, as well as inform and guide the school in its curriculum design and teaching practices.

Currently, there are few teaching tools that specifically exist in Quadrant 4. Computers are not great at supporting these open-ended, flexible forms of teaching as yet. We believe that as more tools are developed for Quadrant 4 teaching practices over the coming years, we will see more high-quality teaching being supported through their use, to supplement teachers' strategies in ways that educators have been aspiring to do offline and online since the time of John Dewey.

Gifted teachers use all quadrants, but at the right times with the right students. They are able to move their students 'out of the everyday' to engage and help them to achieve deeper levels of understanding. The provision and use of Quadrant 4 tools are suited to those moments when the teacher sees that it is the 'right time', and has the option to 'release' students to fully immerse themselves in their learning. These types of digital technologies can make those moments more evident for all teachers, not just the gifted ones.

A summary of the types of digital tools associated with each of the quadrants is presented in Table 13.3.

Table 13.3 *Examples of digital tools associated with teaching practice—content quadrants*

QUADRANT	DIGITAL TOOL	FOCUS
1	Interactive whiteboard	Practices of author, publish, consume
2	Virtual Learning Environment	Moving content online, and practices of author, publish, consume, respond, assess, record, compare, review
3	Wiki	Questioning, assessment, feedback and critical thinking
4	Resilience and reasoning tools (due in the future)	Higher-order thinking practices of ask, brainstorm, choose, act, review, find another solution, share, compare

One purpose of this chapter is to debunk the myth that the use of digital technology automatically means a more open, learner-focused education that prepares students for the twenty-first century. Rather, it is the quality of the teaching that makes the biggest difference to student outcomes. The goal of technology is to support, extend and improve the quality of teaching that is provided to every individual student. It is the teachers that matter, not the technology.

Improving student outcomes is a complex process. Digital technologies can support student learning by extending the repertoire of teachers and informing their teaching strategies. Future developments, for instance, might include Google searches especially customised for school education in response to questions such as 'What could work for my class—and this student—today?', as well as more sophisticated systems to track student engagement, achievement and wellbeing. These types of possibilities can provide a scaffold for teachers to improve their teaching.

We need to have inspirational educational goals for the use of digital technologies. Otherwise we risk those technologies being solely used to meet the administrative needs of schools and school systems. While these are necessary functions of an ICT system, they will not bring about improvements in teaching practice and student achievement.

This discussion of the use of digital tools to support and improve teaching reflects our longer-term aspirations for the use of digital technologies. However, today there are a number of pressing practical questions facing educators and educational planners and policymakers about what technology is available and how to make best use of it. In the final section of this chapter, we will overview some important considerations to assist educational leaders in making decisions about technology, especially how to develop and sustain a vibrant virtual learning environment.

WHAT TO LOOK FOR IN A LEARNING PLATFORM

Understanding the interplay between teaching practice and the use of various digital tools—for example, as discussed in terms of the four quadrants above—is vital in determining the type of learning platform (LP) that would be useful or appropriate for your educational setting. This provides the basis for considering a range of design options for LPs.

The basic premise is that LPs should help to organise, expand and streamline the 'teaching, learning and assessment space' occupied by students and teachers. In general terms, the modern LP will provide a house for content (either written by your teachers or purchased and imported), an online page where students go to see that content, and a set of collaborative and class administrative tools. Becta, the key government digital education authority in the UK, lists the core features of LPs as:

- Content management and content sharing
- Class assessment management
- Collaboration and communication
- Assignment and portfolio management
- Interoperability.

In practice, each LP is different due to differences in needs and context, but there are some common functional requirements. These can be aggregated into three areas: content, management and communications.

Content

In effective learning platforms, users create resources to meet the needs of learners. They tag those resources to make them discoverable by others, who can further tailor those resources in terms of content and sequence to meet their personal requirements. This provides efficiencies in staff time needed to find relevant content, and in the re-use of existing content to meet specific needs of learners.

By ensuring content is packaged in a way that can be used on a variety of platforms, the learner can access and transfer content when and where they wish, and in a format of their choice. Further, through allowing the direct submission of students' work for assessment and having systems in place to monitor progress, not only can valuable time be saved, interventions can also be made and feedback given in timely fashion.

Management

Use of the learning platform should provide a means of meeting learners' accessibility needs—both in terms of disability access and for those learners who cannot attend physically.

Second, the ability to assess and map learners' needs to data stored in the organisation's management information system (MIS) provides a sound basis on which to develop individual targets and education plans. This ability to plan lessons and provide a focus for prereading, extension activities, practice activities and discussions around topics allows teachers to plan in a more natural way and keep learners on track and working at their own pace.

The ability to sequence learning activities means that teachers retain control over the learning path. It ensures that the most effective or appropriate path is highlighted, while leaving the learner with opportunities, where appropriate, to choose a different route suited to their targets and interests.

Third, in effective LPs the use of unique learner identifiers means that learners and teachers can be provided with secure information directly relevant to students' individual learning targets and plans. The learner and teacher can be digitally grouped to support collaborative approaches to learning.

A fourth feature of effective management in LPs is the capability for student information (including attendance and performance data) to be transferred between schools and education sectors, thereby supporting smoother transitions and progressions, continued learning portfolio development and more informed longer-term planning.

Finally, worthwhile LPs incorporate elements to manage access rights. These promote efficiency by providing targeted personalised learning resources to those who need them, rather than providing blanket licensing for everyone.

Communications

Effective LPs contain discussion forums, blogs, wikis, email and other messaging facilities to support peer communication and review processes. They are also inclusive of learners not comfortable or unable to participate in face-to-face discussions. A further aspect of communication functionality is the use of audiovisual conferencing to remove geographical barriers and wasted travel time by linking and sharing teaching resources nationally and internationally.

Look at the cultural as well as the technical factors

A key technical element of LPs is their capacity to organise content so that it can be shared and built upon. Therefore, the most valuable tools are those that upload content, organise content and send content to a class. These are often the most used tools and replace the traditional file server for sharing content.

When content (word documents, website links, pdf or any digital file) is uploaded, it needs to have information added so that it can be identified and retrieved when needed. This information is called metadata or 'information about the information'. Metadata can include details about the subject, topic and year level and allows files to be grouped in ways that make sharing easier. (See also Chapter 12.) This capability requires effort to enter and update the content, and this has been one of the barriers to take-up of virtual learning environments. Teachers need more time to upload their Microsoft Word files on to the LP than to save it to a file server. For content that has been 'authored' (that is, done in a web browser), the changes are easy and quick. On the other hand, if teachers use Word or other like applications to create and maintain their content, then additional work is needed to gain the benefits of an organised LP.

But there are more things to consider in choosing an LP than the technical aspects and capabilities. *The implementation of digital technologies in schools is about school change, not purchasing a product.* If your school is new to technology, or has entrenched ICT systems and personnel, the development of a learning platform may well meet with a lukewarm response.

In the initial stages, the implementation of an LP often means that teachers' 'freedom' to have a plethora of files and photocopies is reduced. However, as the school moves through the change process, the isolation, duplication and poor use of resources (often brought about through lack of communication between staff) are reduced. Teachers' private class-rooms become a little more exposed, and an audience is a powerful motivator for change.

As the implementation of the LP progresses, collaboration and management tools become more important. These developments work to support the later stages of implementation to do with systemic integration—for example, linking student achievement data with student background information and developing portfolios that follow the students through their various stages of schooling, and potentially beyond!

Questions to ask when choosing an LP are presented below. These have been adapted from the listing provided at http://ferl.qia.org.uk.

Questions to consider at school or central office level:
- What content should be on the LP?
- Who should be responsible for new and shared content?
- Who decides the metadata?

Questions to ask of potential suppliers:
- Does the LP already contain content, or are materials available separately from the supplier?
- Is the system purely a shell in which you place your own content, or sourced elsewhere?
- How easy is it to write and upload materials?
- Is uploading content to the LP a simple 'drag and drop' process, or more complicated?
- Is it easy to create online tests?
- How much HTML (web authoring) knowledge is required? (Less is better!)
- How easy is it to do administrative tasks, like enrol students onto the LP?

- How open is the system? Does it allow you to share with other resources or systems you might have? Does it 'talk to' your Management Information System? Does it meet the standards?
- Are the other functions (such as communications, student tracking, assessment) easy to use and well designed?
- Is installation, technical support and training included in the purchasing price? Is training face-to-face online, or both?
- Is there an email or web-based user group you can join and monitor before purchase? And if so, what sorts of comments have existing users made?
- Can you get an evaluation version to install and test before buying?
- Is it configurable to the look and feel of your school or education system?
- Does the supplier offer a hosting service, where the LP is hosted on their servers rather than yours, therefore reducing your need to provide technical support internally?
- Which other schools or education systems are using or planning to use the LP that you are considering? Are there reference sites or demonstration courses available?

(http://ferl.qia.org.uk)

The Internet is a good place to look for information on learning platforms. For example, the 'EduTools' site (see http://www.EduTools.info/index.jsp?pj=1) provides reviews of functionality.

EduTools give a comprehensive breakdown of the tools and users' opinions, as the reviews are largely written by the software users, rather than the businesses. The list of comparisons can be overwhelming and sorting out what is important and what can be left until later is essential. The feature listing provided by Ferl (originally an acronym for 'Further Education Resources for Learning') is shown in Table 13.4 (page 162).

As stated previously, the most important first tools of a learning platform (or VLE) are their information organisation tools and class communication tools. Having teachers put the resources for students in a well-organised file server is a good test—if they are not doing that well, then the additional work to add content to an LP will be very difficult for them.

To this end, many schools have started out with a software program that is free and written in Australia called Moodle. This is a basic all-in-one program that competently provides the features that a school starting out with digital LPs will require. The main advantage is the low impact of getting started with Moodle. It can create momentum in moving teachers on to a digital learning platform.

Table 13.4 *Feature listing and user opinions on learning platform tools*

Learner Tools	Support Tools	Technical Specifications
>>Communication Tools	>>Administration Tools	>>Hardware/Software
Discussion Forum	Authentication	Client Browser Required
Discussion Management	Course Authorization	Database Requirements
File Exchange	Registration Integration	UNIX Server
Internal Email	Hosted Services	Windows Server
Online Journal/Notes	>>Course Delivery Tools	>>Company Details/ Licensing
Real-time Chat	Test Types	Company Profile
Whiteboard	Automated Testing Management	Costs / Licensing
>>Productivity Tools	Automated Testing Support	Open Source
Bookmarks	Online Marking Tools	Optional Extras
Calendar/Progress Review	Online Gradebook	
Searching Within Course	Course Management	
Work Offline/Synchronize	Student Tracking	
Orientation/Help	>>Content Development Tools	
>>Student Involvement Tools	Accessibility Compliance	
Groupwork	Content Sharing/Reuse	
Community Networking	Course Templates	
Student Portfolios	Customized Look and Feel	
	Instructional Design Tools	
	Instructional Standards Compliance	

(Source: EduTools 2007, CMS: Feature List. http://www.edutools.info/feature_list.jsp?pj=4)

SUCCESSFUL ICT IN SCHOOLS

There is a wide range of factors that contribute to successful use of ICT in schools. Among the most important is leadership involvement among the school executive, including a close alliance and collegial exchanges between ICT and Teaching and Learning specialists. These day-to-day behaviours and relationships need to be supported by organisational factors such as clear school plans and policies (including ICT plans integrated with overall school and system directions), the optimal use of physical plant and other resources, and the embedding of ICT in critical business areas (Moyle, 2006; Robertson, Webb & Fluck, 2007).

These factors highlight that successful use of ICT is mostly concerned with relationships and attitudes among people and providing the opportunity for them to 'talk about it' at all levels. In planning, then, recommendations should always be focused on the avenues for having the right conversations in a positive and progressive framework.

In other words, successful use of ICT has much to do with developing the right culture within a school or school system. For example, policies often contain aspirational statements like the following:

- 'We are a secondary school that establishes the educational platform for young people to contribute confidently to their world with wisdom, imagination and integrity.'
- 'We provide resources and skills to optimise the learning possibilities via new technologies.'
- 'We permit maximum access, both internal and external, to the school's ICT facilities.'

Key questions in looking at how the culture supports or works against successful use of ICT are:

- At what point do the aspirational goals cease to be the guiding ones and alternative premises become the reasons for how ICT is designed, implemented, supported and used in the classrooms?

and further:

- Who gets to decide what technologies get used in which ways?

Careful balancing of the roles and responsibilities of school executive, teacher leaders, ICT specialists and system officers and policymakers is needed to develop and sustain a conducive school culture where teachers are effectively engaged in developments—rather than made to feel powerless in the face of successive waves of ICT rollouts and upgrades.

For example, if we have a goal of permitting maximum access and are aiming to develop people of wisdom and integrity, what would be the aspects of a school or system network that might help reflect this? Current networks may be well built, secure and controlled. But too often they tend to be based on a negative premise of 'don't allow people to do things if they do not have explicit permission to do those things'. Another example is where schools encourage their teachers to explore and develop their capabilities with digital technologies, but their ICT policies restrict staff by not allowing them to override filters.

School and system networks may have the highest-quality equipment, expensive and robust storage arrays and servers, and be founded—like all good business networks—on the principles of safety, control and efficient administration. However, in our experience, quality teaching requires flexibility, adaptability, trust, openness, guidelines and guidance and rarely works well under tight control and direction.

The best outcomes for students involve an appropriate balance and alignment among the teaching, technology and policy elements of the school and system operation, but that is not always evidenced. When considering implementation of digital technologies, it can be enlightening to see which of the areas leads or drives decisions in the other. For example, to what extent does *the technology* drive *the policy*, which in turn influences *the teaching*? Or is the alternative direction possible?

This is in no way a criticism of the IT staff. They are working to a set of goals that the school or education authority has set down. However, in an effective education network there is always the need for flexibility. By having the conversation about what is allowed or not (that is, what is driving the functional boundaries) in a proportioned manner, you can find an appropriate balance between IT needs, school policy and teacher needs.

Nothing to fear but fear itself

Fear of the unknown is all too often the driver, as well as the 'frustrater', of policy. To deal with this, the impacts of policies need to be carefully considered and explained. For example, the impact of return on equipment costs and on the tools available for teachers, and the opportunities for extended and engaged learning for students should be made clear. This provides the framework for the executive to do the job they are hired to do—that is make judgements.

Consider this example: If there was a 10 per cent chance that a student was going to bring a bomb to school, it would provide a different outcome to if there was only a 0.000005 chance of this occurring. The judgement on the level of concern would again change if the bomb was to just spray a small amount of confetti. Would you set an explosives expert up to swipe every child every day if there was a 0.000005 chance of confetti or a 10 per cent chance of injury? In other words, the combination of the likelihood of something occurring along with the impact of it occurring are core pieces of information that executives require to be able to make judgement.

With digital technologies it is difficult to understand both the likelihood and the impact of policy decisions. Therefore, it is often best for decisions to sit within a review cycle rather than to be set in stone. This can allow for decisions to be reviewed and change.

Let us consider an example of how ICT policy affects teachers:

> There was a set of teachers who wished to use sound bites with their classes. However, because of lack of access to a CD burner, they had to ask the IT or Media department to do so. As a consequence, the time frames were lengthy. Furthermore, when the CDs were eventually burned, the network was not able to meet the teachers' aims. If the teachers had been given a $50 CD burner, then the workload for both the IT and Media departments would have been reduced, and the opportunities for the students would have increased.

This example highlights the principle:

Where a teacher can demonstrate their competency in a technology and a desire to undertake an activity, the bias should be to support that teacher to undertake that activity.

This involves wherever possible, devolving decision making to a person or group whose key performance indicators are about successful teaching and learning rather than controlling and management.

GUIDELINES FOR SCHOOL AND EDUCATION SYSTEM LEADERS

An essential factor in successful development and implementation of digital technologies is engagement by school and education authority leaders in these key decisions. These individuals are the ones responsible for developing a cohesive organisational culture. It is the organisational culture that drives teaching practice and student learning, and it is the enhancement of teaching and learning that needs to drive the consideration and implementation of digital technologies in educational settings. Leaders at the school level (school executive and leading teachers, and at the system authority level), officers, managers and directors require more than a passing understanding of the technical and educational issues associated with the take-up of digital technologies.

Second, it is important to plan and to be realistic. A useful way to commence planning is to assess where you are. In this respect, we would recommend the Becta *Self-review Framework: An introduction* (see http://school.becta.org.uk). From there, a powerful way to model the use of digital technology is to do your plans as wikis, not word documents—or at least have a wiki element. In this way, ICT plans become spaces for teachers or system officers to talk about the change plan. They become active and lively rather than neglected and dusty.

Finally, make sure that you match the technology in your setting to your aspirations for teaching and learning, and for your organisation as a whole. Know what the technology can do, but have the pedagogy to drive the technology—not the other way around. The 'wild wonderful web' continues to throw innovation after innovation at us. Given the complexity and pace of change in education systems compared with that of the Internet, it can often feel like you are only just coming to grips with the last innovation when the next one hits you.

WHAT'S NEXT?

Web 2.0 brings the next generation of opportunities (and headaches!) to educational leaders, and it is already encouraging discussions around why we structure our schools the way we do. For example, 'school 2.0' (http://www.school2-0.org/), outlines the proposed changes to schooling, schoolwork, the school community and the school systems.

In a world where students are publishing regularly to their peer groups and finding their own (often unguided) way in the digital world, the question is how might we take innovative tools available on the Internet and create a set of tools that supports the types of creative and engaging teaching and learning, especially those explained earlier under Quadrants 3 and 4.

The tools that we have discussed in this chapter have only been around for less than 10 years, and the Web 2.0 tools discussed above have been around for two years. It is a safe bet that they will continue to change significantly and quickly over coming years. The question is: How can schools and education systems adapt to take advantage of emerging technologies? Our students really need us to make that change.

14

PREPARING YOUR TEACHERS AND YOURSELF FOR A DIGITAL SCHOOL

John Hodgkinson

In these early stages of the twenty-first century, new demands and opportunities are emerging for students and schools as a consequence of global networking—or what Friedman (2006) calls 'the flattened, globalised world').

One of the key responsibilities of educational leaders is to ensure that teachers are well prepared to work in ways that make appropriate use of digital technologies. To do that, principals and system officers must not only understand the needs of staff but also appreciate the value and potential of digital technologies, and be able to lead and manage the processes of change required to position their schools to educate the young people in their care using those technologies to their best effect.

In a digital school, digital technologies form an integral part of everyday functions and operations. These technologies are important resources for supporting the delivery of the curriculum and the achievement of outcomes desired by the school community, governments and other important stakeholders. They should be integrated rather than viewed as 'add-ons' or ends in themselves. And while they may appear complex, even daunting, their role after all is simply to support learning and teaching. Technology is no substitute for the relationship between the teacher and the student. The quality of that relationship has been consistently shown to be one of the most critical elements—if not *the* most critical element—in the success of the student.

Ensuring teachers have the requisite knowledge, skills and attributes is difficult. Experienced teachers have an established repertoire of teaching practices and ways of working in the school. Requiring teachers to discard—or alter—significant amounts of their intellectual capital, often built up over many years, will have a profound impact on them. This is especially so in these times when there is a workforce in schools with a high median age. Requiring teachers to learn a new set of skills will be easy for some and difficult for many. Digital technologies can be intimidating for people who were born before the digital era.

Given the different experiences, ages and outlooks of teaching staff, and considering the life opportunities of students that are at stake, careful and wise management of the change process is called for. Get the change process wrong, and you will achieve mundane compliance at best. Get it right, and you will boost the creativity and performance of both staff and students.

This chapter is aimed at school executive with responsibilities for staffing and presents an overview of their strategic role in staff development. The purpose is to assist school leaders to make decisions suited to their particular situations and staff. The focus of the chapter is based on the understanding that we are preparing the young people in the schools' care for *their* future, not ours. Their future will stretch to at least the 2090s. We can have little idea of the details of that time. But we can say with reasonable certainty that it will be different from these early years of the twenty-first century. Our students' futures will involve the use of new technologies in dealing with new global issues, new local issues, new societal issues, and new ways of working alone and with others.

In this context it is essential that as educators we guide young people to develop the capabilities that will help them change and adapt themselves and their environments to that future.

NO 'SILVER BULLETS'

There are no 'silver bullets'—or simple solutions—for ensuring staff are well prepared to teach the essential knowledge, skills, understanding and values in ways that result in high engagement and achievement of all students in all settings. Each of us tends to develop our own strategies.

We are wary of the trap of adopting someone else's solutions, preferring to adapt what is useful to suit our own context and staff needs.

This makes sense because every school is different—every school has a different combination of staff, students, facilities and resources. Also, every member of the school community is different, with differing life and work experiences, differing knowledge and skills, and differing ways of working.

If school leaders are looking for all staff to move at the same rate in integrating digital technologies into their practice, they will be frustrated and disappointed. A school could consist of at least three different 'generations' of teachers, each needing the different mix of professional learning and personal support and challenge to change their beliefs and practices.

One way of dealing with this diversity of staff background in planning for professional learning is to consider some questions along the following lines:

1   The preferred future for your students, your school and your teachers:
    • What is your preferred future?
    • To what extent is this shared by members of your school community?
    • If you have no clear picture as yet, how do you intend to develop one?
    • What will be the principles underlying the process for developing a preferred future?
2   Your teacher demographics:
    • What is their age profile?
    • What are their knowledge and skill levels?
    • What are their personal attributes, aspirations and preferences, particularly when it comes to dealing with change?
    The message here is 'know your teachers' before you provide support or apply pressure for them to change. For example, a summary of the characteristics of 'digital natives' (those under 25 years of age) and 'digital immigrants' (those over 25 years of age), shown in Table 14.1, provides some interesting comparisons.
3   The culture of professional learning in your school or system:
    • What programs and processes are in place for teachers to acquire new knowledge and skills?
    • Are they encouraged and supported to practise these new areas of knowledge and skill?
    • Are they encouraged and supported in taking risks with new ways of working?

Table 14.1 *Comparing digital natives and digital immigrants*

DIGITAL NATIVES (UNDER 25 YEARS)	DIGITAL IMMIGRANTS (OVER 25 YEARS)
Grew up with ICT as a normal part of life	Have learned to use digital technology
Are closest to the way students think and learn	Think and process information in a more 'linear' way than their students or digital natives
Are comfortable with the instantaneous nature of their lives	Need time to think
Have a higher 'muscle twitch speed' than their elders had at the same age	Have a lower 'muscle twitch speed' than digital natives
Are social networkers	Still print emails and talk about ICT objects as 'machines'

(Source: Prensky 2001)

- Is professional learning seen as an ongoing and integrated element of their work or a series of disconnected one-off activities?

Teachers need opportunities to connect their learning to past experiences, current demands and opportunities, and future needs and possibilities. The design and delivery of professional learning programs at school and system level should reflect this.

There will be other issues to consider. These include:

- ICT hardware and software. What resources (including funds, facilities, support staff) are available/needed? How can these be most effectively and efficiently sourced, purchased, prioritised and allocated. There will also be strategic issues with the who, what, where, when and for what purpose. Who will make those decisions, and what criteria will be used to ensure equity? And most importantly: Can the system that is being put in place be scaled up without major rebuilding?
- Accessibility of the ICT. Who will have access to what, when and where? Who will make those decisions, and what criteria will be used?
- Universal, fast and reliable connectivity and capacity. People become frustrated with delays. Fast and reliable connections within the school and to the outside are critical to success. Without proper connectivity and capacity, changing work practices will be much more difficult.
- Digital literacy of teachers. The aim is for teachers to have the confidence and competence to use ICT as a normal part of their everyday work. This involves the right mix of knowledge and skills to work with current

technology, as well as the capability to move with and incorporate appropriate ICT changes into the future. Teachers also need to feel that any shortcomings or problems they have will be managed in a confidential way.

- Access to high-quality learning resources. The quality of the resources available for teachers to embed ICT in their normal work practices is critical. In the early stages of development of a digital school, most teachers will not have the skills needed to develop their own resources. Learning resources available from outside the school for student use must be carefully piloted and evaluated before decisions about implementation are taken.

- Location-specific factors. What are the protocols in your school for undertaking a major change such as the design and implementation of digital technology at your school? Who are the influential people in the school community? Who needs to be involved? How can staff be involved in the way that best meets their needs? How can parents be involved to enhance their understanding and support? What factors about the school community will support, and what will hinder, the changes?

- Time for teachers to learn and become comfortable with using ICT. Teachers need time to reflect on their work, the way they can incorporate digital technologies, and the changes they need to make. Teachers require opportunities to explore and practise using technology until they can use it as easily as they have used a stick of chalk or a whiteboard marker in the past. They need time to plan, to trial, to evaluate and to develop resources, and the cost of this time must be included in the school or system budget. Inadequate provision of time for learning means the teachers, the technology and, eventually, the students are 'short-changed'.

Combined with these issues and factors associated with the introduction and use of digital technologies are two further areas with implications for teachers' work. These concern: (1) the emergence of Web 2.0 technologies and their implications for curriculum design, and (2) the policies and organisational arrangements in place with regard to data storage, intellectual property and knowledge management.

In planning professional learning for teachers, these two areas also deserve careful attention.

1 *Teacher awareness of Web 2.0 technologies—curriculum design implications.* Do you know how many of your teachers use Web 2.0

or related technologies—in either their personal or professional life? These technologies include wikis, blogs, MySpace, Facebook, Bebo, MP3s, Instant Messaging, YouTube, Second Life, and Google Scholar. Most of these technologies did not exist 10 years ago, but they are in common use throughout society today, especially by young people. As the use of Web 2.0 technologies becomes more widespread teachers will need to re-think the curriculum content and methodology for its delivery. Traditional curriculum was linear in its organisation, with silos and pigeon holes—also called 'subjects'. The curriculum of the future will be organised using networks and integration and the language of curriculum will be different.

2   *Teacher facility with data storage, intellectual property and knowledge management.* How do you currently store data in your school? Who owns it? How is it accessed? By whom? For what purpose? And what plans do you have for developing policies and organisational arrangements on data storage and associated issues like intellectual property and knowledge management into the future? Common forms of data storage at present include:
   * computer tapes or cassettes
   * CD
   * DVD
   * USB drive
   * online storage—free or hired or your own server.
   The era of the CD has almost passed. Online storage will be the way of the future. As these trends unfold, teachers' facility to 'navigate the data storage landscape' at school and at system level will become a more important professional capability—particularly with the emerging issues of intellectual property and appropriate use protocols associated with the advent of collaborative digital workspaces.

YOUR ROLE AS A 'ROLE MODEL'

The ways in which you use digital technologies in your day-to-day work send a powerful message to staff about the priority and value that you place on developing knowledge and skills in ICT. Using technology to provide information as well as seek comment or feedback is one way of modelling. Working with staff on the development of online resources or software designs (for example, in student assessment and reporting) is another example—particularly where those innovations serve to ease the administrative burden on staff or excite their curiosity about engaging students in different ways.

Another aspect of modelling is shown by the ways in which you communicate with colleagues—locally, regionally, nationally and globally. The process of designing a digital school and implementing the design successfully cannot be undertaken in isolation. Networking with other individuals and schools is a critical element in successfully achieving the goal. Do not limit this networking to your local area, or even to your system or state or nation. ICT allows you to network with schools and people around the world. Use networking to model learning for your staff.

Develop yourself to be a successful leader

To successfully plan and implement the design for your digital school, you must be competent and comfortable in your role as the leader of the school. To lead the digital school, you must have a clear vision of your goal and share it with your school community—all those involved in and with the school. Unless you have a goal that can be defined and shared, others will not be willing to join you on the journey.

You must know and understand your school community. Who has influence and power? This is not so much about positional authority, but rather about the influence and power of certain individuals and groups in the school community. Who do people follow and in which direction? How can you use this to achieve useful outcomes for the school?

Third, you must know the national and international trends in ICT and in education. An essential element in the design of the digital school is a future orientation. What do you know about how ICT will change into the future, and how young people will use it? How can those uses be adapted to enhance their learning?

Fourth, you must know how to lead and manage. Leading is about moving the school community towards achieving desired ends. Managing is about ensuring that the environment, the processes and the procedures that will make that happen are in place.

Fifth, you must know how to influence and persuade. Positional power will achieve minimal compliance at best. If done with judgement and wisdom, influencing and persuasion will achieve commitment. Persuasion does not happen by chance. To be successful, you must be credible; people must feel that they can believe you. You must make good sense; your arguments must be rational and logical. You must keep your word; integrity and honesty are critical. Do not promise anything that you cannot deliver. You must win their hearts before you can win their minds.

SUCCESSFUL CHANGE THROUGH PROFESSIONAL LEARNING

Professional learning is a change process. To achieve the types of outcomes desired for and by your staff, the approaches and program designs for professional learning need to be informed by research about successful change.

Fullan (2007, p. 5) identifies elements for successful change as follows:

1 Define 'closing the gap' as the overarching goal.
2 Attend initially to the three basics: deprivatisation of practice, learning in context, and lateral capacity building.
3 Be driven by tapping into people's dignity and sense of respect.
4 Ensure that the best people are working on the problem.
5 Recognise that all successful strategies are socially based.
6 Assume that lack of capacity is the initial problem and then work on it continually.
7 Stay the course through continuity of good direction by leveraging leadership.
8 Build internal accountability linked to external accountability.
9 Establish conditions for the evolution of positive pressure.
10 Use the previous nine strategies to build public confidence.

These ten elements cover similar areas to issues and principles of leadership that I have described—having a goal, working with the professionalism of the staff, and providing a conducive environment in which people can learn and change. These elements provide a guide for evaluating your professional learning activities, packages and programs.

Tips for successful staff development

Even though the professional learning must be tailored to the context of different teachers and school communities, the following list can be used as a general guide for successful staff development in the use of digital technologies.

1 Remember that professional learning is task-specific and role-specific, and should be focused on the ways that ICT is used and how to use it.

2   Plan professional learning by involving the groups of the teaching, support and administrative staff who will be using it.

3   Individualise professional learning to suit each person's needs and state of readiness for learning and change. This means organising the learning in ways that are sensitive to individuals' needs, including trust, confidentiality, individual level of confidence, privacy and differences in learning style.

4   Have the 'key influencers' of the relevant staff groups lead professional learning.

5   Make sufficient time available to staff to learn, practise and apply the new knowledge and skills in an environment where they are encouraged to take risks and supported when they make mistakes. Different people will require different amounts of time to learn and implement the learning.

6   Accept that professional learning is ongoing, not a one-off event.

7   Ensure professional learning is followed up with ongoing support, for example, through a help desk or online manuals, with that support tailored to suit the needs of the person and their role in the school.

8   Evaluate and redevelop approaches to professional learning through feedback from the participants and with input from the local (and possibly external) designers and advisers involved in planning the future of your school.

9   Celebrate the outcomes of professional learning. Find ways to show the staff that the changes they make to their knowledge, skills and practices are valuable and valued.

CONCLUSION

The preparation and professional learning of staff to teach and work in schools of today and tomorrow require focused attention on the value and use of digital technologies. As the leader of the school, you need to appreciate the context faced by your staff and students as they go about the core activities of teaching and learning. You need to be aware of the planning issues facing the school community and be prepared to shape and model the processes for embedding digital technologies.

As a leader, you need to understand change and the characteristics of successful professional learning. At times you need to influence and persuade, as well as review and evaluate what is happening. Do not allow yourself to become frustrated when members of staff do not make the progress you expect. Rather take the time to reflect, to consult and to plan and carefully implement the changes to achieve the ends you and your school community desire.

CHAPTER 15

PRINCIPLES AND GUIDELINES FOR CREATING A DIGITAL SCHOOL

Mal Lee & Michael Gaffney

The shift to a digital operational mode offers schools immense opportunities to provide students with a quality education for the twenty-first century. By 'going digital', schooling takes on different forms to what we have known to this point in the history of education. It is an exciting time to be an educational leader! It is also time for acumen; for taking a fresh look at the working of schools; for envisioning new possibilities; and assessing and developing one's and others' capabilities to bring those possibilities to fruition.

In this chapter, we will overview the principles and factors to be addressed in developing a digital school, and provide guidelines to assist you in your situation. Our aim is to encourage you to move from *reflection* on the ideas that have been presented by the various contributors to *action*; from consideration of the theories and concepts of digital schooling to the strategies and practices that will bring those elements to life in real school settings with real teachers and students.

OPERATE HOLISTICALLY

By now it will be apparent how important it is to think holistically, that is, having the mindset that not only removes artificial divisions between the learning in the school and the home, and between the school's educational and administrative operations, but also sees the relationships and synergies between them. In a networked school community dependent on a shared digital infrastructure it is imperative the total operations are always borne in mind.

The same holistic thinking and operational mode apply to education authorities. Many authorities are at least as segmented as schools—internally operating along divisional lines and externally functioning in relative isolation to other education systems. One consequence is that schools have to contend with the challenge of competing and, at times, seemingly contradictory system priorities and policies—for example, when curriculum expectations are thwarted by access in infrastructure and connectivity, or when aspirations for personalised learning confront the industrial realities of teaching loads and 'allowable' class sizes.

Integrated planning

The holistic perspective should be a fundamental principle of school and system planning. Sample questions about evidence of holistic planning in your situation include:

- Has your organisation adopted planning processes where information from different groups flows effectively across the organisation to inform decision making; or is planning divided among different committees, with little overlap of personnel, handling distinct responsibilities?
- Does the ICT group address the technical issues without sufficient consideration of the human or educational variables?
- Does the school marketing team operate without input from the ICT team?

Your answers to these questions indicate the extent to which your organisation has a planning model in place appropriate for contemporary networked development. They also allow you to assess the extent to which present arrangements inhibit holistic integrated planning and development.

One way of approaching the tasks of planning with digital technologies is to use those technologies in the actual planning process. Tapscott (2007) indicates that there are increasing opportunities to use emerging, online collaborative technologies in the daily operations of the school. For example, he suggests that wikis are an excellent policy development tool, and blogs can be readily used as a reflective tool with staff and students.

Personal professional learning

What do you need to know and how can you enhance your awareness of the digital technologies that would be of value to your educational setting? Do you have an appropriate working understanding of the digital resources that are being used and are currently available?

To this point there have been insufficient opportunities for existing and potential school and education authority leaders to gain and maintain an appropriate level of understanding about digital technologies available to schools. While we are conscious of the multiple demands on educational leaders, it is now apparent if one is to shape and use the digital resources in ways that in the end benefit students' learning, then a working knowledge of the technology is vital.

We suggest that the best way to develop that knowledge is through on-the-job, hands-on experience, and to supplement it with the occasional concerted external expert advice and training courses. For example, our experience has demonstrated the near impossibility of explaining the potential of an interactive whiteboard (let alone an integrated, web-based database-driven communications, content management and function management system!) to those with little experience with the technology. You need to give people the opportunity to 'have a go' at using the technologies, and provide them with the security and trust to take risks and make mistakes.

Appropriate resources for on-the-job learning and staff training need to be included in annual budgets, while bearing in mind that as the technology becomes more sophisticated and multifaceted, the need for professional learning grows.

Exercise 15.1
Auditing your knowledge and use of digital technology

Using a spreadsheet, list all the digital technologies used or likely to be used by your school(s). Include the hardware and software, the key systems and web facilities.

Beside each, indicate the extent to which you have used that technology, and your level of understanding of the implications of using that technology. For each technology where your understanding is low, jot down ways you could learn more about its potential and use (for example, consult workplace colleagues, 'Google' the term, search Wikipedia ...).

Contemporary learning

Curriculum change and policy development are a feature of professional life in most schools and education authorities. However, the pace of change in the digital world is such that the school's instructional program may well need refining more regularly. Consider, for example, online social networking. This technology was virtually non-existent in 2005 and yet within three years has become a global phenomenon and a normal part of young people's lives across the developed world.

While we understand that schools have to operate within the curriculum, assessment and reporting policies set by their education jurisdictions, there is always some latitude to better align the 'delivered curriculum' or instructional program to the learning opportunities and demands of the contemporary world. With this possibility in mind, consider the following questions:

- How relevant is your instructional program to students' everyday real and virtual lives?
- Do teaching practices provide appropriate opportunity for students to achieve essential and worthwhile contemporary learning outcomes?
- Does your instructional program 'stand alone' within your school, or is it networked to recognise that learning is happening outside the classroom, in the home and in the community?

Home–school nexus

In 2008, the majority of schools continue to operate as isolated entities, certainly in terms of taking account of students' learning that occurs outside the classroom walls. A key principle of leading a digital school is developing the connection between students' homes and their schools. From this perspective, consider the following questions:

- What moves has your organisation made to create a networked school community through the use of technology?
- Do you have a policy or plan to create such a community; or have your efforts—at least to this point—been rather spasmodic without any overarching framework?

Creating a networked school community begins with developing a strong home–school nexus, but can extend beyond this to include, for example, education providers such as institutes of technology and universities, sister schools, national and international online education communities, and local and global community agencies.

Many of the facilities you put in place to forge that nexus with the home can equally be used with the other parts of your networked community.

Analysing the situation

To create and sustain a digital school, it is wise to conduct a detailed situational analysis of the present operations, the strategic foundations (such as organisational vision, philosophy, agreed principles), and organisational performance. The results can be used to identify the strengths as well as those facets needing attention.

Most analyses can be undertaken internally, but it is often a good idea to involve a critical friend or external evaluator. Some additional validity is possible where a group or network of schools use the same critical friends or external analysts.

Identifying the key variables and having key staff examine the school performance against key performance indicators (KPIs) is an effective whole-school development exercise. In selecting the areas to analyse, it is important to look at human as well as technical variables. History shows that while attention is usually focused on the actual digital technologies, the reality is that variables like planning, funding, leadership, teacher usage of the digital technology, staffing, staff organisation, working conditions and staff development are as important as the actual infrastructure and ICT support.

Exercise 15.2 Conducting a situational analysis

As a sample situational analysis, identify the percentage of:
- teaching staff using the digital technology to varying extents in their everyday teaching
- teaching rooms with ready broadband access
- teaching time in the year when the school's network is down.

Can you immediately provide the current percentage for each of those KPIs?
If you have to check, note how long it takes to find an answer.

An important part of any situational analysis is to talk with staff and elicit their concerns and frustrations with the technology, and the improvements they would like. Once you know your scene, you can then begin prioritising your efforts, conscious at all times of the increasing interplay of the variables.

Total teacher usage

Central to the development of a digital school is having all teachers (and by 'all' we do mean 100 per cent of the teachers) using the appropriate digital technology in their everyday teaching. Achieve that and not only will all students also use the tools, but the growing expectations of the staff and the students will stimulate the sustained growth of the digital school.

With total teacher usage, the next, very real challenge is to continue to enhance the quality and effectiveness of the teaching and to do your utmost to improve the learning of every student in your care.

Visit the pathfinders

Visiting schools that have achieved total teacher usage of the digital technology or are operating to varying extents as digital schools is a powerful means of professional learning and of informing your planning. There can be much to discern about the leadership of those schools as the differences between those strong on the rhetoric and those that are actually going forward will be evident.

The Australian schools highlighted in the case studies presented in this book may be an option for some, but there are increasing numbers of comparable schools throughout the developed world. While still in a minority, there ought to be pathfinder schools nearby that you can visit.

DIGITAL INTEGRATION

One of the significant challenges for traditional schools is to achieve digital integration throughout the organisation. A major impediment is the segmented organisational units within the school, the propensity for each unit (or dare we say 'empire'?) to look only to its domain, to guard its patch and demand annually 'its share' of the budget. That kind of organisational structure and associated middle-manager leadership—within schools and education authorities—has not only spawned the growth and retention of separate systems, but also inhibited the emergence of schools where the leadership team thinks holistically and is comfortable with developing an integrated learning community.

Converging digital technologies can combat—at least to some extent—the tendencies for segmentation in school organisations through using a common ICT infrastructure that enables all members of the school community to make use of the systems wherever they have web access.

As a way of assessing the level, or the potential for digital integration in your setting, you might ask whether your existing organisational model is conducive to the development of a digital school; that is, consistent with the attributes mentioned at the end of Chapter 1.

As a further task, you might like to undertake Exercise 15.3 where you are asked to list all the databases, large and small, used by your organisation. Completing this task will provide you with valuable information about the present situation in your school/education authority and some insights about the challenges ahead.

Exercise 15.3

Compile a spreadsheet of *all* the databases, small and large, currently used by the school. Include:
- those hosted within the school, and those externally hosted
- those that are stand-alone, networked and web-based.

Depending on the size of the school, you might need to offline someone to handle the task.

In preparing the spreadsheet:
- describe the purpose of each; that is, library, accounts, hall bookings, ex-students' association, etc
- name the type of database used
- indicate if it is web-based
- identify with each who/which area is responsible for operating and maintaining that database
- indicate which databases are automatically upgraded when edits are made to the master database.

Upon completion of the task, identify what the school needs to do to integrate all the operations, and make all the services readily accessible through a common web-based login to all the relevant members of the networked school community. At the same time identify which of the database services can best be externally hosted, and which internally.

Staffing

Secondary and K–12 schools are staffed with people with specialist expertise and a commitment to their area of teaching. However, some do not have the knowledge and skill sets needed to work in or lead a digital school. In seeking to develop a digital school, you need people who possess or who are willing and capable of acquiring the requisite skills and understanding.

We appreciate the difficulties of changing key personnel, and do not for one moment want to appear inhumane, but the bottom line—as Greg Whitby indicated in Chapter 9—is that a digital school calls for a different skill set from staff.

Traditionally the professional positions in schools have been filled by teachers, or by former teachers. In digital schools, there is the need for other professionals, each with particular expertise to handle diverse functions. These include business operations, marketing, network management and ICT support. With this in mind, consider the following questions:

- Do you need to rework your mix of educational and other professionals? Do you have the capability and authority to do so, or do you need to present the case to your local education system authority?
- Given that quality network managers and ICT support staff with the desired credentials are much desired in many quarters, do you have the facility to remunerate those 'other professionals' at the market rate, or do you have to make do with less available expertise, at least for a time?
- Do your duty statements for educational and support staff embody the desired skills and understanding? What qualities and competencies are you expecting of the new teachers that you employ?
- Are there positions that you no longer need?

These are a few of the questions to consider as you seek to staff and develop your digital school.

Working conditions

Allied to the question of staff capability is the importance of establishing the appropriate operational parameters and working conditions for staff employed in a digital school. This is a very complex area because the vast majority of working conditions and enterprise agreements used with teachers have emerged from the traditional, paper-based school organisational model.

The networked and digital technology opens the way for significantly different working conditions. Currently early adopting teachers across the world are exploring the options. Some of these options might enhance the student learning, while others will simply overburden already committed teachers. For instance, we are already finding technology companies promoting 24/7/365 teaching support!

In this changing context, it is imperative that school and education authority leaders work with their staff and relevant unions to identify the desired operational parameters for teachers and associated administrative and support staff working within a digital school. We encourage you to make best use of the technology and vary the working arrangements accordingly, but always keep in mind the need to formalise those arrangements. For example, we believe that currently very little thought is being given to additional demands being placed on staff by administrative emails—sometimes sent at any time of day or point in the year, and expecting instant response.

Now is the time to stop, reflect and identify the desired operational parameters for working within the digital mode. As an aside, one of us learned some time ago about the importance of establishing the desired operational parameters. When conducting one of the world's earliest online teacher's conferences in 1995, phone calls for support came in from across the globe at all hours of the day and night! He very quickly moved to set the support parameters within which folk were happy to work!

One suggested way of beginning to address the issues of changing work conditions and operational parameters is described in Exercise 15.4.

Exercise 15.4

Conduct focus groups—with key groups of staff—to discuss the impact of the shift to the use of digital technology upon their working conditions. Ask staff to identify those developments that are:

- easing their workload, or making their work more efficient
- adding unnecessarily to their workload.

Also ask staff about the developments that they would wish to see, the new operational parameters they would like explored, and also the ways of old that should be dispensed with.

We suggest that you hold discussions with:

- the executive team
- the administrative and support staff
- the information technology/services staff
- teacher groups, drawn from the various parts of the school.

Staff development

Ongoing development of staff is an essential component of leading a digital school. One key aspect of staff development is the provision of timely support for the teachers as they begin to use digital teaching resources.

Effective models of staff development need to go well beyond the 'off-site short course' to ensure sustained staff learning and support. One strategy for looking at the appropriateness of your staff development model is described in Exercise 15.5.

Exercise 15.5

Identify the funding set aside in this year's school budget for professional development of staff. In determining the amount, make sure that you include 'hidden' costs such as:

* the time release provided to staff mentors
* the relief teaching time provided to enable teachers to test new technology
* the proportion of the library staffing allocation set aside for the development of the school staff.

What funding has been set aside for the leadership team, the teaching staff and the ICT staff?

What other avenues and sources of funding are available for professional development?

ICT infrastructure

Without a quality and highly reliable school ICT infrastructure with the appropriate digital storage, network backup and disaster proofing that is regularly updated, the development of a digital school cannot be sustained. Following is a recap of the key components:

Network

The importance of quality 'plumbing' cannot be overstated in light of infrastructure growing apace and technology becoming more sophisticated. In 'user' terms, you need a network with high-speed Internet access to each teaching room, which operates 100 per cent—not 95 per cent—of the class time during the total teaching year, and ideally beyond.

In assessing the quality of your network, it is worth considering these questions:

* Can your network provide a 100 per cent level of reliability and, if not, what has to be done to ensure it can?
* Are you able to store and back up the growing body of digital holdings?

- Can your network operate with a loss of power from the grid?
- What would happen to the school's vital digital holdings if there was a fire, vandal attack or storm damage?

In a similar vein, Peter Murray (see Chapters 10 and 11) urges principals to ask questions of their 'IT' coordinator. A sample list is presented below. We suggest that you try them out with yours.

TEN QUESTIONS TO ASK YOUR 'IT' COORDINATOR

1 What is your backup strategy?
2 Can our web server be hacked and what is our security strategy?
3 Are we retaining email independent of users?
4 Are we considering server 'virtualisation'?
5 Are we deploying scalable infrastructure?
6 What remote desktop solutions are we using?
7 What strategies are we using to implement a simple authentication mechanism?
8 What incident tracking systems are we using?
9 Are we using ITIL philosophies?
10 Are we considering Apple and/or Open Source solutions?

(Source: Peter Murray)

Servers and hosting

The decision about where to host services (internally or externally or some variation thereof) has significant implications for the development of your infrastructure, administration and communications systems, ICT support model and budget. Have you examined the best way forward? Also remember, by going digital, you do become more dependent on technology. It is vital therefore that the requisite 'insurance' is taken.

Instructional technology

Some questions to consider in relation to the choice and use of instructional technologies include:

- Who makes decisions about which instructional technologies are chosen? Is it the ICT coordinator, the business manager, individual teachers or the school leadership?

- What criteria are used to make the choice, and how do they relate to the desired teacher and student use of the technology?
- What influence do teachers have in the choice of teaching software?

In the traditional paper-based school, teachers had considerable say in the choice of texts and library books. Do they have a similar say in relation to digital teaching resources? Of note in this regard is the UK education policy initiative to provide teachers with £200 of credit each year to acquire the desired software. Does your school or education system have a comparable form of direct teacher support?

Technology in the home

In reflecting on your ICT infrastructure, what thought have you given to taking advantage of the digital technology within the home? Are you unnecessarily duplicating some of that technology? Most of the contributing authors to this book share Roger Hayward's (see Chapter 7) misgivings about laptops. It is appreciated that 'ubiquitous computing' is all the rage in the USA, but aside from making some technology corporations and politicians happy, we wonder if better educational returns could be achieved by creating networked school communities that build on the technology in the home.

ICT support

The attainment of 100 per cent 'up time' depends not only on the technology, but also on the ICT support arrangements.

It is now clear that as the networks become more sophisticated and the reliance upon them increases, so will the need for quality ICT support. Some of this will be provided 'in-house'; some will probably need to be supplied from external agencies.

Historically, the traditional school staffing formulas have frustrated the engagement of quality ICT support for schools. In early 2008, many schools still rely on its dedicated teachers—often with only limited technical expertise—to maintain its infrastructure.

It is incumbent on school and education authority leaders to institute a model for the years ahead that will provide schools not only with the requisite ICT support, but also with the expertise to enable the schools to meet future needs with the desired functionality and reliability.

What is your situation? Are you, like many schools, dependent on one person whose leaving could place the school's operations at risk?

Information services—information management

The last decade has seen many schools and education authorities reduce their school library personnel, ironically at a time when the need for information professionals in schools has been growing apace.

As highlighted in Karen Bonanno's Chapter 12, it is vital that the school—possibly in conjunction with the education authority—provide its community with the appropriate information services support, which includes a whole-school information management regime able to accommodate the burgeoning amounts of digital information generated or used by the digital school.

Central to these operations will be an astute information professional, or (very likely) a team. In most situations those people will be teacher librarians or school librarians.

In the research for their book, *A History of the Use of Instructional Technology in Schools*, Lee and Winzenried (2008) observed that in general terms, school librarians have had to change their role more than any other part of the teaching force, and thus have become very astute in appreciating the changing information needs of schools. That knowledge ought to be capitalised upon in developing the digital school. Some questions to consider are:

- Do you have in place the personnel and the systems to accommodate this vital area?
- Have you got the policies and the systems to ensure the school is managing its digital assets appropriately—and within the local laws?
- Do you have the library and ICT staff competing to control the school's information and, if so, are you at a point where you need to restructure operations to provide the desired support for the future?

Within a complex digital information landscape, school leaders are going to have to consider and plan for the rapid evolution of the Web as a global collaborative information platform. If Web 1.0 is about 'read' and Web 2.0 is about 'read/write', what will Web 3.0 be? If students and teachers can pull information from the Web and be creators, editors and sharers of information within Web 2.0, then what will be their capabilities in Web 3.0? How will a digital school progress to manage and service the information needs of the school community in those circumstances?

The semantic web has been muted as an extension to the Web, whereby 'web content can be expressed not only in natural language, but also in a format that can be read and used by software agents, thus permitting them to find, share and integrate information more easily' (Wikipedia, 2008e).

Currently, we are able to access 'mash-ups', which are a recombination of web-based multimedia digital formats from a range of sources. The philosophy of Web 3.0 may well be dynamic information collections that are constantly evolving to meet user needs.

Within a digital school, intelligent collecting of information needs to be in harmony with the creation and use of information. The skills and capabilities of those trained in the library and information profession, such as teacher librarians, will be of paramount importance in the development of the digital school's information and service systems.

DIGITAL ADMINISTRATION AND COMMUNICATIONS SYSTEMS

One vital aspect of the digital school that was not addressed in depth earlier was the school's digital administrations and communications systems.

Ideally schools need web-based, common database-driven systems that can be accessed through the one 'log in' by all members of the school's networked community. Those systems should be highly user friendly and, most importantly, should enhance the organisation's efficiency and save all members of the school community time handling the mundane clerical tasks.

Sadly, in 2008, many of the systems in schools leave much to be desired and invariably add to the staff's workload and frustrations. Moreover, most do not provide the decision makers ready information on the effectiveness of the many operations undertaken in a school day. At this point most school administration and communications fall well behind their counterparts in small business. In 2008, staff should be able to take advantage of the employer self service (ESS) human resource management systems, while school and education authority leaders should be able to secure an instant understanding of the state of play of every formal request.

Does your existing system allow you to identify the current situation in the handling of a request, or allow you to swiftly communicate electronically with any subset of your school community?

If it does not, you should be on the lookout—possibly the warpath—to identify an appropriately priced system that does. We are talking about what is now old technology, but for some reason schools would appear to have missed out.

Learning platforms

As Ingvarson and Gaffney indicated in Chapter 13, one of the most important decisions that school and education authority leaders have to make concerns the shape and functionality of their online learning platforms. These can very easily become immensely expensive white elephants.

As Lee and Winzenried (2008) and Becta (2007) indicate, despite the immense hype and proselytising by the advocates, actual teacher and student use of the systems and of the myriad features therein is still minuscule. While it is appreciated that use could be markedly constrained by the failure by schools to successfully address the factors facilitating total teacher use of the instructional technology, one needs to consider very carefully the alternatives, possibly better and significantly less-expensive options emerging in Web 2.0.

We suggest that you look very closely at the actual student and teacher use of the existing online student portal systems, identify the better-used portions, and then decide if a significant outlay of monies can be justified educationally.

Related to this is the propensity of some school and system leaders to assume that all schools and education systems should be using e-Portfolios—the student's digital collection of work undertaken—where all the data is stored on the school's or authority's network. We would strongly argue that you do not contemplate moving into this arena until undertaking in-depth research and becoming aware of the potential challenges, costs and actual educational benefits of such a move. This is a hard one!

BUDGET

Ingle Farm Primary School, discussed in Chapter 8, is a low socioeconomic government primary school that has been able to become a pathfinding digital school. We can name a number of similar schools. Indeed we contend that virtually every school in the developed world could become a digital school if a wise principal so decides.

However, in making this observation we are also conscious most schools in the developed world have only around 2.5–3.0 per cent of their total annual budget to spend on digital technology, and that many are also constrained in their use of those limited resources by the local education system authorities.

While the pathfinders have shown it is possible to become 'digital', the other reality is that schools in comparison to other information-rich industries have grossly inadequate funding for both the technology and the associated staff development. While some governments are prepared to inject supplementary funds, if all schools are to become digital and continue to make best use of the ever-more sophisticated technology, a greater proportion of the recurrent funding does need to be made available for that purpose.

However, in saying this, we urge governments, education authorities and schools to look closely at the current school buying patterns and identify where savings can be made when schools shift from a paper to digitally based mode. Of some note in this regard is the finding that schools that use interactive whiteboards have been able to markedly reduce their considerable annual photocopying expenses.

As a second step, we recommend that educational leaders and policymakers critically evaluate the present spending on ICT, and give careful consideration to issues associated with the total cost of ownership. For example, school laptop programs—even when 'part subsidised' by parents— are immensely expensive, as well as being of questionable educational value. There is not only the cost of acquisition, and replacement every three to four years, but also the attuning of the school's infrastructure to accommodate the laptops and the considerable cost of support. One only has to look at the special powered student lockers bought by some schools to house the students' laptops to appreciate the consequences. By contrast, schools using interactive whiteboards do not need to consider replacing them for another 10 to 12 years, or paying immense annual software licence fees. The personal computer strategy, with its three-to-four-year outlay of very considerable monies, is not the only one open to digital schools.

Has your school done an in-depth analysis of its current ICT expenditure and ascertained if it is in fact sustainable, or desirable? Ways of approaching this question are suggested in Exercises 15.6 and 15.7.

Exercise 15.6 Analysing expenditure on digital technologies

Bring your leadership team together and ask each person to identify <u>three</u> areas where they believe significant financial savings can be made in the shift from a paper-based mode to a digital mode of school operation.

Exercise 15.7 Evaluating the use of instructional technologies

- Which of your instructional technologies are the most used in teaching and learning? [By 'instructional technologies' we mean those technologies used by teachers to supplement their voice in their teaching.]
- Which of your digital instructional technologies—hardware and software—are most used? What data have you to support that belief?
- Which technologies are now obsolete and could be done away with?

EVALUATION AND REFLECTION

Does your school or education authority engage in regular evaluation and reflection on the use of digital technology?

Do you involve staff and students in that discourse?

To what extent have you and your colleagues been able to 'de-mythologise' the use of ICT and come to see it as another tool to help enhance teaching and improve student learning?

Lee and Winzenried (2008) found few published school-based studies (even those about schools with annual ICT budgets well over $1 million!) that seriously evaluated expenditure on ICT. That finding is consistent with the experience of our contributing authors.

In most instances professional educators can soon ascertain the worth of a strategy or a tool, particularly if they involve their very ICT savvy clients in the discussion. It is therefore of concern that so few evaluations of the technology and of the processes used to implement them appear to be taking place. Related to this, some questions to consider are:

- Has your school analysed the effectiveness of implementation of digital technologies and the outcomes produced, and then reflected on the educational or administrative value of its investment?
- Do you have Key Performance Indicators against which to evaluate school performance in moving towards a digitally based mode of operation?

Take advantage of the 'politicking'

One of the realities of governments—national and regional—is that every so often (invariably near an election) funding is made available for technology. It happened with TVs, with video recorders, and now with personal computers and other forms of infrastructure and digital tools.

Historically, most of the funding is for items that will provide good media coverage and often does not fund basics like staff development or infrastructure and support. Notwithstanding, the leader of a digital school ought to seek to get a fair share of that money—and work to ensure that its expenditure is used to best effect and reported against its impact on student outcomes.

Celebrate the successes

The digital mode of operation offers schools immense and exciting possibilities. In the hands of astute educational leaders, it provides the opportunity to create effective, engaging networked school communities that educate young people for the contemporary world.

But the efforts that need to be expended in realising this potential are substantial. Therefore, when your 'KPIs' are reached, take the opportunity to celebrate your success. Staff will have put in immense effort and many will have dramatically enhanced their teaching. Take the time to savour those achievements.

When you reflect on your leadership—whether it be in schools, in education authority offices, or in other settings—your experience will invoke some special memories and the satisfaction that you have made a meaningful and positive difference to the lives and learning of others in these changing times.

APPENDIX

PRECURSORS TO PLANNING: TEMPLATES FOR DISCUSSION GROUPS

1 SELF-EVALUATION FOR SCHOOL LEADERS

Answers and reactions to these questions and statements will help illustrate the values, beliefs and attitudes that influence how you approach tasks and people.

- What are your core values and beliefs about schooling and/or learning and teaching?
- Within the parameters of accepted school norms there are various acceptable differences in leadership approach. For example, if forced to choose, do you feel more comfortable with service, tradition and harmonious relationships or setting new direction, innovation and the energy of change?
- Do you see the work you are doing as redefining schooling or building on and improving what exists?
- Do you see your approach modifying current curriculum directions and pedagogical approaches or setting new ones, or both?
- Where in your judgement is the balance between curriculum content and learning process?
- Can you visualise a 'school/schooling of the future'?

Recommended resource
Dr Julia Atkin's paper, 'From Values and Beliefs to Policy and Practice' (1996) outlines how you can gauge values and beliefs at the individual and group level, use them to galvanise group effort, assist in developing policy and practice, and in reviewing success.

2   FOCUS ON LEARNING: CULTURE

Answers to these questions will influence—if not determine—many policy, practice and school cultural issues. Individual reflection needs to be followed by group discussion and reflection to build some acceptable models that define commonality and acceptable diversity at this level about the purposes that are being undertaken.

- What is it you remember from your own education?
- What aspects of human interaction/teaching and learning do not change over time, in spite of the context and technology?
- What is it about learning and human interaction that you would not wish to lose and/or cannot afford to lose as the future unfolds?
- How do you understand the role of teachers? What is the role you would like to see teachers play? What aspects of their current role should be kept? What aspects can be allowed to go?
- Do you see learning as sequentially stepped, or less linear and more web-like, as both, or other?
- How would you combine both linear sequence and web-like connections in the one school culture?
- Is there a reasonably consistent view among students, staff and parents as to what that 'learning moment' looks like? Can it be described in a small set of illustrative examples?
- For most people, intellectual development is central to schooling. What is the place of social, emotional, physical, aesthetic and spiritual development? What are the priorities and relativities for your school?
- What strengths and weaknesses exist in your parent body? In what areas, if any, can the school community decide that parents will take the lead and the school provide the secondary role?
- Salusinszky (2007) suggests that the more technology dominates our lives, the greater the challenge to remain connected to the source of our creativity, solitude and stillness. How would these aspects, if accepted, be described and incorporated in school life?

Group exercise

A tested and successful process for parents and staff is to describe and rank the skills, knowledge, behaviours and attitudes of the perfect Year 12 student graduating from your school in 2026—that is today's babies; or choose a nearer date based on when the students of parents involved in the discussion leave the school.

The list is easy to determine as positive human qualities are almost universal. However, the ranking exercise is vital. For example, would creative and critical thinking skills rank above respect for authority? If so, what influence does this have for teaching and learning and school culture, policy and practice?

3 FOCUS ON LEARNING: EVIDENCE OF QUALITY

What evidence shows that quality learning is occurring? Will basic skills tests be the only or best measure? What other data can you collect?

The following points are drawn from Dr Julia Atkin's work.

It is generally agreed that quality learning results in:

- increased confidence and skills
- enthusiasm to share and express learning
- increased independence; increased self-direction
- growth and progress.

The learner is:

- willing to ask for help
- able to put learning into practice
- able to question further
- able to define problems and experiment with new ways to solve
- prepared and able to interact with others
- able to recognise when it is appropriate to work interdependently
- actively involved
- increasingly self-directed.

The learner experiences:

- a sense of achievement and success
- good feelings about self
- the learning as relevant
- valuing of the learning/expressing by others and/or self
- pride in achievement/learning
- affirmation in own way of knowing and being.

What data can you gather that will assist in making judgements in these areas?

What learning occurring outside the classroom can you leverage off?

Resources
See Resources at the end of the next section, 'Focus on teaching'.

4 FOCUS ON TEACHING

Quality of teaching is the most significant influence on student outcomes, outside of who students are and what their parents/family provide.

- Staff are finite in number in your school. What is the most effective way to use their skills? What is the most efficient manner to use their energies and time? What can be given priority—especially professional learning resources under your vision and values?
- What aspects of current classroom practice need to be improved? What is good practice and should be kept?
- How many of your current staff will you have with you in three years? Five years?
- What is the current rate of staff turnover?
- What groups of teachers come and go?
- What use of teacher time can be discontinued? Is it possible to move non-teaching tasks to non-teaching staff?
- Do you control staffing? If so, what staffing profile would best fit your purposes?
- What does your staff capabilities audit look like, especially in the areas of cognitive research, learning and pedagogy, and the use of ICT in teaching and learning?
- What are staff professional learning needs relative to your agreed commonality and acceptable diversity in the area of values and beliefs about teaching, learning and the purposes of schooling?
- What is your school record of moving from professional learning to implementation? If, like many, it is not good, why? How can it be improved?
- Who are the key people in your school? What are their skills and values?
- Who are the early adopters who will showcase best practice? Provide these groups with quality resources and support in the initial phases. This is an agreed school plan and those able and willing to lead need to be supported and seen to be supported.
- Who are the best senior staff for supporting teachers in teaching and learning using digital technologies?

Resources

Consider the following resources:

Dimensions of Learning (http://www.mcrel.org/dimensions/whathow. asp)—a model that uses knowledge about learning to define the learning process. Its premise is that the five dimensions of learning are essential to successful learning. The dimensions are:

a   Attitudes and perceptions
b   Acquire and integrate knowledge
c   Extend and refine knowledge
d   Use knowledge meaningfully
e   Productive habits of mind

Teaching for Understanding (http://learnweb.harvard.edu/ALPS/tfu/) is a part of Active Learning Practice for Schools (ALPs). ALPS is an electronic community dedicated to the improvement and advancement of educational instruction and practice. They aim to create an online collaborative environment between teachers and administrators from around the world with educational researchers, professors and curriculum designers at Harvard's Graduate School of Education (http://gseweb.harvard.edu/) and Project Zero (http://www.pz.harvard. edu/index.cfm).

Herrmann Whole Brain Learning (http://www.herrmann.com.au/index. htm) or (http://www.hbdi.com/home/index.cfm). People learn in many different ways. The brain is the source of who we are and how we learn. Ned Herrmann (1988) combined research on right brain/left brain differences with research on the Triune brain to create a metaphorical model to explain the process of thinking and learning. Depending on which aspects we engage, our learning processes can be very different. Brain dominance leads to thinking style preferences, which impact what we pay attention to and how and what we learn naturally.

Integral Learning Model (http://www.learning-by-design.com/; http:// www.learningtolearn.sa.edu.au/Colleagues/pages/default/atkin/; http://www.learningtolearn.sa.edu.au/Colleagues/files/links/ IntegralLearning.pdf). Dr Julia Atkin is an education and learning consultant. Her work with educators over many years focused on reflection and dialogue around two key questions: What is powerful learning? and What is powerful to learn? Julia's approach bridges the gap between theory and practice. In October 2003, The Bulletin named Julia as one of Australia's Smart 100—a list of 100 people, ten in 10 fields, making a difference to Australian society through innovation.

Five Minds for the Future by H. Gardner (2006). (See Bibliography) The International Congress for Schools Effectiveness and Improvement (http://www.icsei.net/)—the desire to make schools more effective through a continuous quest to better understand what the big ideas mean, both theoretically and in practice. Effectiveness studies gave birth to this movement just over two decades ago, a period that has amassed an impressive body of knowledge on effective schools, effective leadership, effective teaching and how those interplay with one another to enhance student learning. The School Improvement movement emerged, seeking to apply the lessons learned while urging caution on policy makers overly keen to apply simplistic remedies.

5   DIGITAL COMPONENTS

- What has been invested in ICT over the last five years? What returns have been seen on that investment? Where has learning improved? What improvements in teacher effectiveness or efficiency have been noted? What data supports anecdotal evidence? If that money had been invested in other ways, could the returns have been different? For example, if a different range of digital technologies had been used, would different results have been seen? What if those monies had been expended on resources other than digital?
- What are the technological opportunities that currently exist, and what may be coming? What risks do you run in moving towards these new technologies, and what risks are run in not moving?
- What bandwidth and network infrastructure currently exist? What bandwidth do you need for digital video streaming, video conferencing, a large repertoire of podcasts? Are there more bandwidth intensive uses for your network? How is the network used and how might that use be improved?
- Does the 'pipe' into and out of the school match your internal capacities? If not, what options are open to you?
- Have you banned portable devices such as mobile phones and iPods or are you endeavouring to find ways to use them productively? Why was this decision made?
- How can you use and build on the popularity of blogs, social network-ing, mobile phones and iPods?

- What technologies are currently used in teaching and learning? Why are these used and others not? Do they achieve their purposes? Are their purposes explicit?
- Much of the material accessed by students and staff digitally is unedited, not refereed and often anonymous. What learning processes, policies and practices are needed to have staff and students scrutinise all material?
- Arguably one of the great risks for schools regarding their duty of care and for student wellbeing is the propensity of the Internet to encourage both freedom of action and words with anonymity. To be able to remain unaccountable for one's words and actions is not a socially positive manner in which to interact with others. What processes does your school use to build positive social habits? How does a school moderate such human propensities amplified by the Internet?
- Do teachers have access to appropriate digital resources for teaching and management; for example, personal computer, key software applications, email, personal portal, portable digital storage, ISP access at home capable of supporting school commitments?
- Do students have access to appropriate digital resources for learning and building of knowledge?

Resources

Learning in an Online World (series), published by Curriculum Corporation for MCEETYA (Ministerial Council on Education, Employment, Training and Youth Affairs)

- *Bandwidth Action Plan* (2003)
- *Contemporary Learning* (2005)
- *Content Specifications Framework* (2006)
- *Content Strategy* (2004)
- *Learning Architecture Framework* (2003)
- *Learning Architecture Framework: Tasmanian Case Study* (2004)
- *Leadership Strategy* (2006)
- *Online Curriculum Content Investment Agreement 2006–08* (2006)

A very good resource is to visit other schools, see what they are doing, offer reciprocal visiting rights and share experiences. Visit local schools across all sectors; all have something to offer and often the differences are not as large as expected. Where possible, venture further afield and repeat the reciprocal and discursive behaviours.

BIBLIOGRAPHY

AAPT. (2007). *Research finds new technology is challenging the Australian family*. Retrieved March 31, 2008, from http://home.aapt.com.au/ At_AAPT/What_s_news/2007/Research_finds_new_technology_is_ challenging_the_Australian_family.html

Abram, S. (2005). Web 2.0, Library 2.0, and Librarian 2.0: Preparing for the 2.0 world. *SirsiDynix OneSource* e-newsletter. Retrieved January 9, 2008, from http://www.imakenews.com/sirsi/e_article000505688. cfm?x=b6yRqLJ,b2rpQhRM.

Abram, S., & Luther, J. (2004). *Born with a chip*. Available from http://www. libraryjournal.com/article/CA411572.html.

Anderson, P. (2007). What is Web 2.0? Ideas, technologies and implications for education, *JISC Technology & Standards Watch Report*. Retrieved January 10, 2008, from http://www.jisc.ac.uk/media/documents/ techwatch/tsw0701b.pdf.

Anderson, R.E., & Becker, H.J. (1999). Teaching, learning and computing: 1998 national survey. University of California and University of Minnesota: Center for Research on Information Technology and Organizations.

Appleyard, B. (2007, April 23). Anarchy of distance. *The Australian*, News Corporation, p. 12.

Association for Library Collections & Technical Services. (1999). *Task force on metadata: Summary report*. American Library Association. Retrieved January 9, 2008, from http://www.libraries.psu.edu/tas/jca/ccda/tf-meta3.html.

Atkin, J. (1996). *From values and beliefs to policy and practice*. Seminar Series No. 54. Jolimont, Victoria: Incorporated Association of Registered Teachers of Victoria.

Atkin, J. (1997). *Enhancing learning with information technology: Promises, pitfalls and practicalities*. Seminar Series No. 70. Jolimont, Victoria: Incorporated Association of Registered Teachers of Victoria.

Atkin, J. (1999). Connected learning: The challenge for communities and individuals. Unpublished paper.

Australian Communications and Media Authority. (2007, December). *Media and communications in Australian families*. Canberra. Available from http://www.acma.gov.au/webwr/_assets/main/lib101058/media_and_society_report_2007.pdf
This study provides a comprehensive picture of the use of all types of digital technology in the home in a developed nation in 2007. While Australian, the trends described provide all school leaders with an appreciation of the technologies being embraced by the young in the developed world.

Australian Copyright Council. (1994–2008). *Education and teaching, Redfern, NSW*. Retrieved January 14, 2008, from http://www.copyright.org.au/information/specialinterest/education.htm.

Barber, M., & Mourshed, M. (2007). *How the world's best performing school systems come out on top*. McKinsey & Company. Available from http://www.mckinsey.com/clientservice/socialsector/resources/pdf/Worlds_School_Systems_Final.pdf.

Barlow, J.P. (1995, December). In N. Tunbridge, The cyberspace cowboy. *Australian Personal Computer*.

Beare, H. (2001). *Creating the future school*, London: Routledge Falmer.

Beare, H. (2006). *How we envisage schooling in the 21st century: The new imaginary in practice*. London: Specialist Schools and Academies Trust.

Becta. (2005). *The Becta Review 2005: Evidence on the progress of ICT in education*. British Educational Communications and Technology Agency. Retrieved January 2, 2008, from http://www.becta.org.uk/page_documents/research/becta_review_feb05.pdf.
The annual Becta reviews provide an invaluable 'warts and all' in-depth, up-to-date analysis of the many variables associated with developing digital schooling across a nation. A model for all education authorities. The UK is undoubtedly one of the world leaders not only in its investment in digital technology for the education of the young, but also in its use of research to inform the policy development and its willingness to go public with the research. Pleasant absence of 'spin-doctoring'. Can be readily downloaded from the Becta site at http://schools.becta.org.uk.

Becta. (2007). *Harnessing technology review 2007: Progress and impact of technology in education: Summary report*. Available from http://publications.becta.org.uk/display.cfm?resID=33980.

Becta. (2008). *Self review framework introduction*. Retrieved February 8, 2008, from http://schools.becta.org.uk/index.php?section=srf.

Bonanno, K. (2006). Managing information within professional groups. *Access, 20*(1), 27–31. Retrieved January 20, 2008, from http://www.kb.com.au/downloads/InformationManagment.pdf.

Bransford, J.D., Brown, A.L., & Cocking, R.R. (1999). *How people learn: Brain, mind, experience and school*. National Academy of Sciences. Available from http://www.nap.edu/html/howpeople1/.
This book locates the enterprise of schooling within the business of schooling. Schools are about learning and we have to understand how people learn before we confront the issues of improving learning outcomes for all students. This text synthesises decades of best theory and practice. In the first chapter it makes the observation that '... the meaning of knowing has shifted from being able to remember and repeat information to being able to find and use it' (p. 5). As we move from an industrial to a knowledge age model of schooling, it is imperative we understand how learning takes place.

Brown, J. (2000, April). Growing up digital: How the web changes work, education and the ways that people learn. *Change*, 11–20.

Byrk, A., & Schneider, B. (2002). *Trust in schools*. New York: Russell Sage.

Caldwell, B. (1995). Resourcing the transformation of school education: Part 1. *The Practising Administrator, 17*(1), 4–7.

Caldwell, B. (2006). *Re-imagining educational leadership*. Melbourne: ACER Press.

Callahan, R. (1962). *Education and the cult of efficiency*. Chicago: University of Chicago Press.

Candy, P.C. (2004). Linking thinking: Self-directed learning in the digital age. A paper prepared with a grant from the DEST Research Fellowship Scheme. Canberra: Commonwealth of Australia. Retrieved November 30, 2007, from http://www.dest.gov.au/sectors/training_skills/publications_resources/other_publications/linking_thinking.htm.

Capra, F. (1996). *The web of life*. New York: Anchor Books.

Cerf, C., & Navasky, V. (1984). *The experts speak: The definitive compendium of authoritative misinformation*. New York: Pantheon Books.

Collins, J. (2006). *Good to great and the social sectors*. London: Random House.

Combes, B. (2007). Techno savvy or just techno oriented? How do the Net Generation search for information? In J. Bales et al. (Eds.), *Hearts on fire: Sharing the passion*, 22–34. ASLA XX Biennial Conference Proceedings 2007, Australian School Library Association, Canberra, ACT.

Copyright Agency Limited. (2007). Info sheets. Sydney: Copyright Agency Limited. Retrieved January 14, 2008, from http://www.copyright.com.au/information.htm.

Crawford, W., & Gorman, M. (1995). *Future libraries: Dreams, madness and reality.* Chicago: American Library Association.

Creative Commons (2008). *Creative commons.* Retrieved January 14, 2008, from http://creativecommons.org/.

Crosby P. (1980). *Quality is free.* New York: Mentor Books.

Csikszentmihalyi, M. (1990). *Flow: The psychology of optimal experience.* New York: Harper & Row.

Cuban, Dr. L. (1986). *Teachers and machines: The classroom use of technology since 1920.* New York: Teachers College Press.

Cuban, Dr. L. (2000). *So much high-tech money invested, so little use and change in practice: How come?* Available from http://www.edtechnot.com/notarticle1201.html.

Cuban, Dr. L. (2001). *Oversold and underused: Reforming schools through technology, 1998–2000.* Cambridge, MA: Harvard University Press.

Darling-Hammond, L. (1998). Teacher learning that supports student learning. *Strengthening the Teaching Profession, 55*(5), 6–11.

Department of Education and the Arts, Queensland. (2005). *Smart classrooms.* Retrieved January 2, 2008, from http://education.qld.gov.au/smartclassrooms/.

Department of Education, Training and the Arts, Queensland (2006). *Smart classrooms: Professional development framework.* Retrieved January 2, 2008, from http://education.qld.gov.au/smartclassrooms/strategy/tsdev_pd.html.

DfES. (2005). *Harnessing technology: Transforming learning and children's services.* London. Available from http://www.dfes.gov.uk/publications/e-strategy/docs/e-strategy.pdf.

Downes, T., & Fatouros, C. (1995). *Learning in an electronic world: Computers in the classroom.* Newtown: Primary English Teaching Association.

Drake Personnel. (2007). *Great people.* May newsletter, Adelaide edition.

Earl, Dr. L., & Katz, Dr. S. (2001). Leading schools in a data rich world. In Leithwood & Hallinger (Eds.), *International Handbook of Leadership.*

EduTools. (2007). CMS: CMS home. Retrieved March 20, 2008, from http://www.edutools.info/static. jsp?pj=4&page=HOME.

Ellyard, P. (1998a). From cowboy to cosmonaut. *Principal Matters, 9*(3), 15–18.

Ellyard, P. (1998b). *Ideas for the new millennium.* Melbourne: Melbourne University Press.

Ellyard, P. (2001). Imagining the future and getting to it. In C. Barker (Ed.). *Innovation and imagination at work.* AIM Australia Management Today Series, 152–173. Sydney: McGraw Hill.

Ellyard, P. (2004). Becoming a leader first of self, then of others. In J. Marsden (Ed.), *I believe this* (pp. 86–88). Sydney: Random House Australia.

Ellyard, P. (2007). *Designing 2050: Pathways to sustainable prosperity on spaceship Earth.* Melbourne: TPNTXT.

Elmore, R. (2004). *School reform from inside out.* Cambridge: Harvard Education Press.

Elmore, R. (2006). Agency, reciprocity and accountability. In Fuhrman et al., *The public schools.* New York: Oxford University Press.

eMINTS. (2007). *About eMINTS: Professional development for educators by educators.* Retrieved January 2, 2008, from http://www.emints.org/about/index.shtml#results.

eMINTS National Center. (2007). Welcome to eMINTS in Missouri. Retrieved January 2, 2008, from http://missouri.emints.org/.

Evans, J., & Lindsay, W. (2002). *The management and control of quality* (5th ed.). South Western/Thomson.

Fielding, M. (1999, August). Radical collegiality: Affirming teaching as an inclusive professional practice. *Australian Educational Researcher, 26*(2), 1–34.

Finger, G. (2002). Technology and behaviour management: Identifying strategic intents—understanding and creating new environments. In W. Rogers (Ed.), *Teacher leadership and behaviour.* London: Sage Publications.

Finger, G., Jamieson-Proctor, R., & Watson, G. (2006). *Measuring learning with ICTs: An external evaluation of Education Queensland's ICT curriculum integration performance measurement instrument.* Symposium paper, Australian Association for Research in Education Conference—Education Research Creative Dissent: Constructive Solutions, The University of Western Sydney Parramatta Campus, Australia, Nov 27–Dec 1, 2005. Retrieved May 27, 2007, from http://www.aare.edu.au/05pap/abs05.htm#T.

Finger, G., Proctor, R.M.J., & Watson, G. (2003). *Recommendations for the development of an ICT curriculum integration performance measurement instrument: Focusing on student use of ICTs.* Proceedings of the annual conference for the Australian and New Zealand Associations for Research in Education (AARE – NZARE), Auckland, New Zealand.

Finger, G., Russell, G., Jamieson-Proctor, R., & Russell, N. (2007). *Transforming learning with ICT: Making IT happen.* French's Forest, NSW: Pearson Education Australia.

Fitzallen, N., & Brown, N. (2006). *What profiling tells us about ICT and professional practice.* Symposium paper, Australian Association for

Research in Education Conference—Education Research Creative Dissent: Constructive Solutions, The University of Western Sydney Parramatta Campus, Australia, Nov 27–Dec 1, 2005. Retrieved May 27, 2007, from http://www.aare.edu.au/05pap/abs05.htm#T.

Friedman, T. (2006). *The world is flat* (2nd Edition). New York: Farrar, Straus & Giroux.

A must read for all leaders and potential leaders of digital schools. Provides an invaluable insight into the global forces at play and how the confluence of set of developments has changed societies and the workplace globally.

Fullan, M. (2005). Professional learning communities writ large. In R. Dufour, & R. Eaker (Eds.), *On common ground: The power of professional learning communities.* Bloomington, IN: Solution Tree.

Fullan, M. (2007). Retrieved November 30, 2007, from http://www.michaelfullan.ca/resource_assets/07_Keynote.pdf.

Fuller, A. (2007). *Don't waste your breath.* Retrieved November 30, 2007, from http://ww.abc.net.au/talkitup/pdfs/Dont_waste_your_breath.pdf.

Gardner, H. (2007). *Five minds for the future.* Harvard: Harvard Business School Press.

Gee, J.P. (2006). Literacy, learning and video games. *EQ Australia.*

Gee, J.P. (2007). *What video games have to teach us about learning and literacy* (2nd Edition). New York: Palgrave Macmillan.

In both the article and the book Gee provides an interesting insight into the structure of video games and how we can utilise this information to study issues such as learning theory, motivation and the development of expertise. In the book he makes a strong case in favour of video games being more akin to agents of learning (like recreational reading) as opposed to mindless entertainment (like really dumb movies). By using video games to illustrate these ideas he provides some invaluable insights into how we might structure educational 'reform' in more contemporary times.

Gittins, R. (2006, March 22). Cast the die early and reap the reward. *Sydney Morning Herald* (p. 11).

Gliddon, J. (2006, October 17). Get smarter. *Bulletin*, 37–42.

Gore, A. (1994). 'Super highway' speech. Available from http://artcontext.com/calendar/1997/superhig.html.

Grose, M. (2006). *Generation X parents: A social report on parents today.* Workshop paper, AHISA Pastoral Care Conference. Available from www.parentingideas.com.au.

Grossman, L. (2006). Person of the year. *Time Magazine, 51.*

Hargreaves, A. (2003). *Teaching in the knowledge society: Education in the age of insecurity.* Columbia: Columbia University, Teachers College Press.

This book challenges our contemporary notions of schooling by examining what our world looks like in a knowledge age. It emphasises that the purpose of schooling is on the person not the process. This is critical if we are to address the challenges of schooling in today's world. As Hargreaves observes, 'The educational answer to the angst of early adolescents is mainly to be found not in more curriculum, but in stronger community' (p. 61). Hargreaves is insistent that our answers are not to be found in technology but knowing our purpose and exploring new ways of building robust learning communities. He makes the point that teaching is not for the faint-hearted and it '... requires qualities of personal and intellectual maturity that take years to develop' (p. 66).

Hart, S., Brinkman, B., & Blackmore, S. (2003). *How well are we raising our children in the North Metropolitan area? Results of the Early Development Instrument.* North Metropolitan Health Service (WA).

Hay, L. (2006). Student learning through Australian school libraries Part 2: What students define and value as school library support. *Synergy, 4*(2), 27–38. Carlton: School Library Association of Victoria.

Her Majesty's Inspectors of Education. (2005). *The integration of information and communications technology in Scottish schools.* Available from http://www.hmie.gov.uk/documents/publication/EvICT%20Final%2018%20Oct.html.

Herrmann, N. (1988). *The creative brain.* Lake Lure, NC: Brain Tools.

Hodas, S. (1993). Technology refusal and the organisational culture of schools. *Education Policy Analysis Archives, 1*(10). Retrieved January 2, 2008, from http://olam.ed.asu.edu/epaa/v1n10.html.

Hough, M. (2000). Leadership of electronically capable schools. *ACEA Monograph,* (2). Melbourne.

Hough, M. (2001). *Emerging new technologies and their implications for the intellectual capital of organisations.* CIMA Annual Conference: Harnessing and managing intellectual capital, Sydney.

Hough, M. (2004). New technologies and their impact on educators. *ACEA Hot Topic.* Melbourne.

Hough, M. (2006). *Moral values: The bottom line.* Public Sector Reform Conference, Hong Kong.

Hough, M. (2007a). Keynote addresses: *Leading a digital school—the challenges,* and *Next stage: Leading a digital school.* Conference for School Leaders, Sunshine Coast.

Hough, M. (2007b). Keynote addresses: *Teachers as leaders—what is the world that we are preparing them for?,* and *Leading a futures oriented school.* QSite Conference, Moreton Bay College.

Hough, M., & Paine, J. (1997). *Creating quality learning communities.* Macmillan.

Illinois Institute of Design (ID). (2007). *Schools in the digital age.* Illinois Institute of Technology. Available from http://www.id.iit.edu/635/documents/MacArthurFinalReport1.pdf.
A recommended read for all. This high-level think tank that drew on the talents of visionaries like Charles Handy and Gary Hamel provides some very good insights and stimulating ideas.

Inayatullah, S. (1995). Metaphors and the future—An interview by Anna Smith (1995). Metafuture.org Interviews. Retrieved January 2, 2008, from http://www.metafuture.org/interviews/METAPHORSANDTHE FUTURE.htm.

International ICT Literacy Panel. (2002). *Digital transformation: A framework for ICT literacy.* Educational Testing Service.

Jamieson-Proctor, R., & Finger, G. (2006). Relationship between pre-service and practising teachers' confidence and beliefs about using ICT. *Australian Educational Computing—Special Conference Edition, Journal of the Australian Council for Computers in Education, 21*(2), 25–33.

Jamieson-Proctor, R.M., Burnett, P., Finger, G., & Watson, G. (2006). ICT integration and teachers' confidence in using ICT for teaching and learning in Queensland State Schools. *Australian Journal of Educational Technology, 22*(4), 511–530.

Johnson, K.E., & Golombek, P.R. (2002). Inquiry into experience: Teachers' personal and professional growth. In K. Johnson & P. Golombek (Eds.), *Teachers' narrative inquiry as professional development*, ch. 1, pp. 1–14. Cambridge: Cambridge University Press.

Jonassen, D. (1999). *Welcome to the design of constructivist learning environments (CLEs).* Retrieved January 2, 2008, from http://tiger.coe.missouri.edu/~jonassen/courses/CLE/index.html.

Kahane, A. (2004). *Solving tough problems.* San Francisco: Berrett-Koehler.

Kersteen, Z.A., & Linn M.C. (1998). Previous experience and the learning of computer programming: The computer helps those who help themselves. *Journal of Educational Computing Research, 4,* 321–334.

Klein, P.S., Nir-Gal, O., & Darom, E. (2000). The use of computers in kindergarten, with or without adult mediation: Effects on children's cognitive performance and behavior. *Computers in Human Behavior, 16,* 591–608. Elsevier Science.

Kurzweil, R. (1999). *The age of spiritual machines: When computers exceed human intelligence.* New York: Penguin Books.

Ladwig J., & Gore, J. (1998). Nurturing democracy in schools. In J. Smyth, R. Hattam, & M. Lawson (Eds.), *Schooling for a fair go*, pp. 15–26. Leichhardt, NSW: Federation Press.

Laferrierre, T. (1997). Towards well-balanced technology enhanced learning environments: Preparing the ground for choices ahead. Unpublished working paper. Toronto: Council of Ministers of Education Canada.

Layton, T. (2000, September). Digital learning: Why tomorrow's schools must let go of the past. *Electronic School.*

Lee, M. (1996). The educated home. *The Practising Administrator, 3.*

Lee, M. (2000). Chaotic learning: The learning style of the 'Net Generation'. In G. Hart (Ed.), *Readings and resources in global online education.* Melbourne: Whirligig Press.

Lee, M. (2003). Macro ICT trends in schooling. *The Practising Administrator.* (1), 30–32.

Lee, M. (2006a). Digital take-up and phased lift-off. *Australian Educational Leader, 28*(1), 36–37.

Lee, M. (2006b). Managing the school's digital teaching resources and assets. *Australian Educational Leader, 3.*

Lee, M., & Boyle, M. (2004, March). Richardson Primary School: The Richardson Revolution. *Educare News.*

Lee, M., & Winzenried, A. (2006). Interactive whiteboards: Achieving total teacher usage. *Australian Educational Leader, 28*(3), 22–25.

Lee, M., & Winzenried, A. (in press). *A history of the use of instructional technology in schools.* Melbourne: ACER Press.
This work provides a rare, in-depth insight into the factors needing to be addressed to achieve the whole-school teacher use of digital technology in their everyday teaching, as well as the lessons the leaders of digital schools can learn from a century of use of instructional technology.

Leithwood, K., & Riehl, C. (2004). What we know about successful leadership. *The Practising Administrator,* (4), 4–7.

Lemke, L. (2002). Becoming the village: Education across lives. In G. Wells, & G. Claxton (Eds.), *Learning for life in the 21st century.* Oxford: Blackwell.

Levine, M. (2003). *The myth of laziness.* New York: Simon and Schuster.

Lloyd, M. (2006). *Towards a definition of the integration of ICT in the classroom.* Symposium paper. Australian Association for Research in Education Conference—Education Research Creative Dissent: Constructive Solutions, The University of Western Sydney Parramatta Campus, Australia, Nov 27—Dec 1, 2005. Retrieved March 31, 2008, from http://www.aare.edu.au/05pap/llo05120.pdf.

Loader, D. (2006). Re-imaging schooling. *Occasional Paper*, (98). Centre for Strategic Education.

Lorenzo, G. (2007). *Catalysts for change: Information fluency, Web 2.0, Library 2.0, and the new education culture*. Clarence Center, New York: Lorenzo Associates. Retrieved January 8, 2008, from http://www.edpath.com/ stn.htm.

Mackay, H. (1993). *Reinventing Australia: The mind and mood of Australia in the 90s*. Sydney: Angus and Robertson.

Mackay, H. (2004). *The Ipsos Mackay Report*, (5), (6), (7). Regular two-weekly reports on the issues and viewpoints of Australian society as revealed by focus groups.

Mackay, H. (2007). *Advance Australia where?*. Sydney: Hachette Books.

Maddux, C.D., LaMont Johnson, D., & Willis, J.W. (2001). *Educational computing learning with tomorrow's technologies* (3rd Edition). Needham Heights, MA: Allyn & Bacon.

Mallan, K., Lundin, R., Elliott Burns, R., Massey, G., & Russell, A. (2002). *Performing hybridity: Impact of new technologies on the role of teacher-librarians*. A report of research conducted under a QUT Scholarship in the Professions grant. Brisbane: Queensland University of Technology.

Marshall, S.P. (2006). *The power to transform: Leadership that brings learning and schooling to life*. San Francisco: Jossey-Bass.

Martin, R. (2007, June). How successful leaders think. *Harvard Business Review*, 60–67.

Martinez, M.E., & Mead, N.A. (1988). *Computer competence: The first national assessment*. Princeton National Assessment of Educational Progress and Educational Testing Service.

Marzano, R.J. (2003). *What works in schools: Translating research into action*. ASCD Publications.

Masters, J., & Yelland, N. (1996). Geometry in context: implementing a discovery-based technology curriculum with young children. Paper presented at the Australian Computers in Education Conference Get IT, Canberra, ACT.

Mawhinney, H., Haas, J., & Wood, C. (2005). Teachers' collective efficacy beliefs in professional learning communities. *Leading and Managing*, *11*(2), 12–45.

Meredyth, D., Russell, N., Blackwood, L., Thomas, J., & Wise, P. (1998). *Real time: Computers, change and schooling*. Canberra: Department of Education, Training and Youth Affairs.

Milken Exchange on Education Technology. (2005). *Transforming learning through technology: Policy roadmaps for the nation's governors.* Santa Monica, CA: Milken Exchange on Education Technology. Available from https://depts.washington.edu/academy/leadership/files/governors_policy_roadmaps-lead.pdf.

Milojević, I. (2005). *Educational futures: Dominant and contesting visions.* London: Routledge.

Ministerial Council on Education, Employment, Training and Youth Affairs (MCEETYA). (2000). *Learning in an online world: The school action plan for the information economy.* Retrieved January 2, 2008, from http://www.edna.edu.au/edna/webdav/site/myjahiasite/shared/01_learningonline_prog_v1.pdf.

Ministerial Council on Education, Employment, Training and Youth Affairs (MCEETYA). (2003). *Research strategy: Learning in an online world.* Carlton South, Victoria: MCEETYA.

Ministerial Council on Education, Employment, Training and Youth Affairs (MCEETYA). (2005). *Pedagogy strategy: Learning in an online world.* Carlton South, Victoria: Curriculum Corporation. Retrieved January 2, 2008, from http://www.curriculum.edu.au/verve/_resources/pedagogy_strategy_file.pdf.

Ministry of Education. (2003). *Digital Horizons: Learning through ICT* (Revised Edition). Wellington, New Zealand: Learning Media.

Mitchell, L. (2007, February 12). The classroom's great white hope. *The Age,* p. 11.

Moyle, K. (2006). *Leadership and learning with ICT: Voices from the profession.* Available from http://www.appa.asn.au/CMS/uploads/articles/leadership%20and%20learning%20with%20ict.pdf.
An invaluable read for all current and prospective leaders of digital schools. Kathryn Moyle's national study of the readiness of Australian school principals to lead a digital school, and the support they desire, is applicable to school and educational authority leaders globally.

Mumtaz, S. (2000, May 2001). Children's enjoyment and perception of computer use in the home and the school. *Computers and Education, 36*(4), 347–362. Elsevier Science.

Naisbitt, J. (1984). *Megatrends.* London: Futura.

National School Boards Association (NSBA). (1984). Leadership and technology. In National School Board Association (NSBA) (2002), *Why change?* Retrieved January 2, 2008, from http://www.nsba.org/sbot/toolkit/WhyChange.html.

National School Boards Association (NSBA). (2007, August 14). More teens and 'tweens are creating content and connecting online for educational benefits, offering schools new opportunities to use technology reports: New National School Boards Association study. Media release. Retrieved April 7, 2008, from http://onlinepressroom.net/nsba/new/.

NCREL/Metiri Partnership. (2005). *enGauge: 21st century skills for 21st century learners.* NCREL. See www.ncrel.org/engauge/skills.

Neville Freeman Agency. (2006). Open book scenarios: Teaching for uncertain futures. Thought starters. *Teaching Australia.*

North Central Regional Educational Laboratory (NCREL). (2003). *enGauge 21st century skills: Literacy in the digital age.* Illinois: NCREL, and California: Metiri Group. Retrieved January 2, 2008, from http://www.ncrel.org/engauge.

Norwood, G. (2006). *Deeper mind: Maslow's Hierarchy of Needs.* Retrieved January 2, 2008, from http://www.deepermind.com/20maslow.htm.

Oblinger, D.G., & Oblinger, J.L. (2006). *Educating the Net Generation.* Educause. Available from http://www.educause.edu/educatingthenetgen.
This intriguing, web-based publication provides an excellent insight into the thinking and learning of the 'Net Generation'.

OECD. (2005). *Are students ready for a technology-rich world? What PISA studies tell us.* Paris, France: OECD Publishing Programme for International Student Assessment.

Open Source CMS. (2008). Retrieved March 30, 2008, from http://www.opensourcecms.com/index.php?option=com_content&task=view&id=424&Itemid=184&addcomment=1.

Orren, G. (2002). *The strategies of persuasion: The science and art of effective influence.* Notes from a paper delivered at the Conference of the Queensland Secondary Principals Association. Retrieved November 30, 2007, from http://aspa.asn.au/content/view/169/49/.

Peters, T. (2003). *Re-imagine!* London: DK.

Prensky, M. (2001, October). Digital natives, digital immigrants. *On the Horizon, 9*(5). NCB University Press. Retrieved January 5, 2008, from http://www.marcprensky.com/writing/Prensky%20-%20Digital%20Natives,%20Digital%20Immigrants%20-%20Part1.pdf.

Prensky, M. (2006). *Don't bother me Mum, I'm learning.* St Paul, Minnesota: Paragon House.

Queensland College of Teachers. (2006). *Professional standards for teachers.* Retrieved January 2, 2008, from http://www.qct.edu.au/ProfessionalStandards/Overview.htm.

Robertson, M., Webb, W., & Fluck, A. (2007), *Seven steps to ICT integration*. Melbourne: ACER Press.

Robinson, Sir Ken (2007). *Out of our minds: Learning to be creative*. Keynote address, ICP Conference, Auckland.

Roblyer, M.D. (2006). *Integrating educational technology into teaching* (4th ed.). Upper Saddle River, New Jersey: Pearson Merrill Prentice Hall.

Roffe, I. (2004). *Innovation and e-Learning: e-Business for an educational enterprise*. Cardiff: University of Wales Press.

Sachs, J., Russell, N., & Chataway, G. (1990). Technology and education: Forging links with business and industry. In M. Dupe (Ed.), *Making the links: Technology and science, industry and education*. Canberra: Australian Government Publishing Service.

Salusinszky, I. (2007, April 14–15). Lost in conversation. *The Weekend Australian Review, 44*. News Corporation.

Samaras, A. P. (1996). Children's computers. *Childhood Education, 72*, 133–136.

Sanders, R. (2006). The imponderable bloom: Reconsidering the role of technology in education. *Innovate, 2*(6).

Schein, E. (1985). *Organizational culture and leadership: A dynamic view*. San Francisco: Jossey-Bass.

SCIS. (2007). *Schools catalogue information service subject headings*. Last updated October 29, 2007. Melbourne: Curriculum Corporation. Retrieved January 12, 2008, from http://www1.curriculum.edu.au/scis/productinfo/subjectheadings.htm.

Senge, P. (2007, October). *Preparing 21C learners for the 21C world*. Video-conferencing keynote address, ACEL National Conference, Darling Harbour, Sydney.

Sennett, R. (2006). *The culture of the new capitalism*, ch. 1 (Bureaucracy), pp. 15–82. New Haven and London: Yale University Press.

Shalain, L. (1998). *The alphabet versus the goddess: The conflict between word and image*. London: Penguin Compass.

Sheahan, P. (2005). *Generation Y: Thriving and surviving with Generation Y at work*. Hardie Grant.

Sheahan, P. (2007). *Flip*. North Sydney: Random House Australia.

Shelton, M., & Jones, M. (1996). Staff development that works! A tale of 4 T's. *NASSP Bulletin, 80*(582), 99–105.

Siemens, G. (2004). *Connectivism: A learning theory for the digital age*. Retrieved January 2, 2008, from http://www.elearnspace.org/Articles/connectivism.htm.

Spender, D. (2007, May 19–20). Digi-kids and a new way of learning. *Sydney Morning Herald*, Weekend Edition, p. 32.

Tapscott, D. (1998). *Growing up digital*. New York: McGraw Hill.

Tapscott, D. (2007). *Wikinomics*. New York: Atlantic Books.

Taylor, C. (2003). *An introduction to metadata*. Brisbane: The University of Queensland, UQ Library. Retrieved May 27, 2007, from http://www. library.uq.edu.au/iad/ctmeta4.htm.

Taylor, R.P. (1980). (Ed.). *The computer in the school: Tutor, tool, tutee*. New York: Teachers' College Press.

Thian, Dr. Deidre (2007). *What parents want: An Independent Schools Queensland survey: Why did you choose an Independent School?*. Independent Schools Queensland.

Treadwell, M. (2007a). *Teachers @ work*. Retrieved November 30, 2007, from http://teachers.work.co.nz/.

Treadwell, M. (2007b). *The emergent 21st century teacher*. Retrieved November 30, 2007, from http://www.i-learnt.com/.

Trinidad, S., Newhouse, P., & Clarkson, B. (2006). *A framework for leading school change in using ICT: Measuring change*. Symposium paper. Australian Association for Research in Education Conference Education Research Creative Dissent: Constructive Solutions, The University of Western Sydney Parramatta Campus, Australia, Nov 27–Dec 1, 2005.

Truch, E. (2001). Knowledge management: Auditing and reporting intellectual capital. *Journal of General Management* (UK), *26*(3), 26–40.

UK Treasury Briefing Paper. (2007, July). Unpublished handout. Further information can be found at http://schools.becta.org.uk/index. php?section=oe&catcode=ss_es_opp_02&rid=13420.

United Nations Educational, Scientific and Cultural Organisation (UNESCO). (2002). *Information and communication technologies in teacher education: A planning guide*. Paris, France: Division of Higher Education, UNESCO.

US National Schools Board Association. (2007). *New study explores the online behaviors of US teens and tweens*. Available from http://www.nsba.org.

Venezky, R., & Davis, C. (2002, March). *Quo Vademus? The transformation of schooling in a networked world*. OECD/CERI.

Vernez, G., Karam, R., Mariano, L.T., & DeMartini, C. (2006). *Evaluating comprehensive school reform models at scale: Focus on implementation*. Rand Education. Available from http://www.rand.org/pubs/monographs/ MG546/.

Vrasidas, C., & Glass, G.V. (Eds.) 2005. *Preparing teachers to teach with technology* (ch. 1). IAP.

Wallace, J. (1995). The changing world of school leadership: Working in a professional organisation today. *The Practising Administrator, 17*(1), 14–17.

Warner, D. (2006). *Schooling for the knowledge era*. Melbourne: ACER Press.

Watkins, C. (2001). Learning about learning. *Research Matters*, (13). Institute of Education, National School Improvement Network.

Weinbaum, A., Allen, D., Blythe, T., Simon, K., Seidel, S., Rubin, C. (2004). *Teaching as inquiry*. New York: Teachers College Press.

Wheatley, M., (1999). *Leadership and the new science: Discovering order in a chaotic world*. San Francisco: Berrett-Koehler Publishers.

Wikipedia. (2005). Thomas J. Watson. Wikipedia, the free encyclopedia. Wikipedia Foundation. Last edited 05.05, January 2, 2008. Viewed January 2, 2008, at http://en.wikipedia.org/wiki/Thomas_J._Watson. *Contrary to the views of some traditionalists, Wikipedia is an invaluable tool for all school and education authority leaders wanting to secure an understanding of the very latest digital technology, provided one is ever critical. No other free source can provide the currency—and indeed openness—of the Wikipedia entries.*

Wikipedia. (2008a). MySpace. Wikipedia, the free encyclopedia. Wikipedia Foundation. Last edited 20.35, January 4, 2008. Viewed January 8, 2008, at http://en.wikipedia.org/wiki/MySpace.

Wikipedia. (2008b). List of Google products. Wikipedia, the free encyclopedia. Wikipedia Foundation. Last edited 6.09, January 7, 2008. Viewed January 8, 2008, at http://en.wikipedia.org/wiki/List_of_Google_products.

Wikipedia. (2008c). Web 2.0. Wikipedia, the free encyclopedia. Wikipedia Foundation. Last edited 22.24, January 7, 2008. Viewed January 8, 2008, at http://en.wikipedia.org/wiki/Web_2.0.

Wikipedia. (2008d). Web 3.0. Wikipedia, the free encyclopedia. Wikipedia Foundation. Last edited 00.24, January 5, 2008. Viewed January 8, 2008, at http://en.wikipedia.org/wiki/Web_3.0.

Wikipedia. (2008e). Semantic web. Wikipedia, the free encyclopedia. Wikipedia Foundation. Last edited 15:11, February 2, 2008. Viewed February 4, 2008, at http://en.wikipedia.org/wiki/Semantic_Web.

YouTube. (2007). Terms of use. YouTube. Viewed January 14, 2008, at http://www.youtube.com/t/terms.

INDEX